Malcolm Root's
PAGEANT OF TRANSPORT

A Treasury of Transport Paintings from Times Past

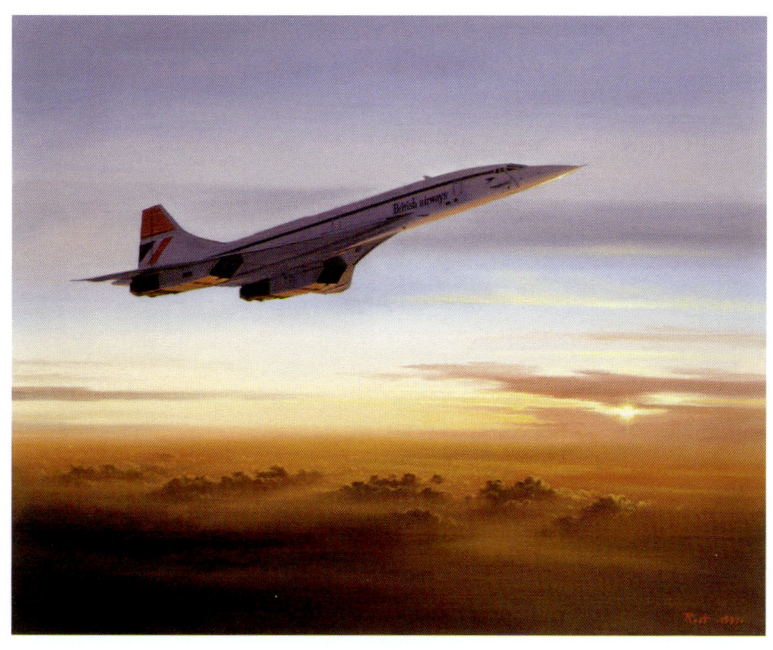

TEXT BY
TOM TYLER

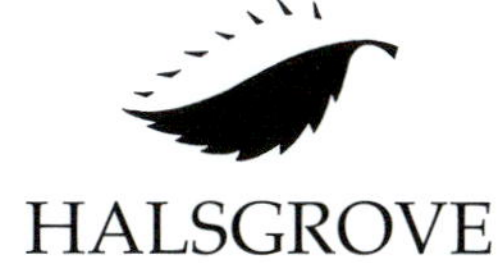

HALSGROVE

First published in 2006 by Halsgrove.
Reprinted 2007
Images © 2006 Malcolm Root
Text © 2006 Tom Tyler

Title page image: **Concorde** (Painted 1999)

Concorde, the world's first successful supersonic airliner, was built jointly in Britain and France, and the first prototype flew on 2 March 1969. Once in service Concorde could cruise at 52 000 feet at a speed of 1350mph which cut the transatlantic flight time by half. On 4 June 2002 Concorde took part in the flypast with the Red Arrows for the Queen's Golden Jubilee celebrations. The streamlined requirement for the aircraft meant a narrow cabin and small passenger-carrying capacity compared to jumbo jets, and the economics of the aircraft thus depended on how much extra passengers would pay for speed and prestige. The answer was 'not enough' and Concorde was taken out of service, sadly, in 2003.

British Library Cataloguing-in-Publication Data
A CIP record for this title is available from the British Library

ISBN 978 1 84114 536 5

HALSGROVE
Halsgrove House
Lower Moor Way
Tiverton, Devon EX16 6SS
T: 01884 243242
F: 01884 243325
www.halsgrove.com

Printed and bound in Italy by D'Auria Industrie Grafiche Spa

Author's Preface

This is the third volume published by Halsgrove of the paintings of Malcolm Root, and even more than the previous two books it demonstrates what a versatile and gifted artist Malcolm is when it comes to portraying all manner of transport subjects. As can be seen by the first three paintings in this book he is always ready to rise to a challenge, and to portray something quite new.

In this book, unlike the first two, the paintings have been arranged principally in chronological order according to the scenes and transport they portray, and thus they become a record of the development of transport in our country down the last ten centuries or so. In places the chronology has been altered a little, and this has been explained in the text.

This pageant of transport is closely interwoven with every other development in the history of our land. The first picture is a military scene, reminding us that warfare, however undesirable, has often acted as the spur to progress in the development of transport, as it has in other fields, like medicine. Conversely, social and domestic changes of a far-reaching nature have often been brought about by the development of transport, such as the coming of the railways.

This development of transport was influenced mainly by two factors. First, the medium to be traversed, and second the motive power available. The three divisions of land, water and air can be further divided into land – road and rail; water – sea and inland waterways, and air. For many centuries, until the coming of the railways, the condition of roads and tracks, or the lack of them altogether, governed the type of wheeled transport in use. In many places there was no possibility of using wheeled transport at all. The arrival of railways, and later the car, changed that situation out of all recognition.

The sea, of course, remained a constant medium, so significant changes were due to size – dictated usually by the shipbuilding materials available, and the motive power that could be harnessed. The building of inland canals, and the opening of rivers to navigation, produced a whole new means of carrying passengers and cargo, the horse-drawn narrow boat.

The air also remained a constant medium, and here the new building materials for aircraft, and in particular the development of more powerful and economical engines, were the factors that produced rapid development.

With regard to motive power, this pageant of transport reminds us how at first manpower and horsepower were complimented by wind and water power, until the great breakthrough came in the eighteenth century with the invention of varieties of steam engines. This was followed in the next century by the invention of the electric motor and different types of internal combustion engine, and finally in the twentieth century came the jet engine and the rocket motor – both incidentally developed largely for military reasons.

In the following succession of brilliant paintings by Malcolm Root we are reminded of this fascinating history of transport by the accuracy and detail of the pictures, and we are better able to appreciate the way that the different forms of transport have developed over the centuries. The book is indeed a Pageant of Transport.

Once again I should like to accord special thanks to those who have helped me with information and inspiration, and especially to Harry Saunders, Bill Ramsey and Bob Mellor and the staff at the Ipswich Transport Museum. Special thanks also go to my daughter who sets up and sorts out my wilful computer, and to my wife for proofreading and much encouragement.

Tom Tyler

Artist's Introduction

In the year 1999 I was asked to paint a series of four pictures for the Wentworth Wooden Jigsaw company. These were to portray historic scenes showing war and conflict, trade and industry, exploration, and finally the expansion of transport. These pictures provided a welcome departure from my normal line of work, and we thought them worthy of inclusion in this book, especially as elements of transport are fundamental to each of the scenes portrayed. The first of these, a castle under siege, took me back to my days at school when we all struggled to draw Saxons, Normans and the obligatory Viking longboat on the plain page next to the text. Had they been judged as comic or cartoon figures we would probably have scored a better mark out of ten! It will not go unnoticed that the final picture of the four, created for the jigsaw and reproduced as the final painting in this book, is entirely devoted to the forms of transport that we are more familiar with today. I find it truly amazing that in just over one hundred years we have progressed from the first man-made flight to landing a man on the moon and further explorations to other planets.

Transport art today is largely, though not exclusively, driven by nostalgia, and for this reason many of the pictures within the book are within living memory of many people. I make no excuses for this as nostalgia has a big influence on the pictures I paint now, and have painted in the past. Whilst on the subject of nostalgia, I have very fond memories of the Ealing Studios films and other film productions of the time. Not only are they a useful source of reference for both vehicles and street scenes, but they also give me inspiration because of the aura of the 1950s which they evoke. 'The Titfield Thunderbolt', 'The Ladykillers' and 'The Iron Maiden' spring to mind. These all lodge themselves in the memory somewhere and re-emerge from time to time. A not so gentle film was 'The Battle of the River Plate' which I was taken to as a child. When I returned home I tried to draw a picture of HMS *Exeter* which must have had over a hundred guns and resembled a porcupine. Not one of my better works of art! Whilst this book places the paintings and the forms of transport they portray in an approximate date order, it is not meant to be a chronology of transport, but more a pageant of transport.

This is the third book of my paintings to be published by Halsgrove, and the third in which Tom Tyler has added to the pictures with his humorous, anecdotal and factual text. For this I am truly grateful, as he is a pleasure to work with. I would also like to take this opportunity to thank Geoff Mills for his information on buses, Dave Bevan with matters pertaining to trams and Duncan Swift on matters relating to aircraft. I would also like to thank Neville Stead and all the other excellent photographers too numerous to mention by name who have helped me with photographs for reference. Once again Redwood Photographic has provided me with top-class transparencies without which the reproduction would have been much the poorer. My wife, Meryl, rarely gets a mention, but without her this book would not have been published. Finally I would like to thank all the owners of the paintings for their help and cooperation.

Malcolm Root

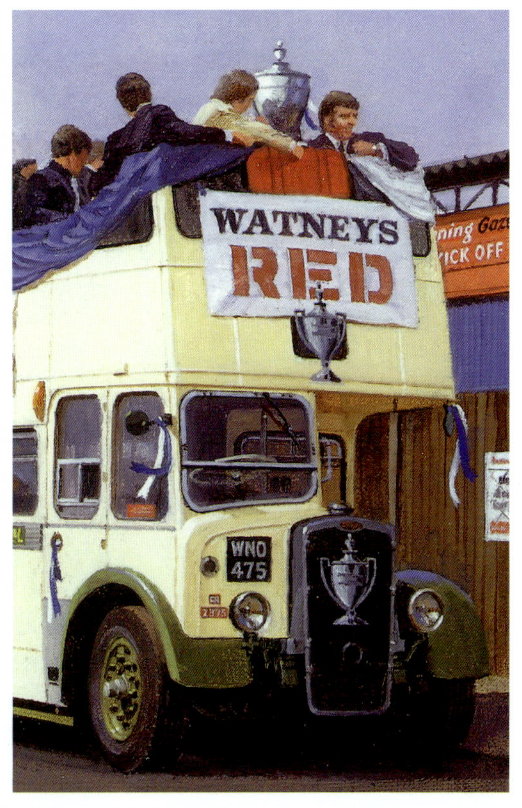

The Paintings

Forging Nations in Conflict – Millennium 1
Painted 1999

This is the first of the four paintings which Malcolm produced to celebrate the Millennium in 2000 AD, and which were designed to be used as images for jigsaw puzzles. The theme of the painting covered the period from AD1000–1250, and has the title 'Forging Nations in Conflict' as this was felt by the author to be the dominant historical subject for this period. The painting shows two upper scenes, one of William the Conqueror on horseback leading his army, and the other shows a Christian Knight on Crusade fighting with a Saracen adversary.

The main scene in the picture shows a full-scale siege of a medieval castle taking place. From a transport point of view the painting is an interesting curtain-raiser. There is only one wheel to be seen. Gone are the chariots of King Solomon and Boudicca and the Romans. Most travel is on foot or on horseback, certainly as far as the military is concerned. There is, however, the interesting siege tower. This was a wooden vertical structure on wheels, with platforms at different heights, connected by internal ladders. At the top was a drawbridge which could be let down across the castle wall, to allow soldiers to gain access to the battlements. The tower was filled with soldiers, and then pushed forward along some kind of causeway to the castle wall. The whole operation was decidedly uncomfortable for the attacking force as the tower pushers were very exposed to missiles from the castle walls, and the whole tower structure was highly inflammable, a weakness the defenders on the castle walls would try to exploit.

The siege tower can be seen, however, as the forerunner of the armoured personnel carrier, and reminds us how military requirements often led to new developments in transport. Horse-drawn cannon not only led to developments in wheel construction, but also to a demand for improved roads, which were a great benefit to other wheeled traffic. The pace of improvement would be very slow, largely due to the materials at hand, and it would be a long while before Britain's roads were again as good as those at the time of the Roman occupation.

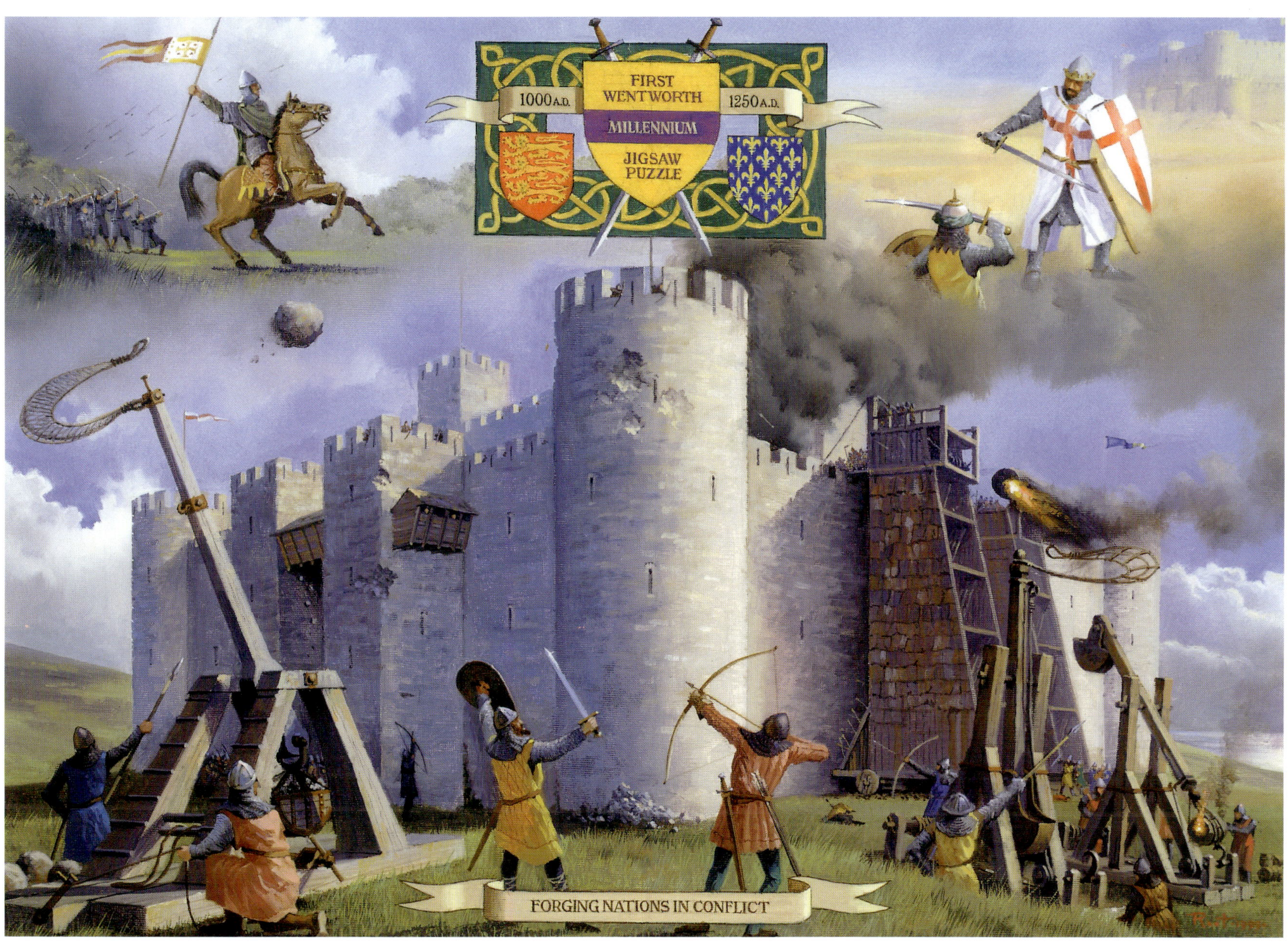
1000 A.D.
1250 A.D.
FIRST
WENTWORTH
MILLENNIUM
JIGSAW
PUZZLE
FORGING NATIONS IN CONFLICT

Developing Industry and Trade – Millennium 2
Painted 1999

In our second painting in Malcolm Root's Millennium series, the theme is 'Developing Industry and Trade'. This title, for the period AD1250–1500 may come as a surprise, as the Industrial Revolution is usually dated in the eighteenth and nineteenth centuries. In fact, most of the important ingredients of the development of industry and trade occurred during this period, and it was only the harnessing of steam power which caused the huge acceleration of industrial development in the later 1700s. Meanwhile, as our picture shows, wind and water power were being used to good effect much earlier, and a wide variety of industrial plant was being powered with windmills and water wheels.

In England the condition of the roads had improved little over the centuries and there was thus little incentive to develop more sophisticated land transport. The cart in the picture being used to ferry sacks of corn to the windmill for grinding is a fairly primitive one-manpower model, though many larger carts were pulled by horses. Horse-drawn litters were also used by the wealthy for travel, and during this period horse-drawn carriages were also developed and improved, though again bad roads often limited their use.

It was at sea that the most significant development took place during this period. The English were an Island Race, and thus ships were of the utmost importance both for warfare and trade. With improved shipbuilding skills and better materials vessels became larger, with more sophisticated sails and rigging. Warships could carry as many as 180 of the guns and cannons which had been developed for naval warfare, as well as hundreds of sailors and soldiers. As our picture shows, trading ships also grew in size and tonnage, enabling much larger cargoes to be carried, and the quayside crane testifies to this new situation. Better sails and rigging enabled ships to sail closer to the wind and to cope with wind conditions which previously would have confined ships to harbour.

Progress in developing transport remained slow during this period. Because political instability absorbed a lot of energy, warring factions diverted attention away from improvements to the country's infrastructure, and most people's energies had to be devoted to finding enough food to eat and keeping a roof over their heads. Travelling was a luxury reserved for the rich, or those with military requirements, and the best means of land travel was still to ride a good horse!

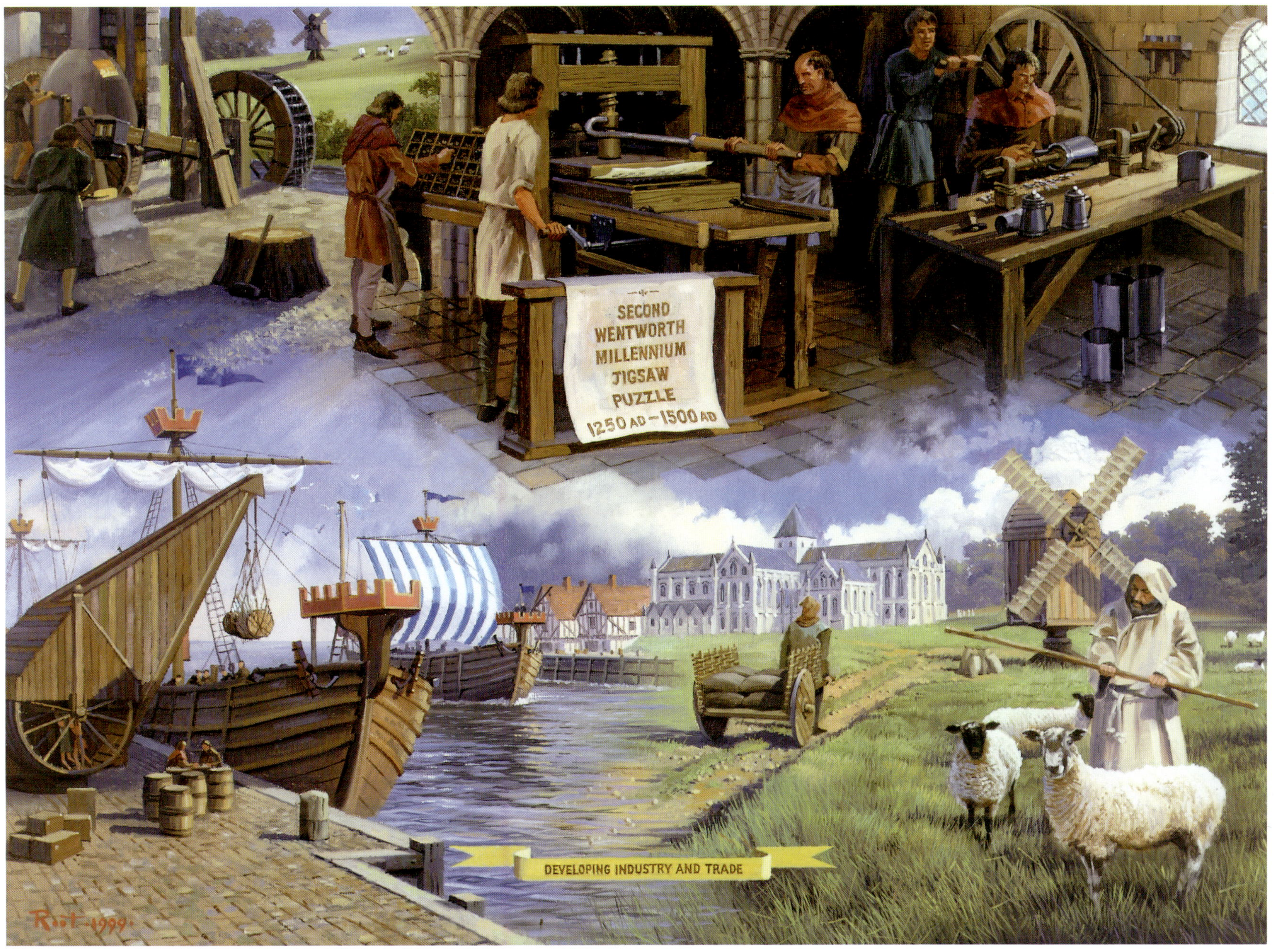

SECOND
WENTWORTH
MILLENNIUM
JIGSAW
PUZZLE
1250 AD – 1500 AD
DEVELOPING INDUSTRY AND TRADE
Root 1999

Exploring the World – Millennium 3
Painted 2000

During this important period, roads continued to be awful, and on one occasion King James II's coach overturned, throwing the King and Queen out into the mud! Coaches became a bit more comfortable, but still continued to be cumbersome vehicles which were the property of the very rich. The two-manpower sedan chair was a help in larger towns and cities. Guns became larger and heavier, and needed large teams of horses to pull them about the countryside. The horse continued to be the main means of transport, but a change would come with turnpike roads being constructed, and swifter private carriages and stagecoaches.

At sea the situation was entirely different, and this was due to a number of powerful incentives. First, England's defence was more and more vital, as the defeat of the Spanish Armada in 1588 demonstrated. It was the superior sailing and handling qualities of the English ships which played a large part in this notable victory. Second, exploration of the newly-discovered countries in the world brought new opportunities for trade, and the possibility of gold, silver, jewels and valuable spices. Third, such exploration, coupled with a bit of freebooting or piracy, depending on which side you were on, enabled the English to weaken their European rivals, and win glory for themselves at home.

This painting gives us a vivid reminder of the ingredients which were so important. The *Golden Hind*, though small, was a sophisticated ship for her time, commanded by a genius of great courage and daring, Sir Francis Drake, and with a very able crew. Queen Elizabeth rewarded him with knighthood on his ship at Deptford when he returned from his circumnavigation of the world. Drake was also a skillful navigator, but it was John Harrison, also seen in the picture, who produced the accurate timepieces which enabled ship's navigators to calculate longitude with the necessary accuracy. As a result Captain James Cook was able to explore the Pacific Ocean, opening up and claiming new lands like Australia and New Zealand, and also to produce accurate charts to direct those who followed him.

In this period the foundations of Britain's overseas empire were laid down, and valuable trade increased enormously with the import of raw materials which helped to accelerate the Industrial Revolution. By 1750 the way was prepared for a giant leap forward in both land and sea transport.

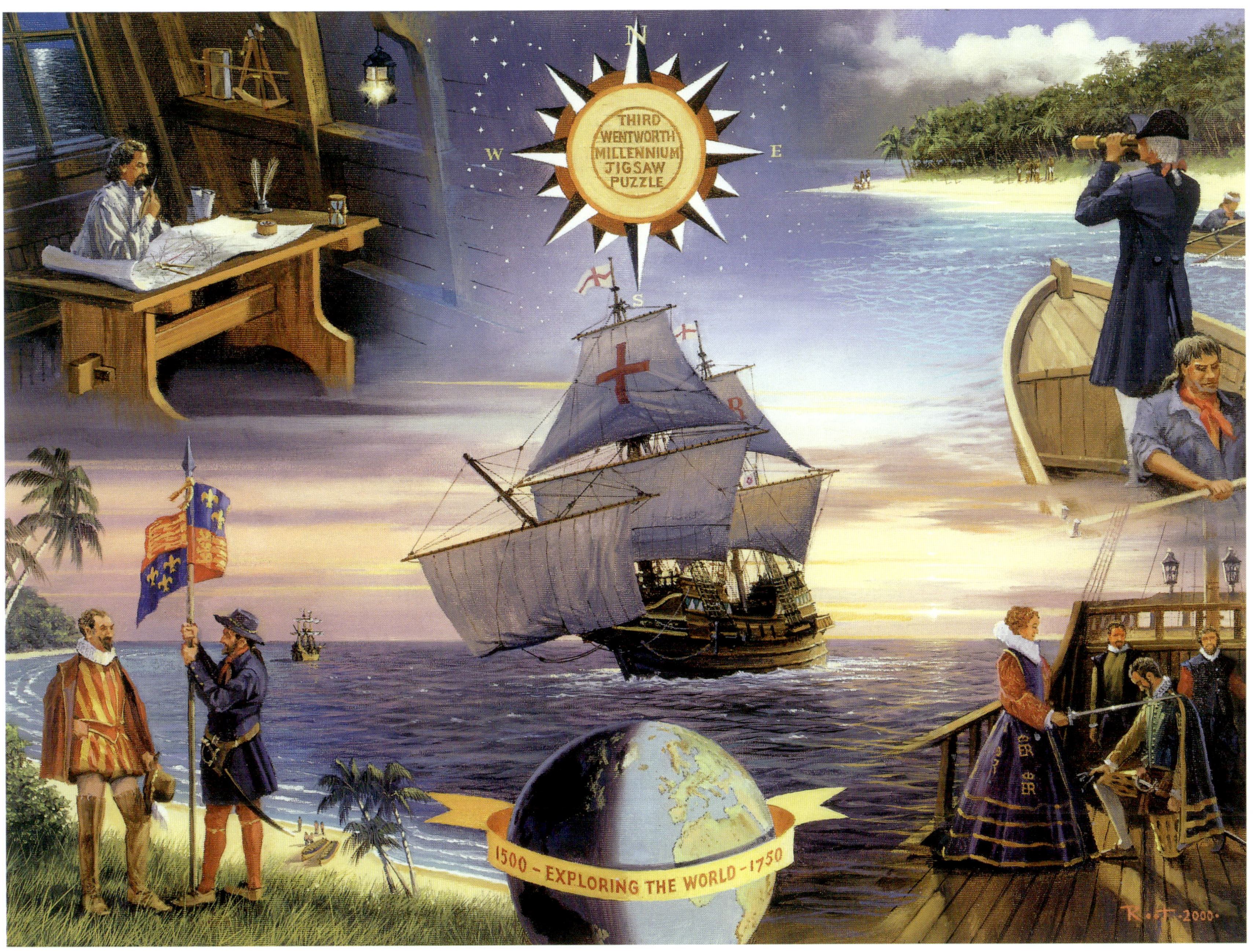
N
W
E
THIRD
WENTWORTH
MILLENNIUM
JIGSAW
PUZZLE
S
1500 ~ EXPLORING THE WORLD ~ 1750

High Road to Aberfeldy
Painted 2004

We have seen in the last two paintings how sailing ships developed, and later on will discover the changes that came with steam propulsion. On land there was little progress, especially for ordinary people, though rich young men could dash along bad roads in their curricles. By the start of the nineteenth century Richard Trevithick had constructed a small locomotive which would pull a carriage round a circular track. He used it as a sort of funfair attraction, but it was the forerunner of a huge development, the railways. George Stephenson is rightly credited with pioneering a huge step forward with the opening of the Stockton & Darlington Railway in 1825, the economic benefits of which were immediately apparent, as the cost of carrying minerals dropped from 7d to 1½d per ton per mile, a huge saving.

By the end of the nineteenth century the railway network, with its main lines and small branchlines provided the British Isles with a lifeline of communications and transport. The locomotive in this picture dates from 1900, though the scene is actually post-1948, in the British Railways era. This is the branchline that runs from Ballinluig via Grandtully to Aberfeldy, north of Perth in east Scotland. As can be seen the countryside is stunningly beautiful on a sunny day, and Malcolm has captured the light and shade to perfection.

The tank locomotive is an 0-4-4T ex Caledonian Railway 439 class, numbered 55200, and designed by McIntosh. With a modest boiler pressure of 180lbs/square inch, it had a tractive effort of 18 680lbs, and weighed in at 53 tons. It was ideal for use on small branchlines and, in 1960, sixty years after they were built, over forty of the class were still in service. The train is also a reminder of the first days of the railway, for the inaugural train on the Stockton & Darlington Railway was also mixed freight and passenger, though the passengers were carried in converted trucks. On branchlines especially, the trains consisted of strange mixtures as the railways undertook to carry anything and everything. Many trains would have 'Private Owner' wagons as part of their stock. The development of railways forms a very important part of our pageant.

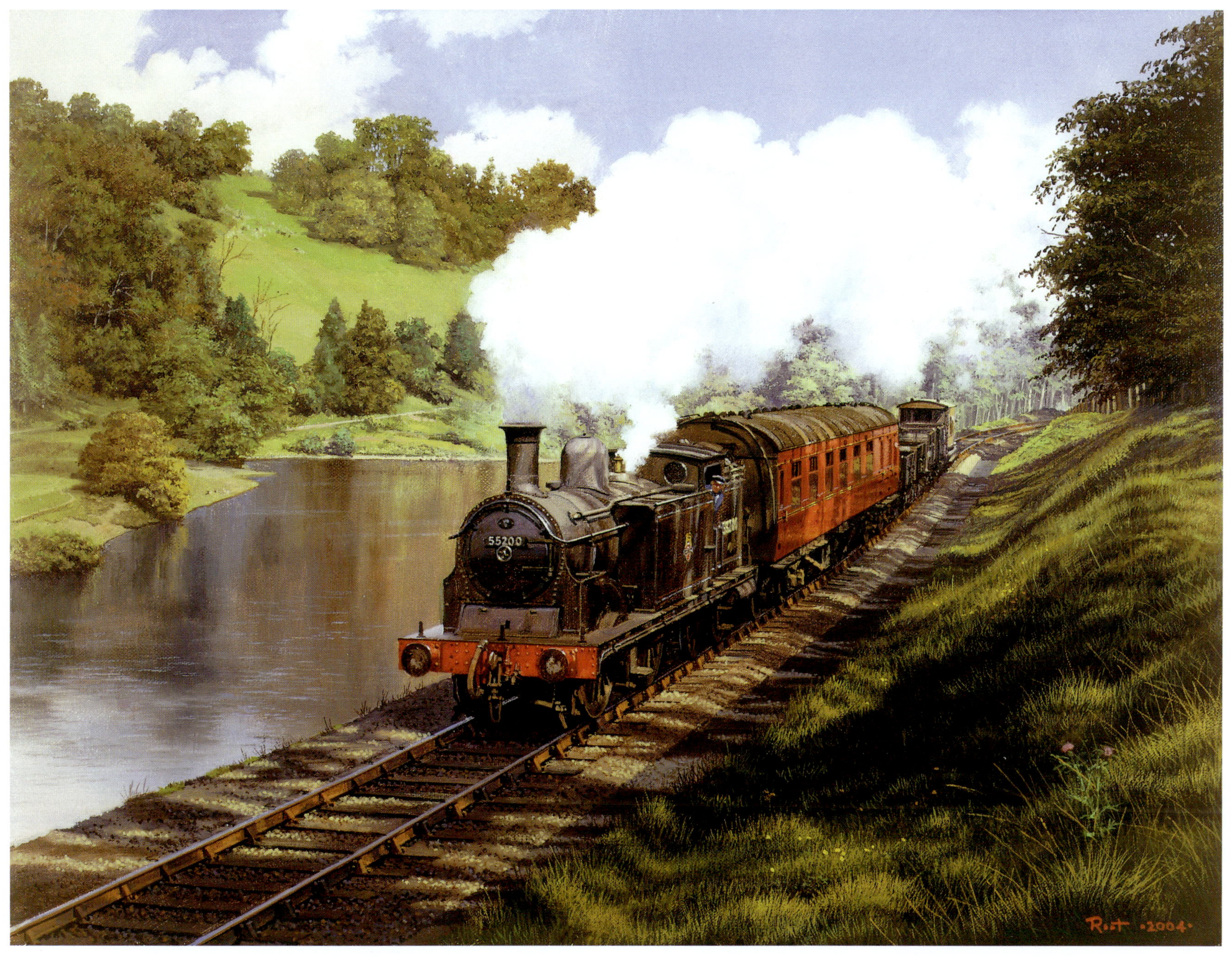

Steam Up at Dawn
Painted 1996

When steam was first harnessed to drive machinery in the eighteenth century the engines were stationary beam engines. But the need for better transport was so great that before long a beam engine was mounted on wheels to pull trucks on the existing tramways. Harnessing steam for road travel posed greater problems, partly because of the gradients and road surfaces.

The traction engine, developed at the end of the nineteenth century, was handicapped for a number of reasons. The nature of the steam engine meant that it was heavy in relation to its power. This didn't matter so much in a ship or on rails, but for a road vehicle it was a big problem. In addition to the weight of the engine you then had to add in the weight of heavy fuel, in this instance coal and also water. An average traction engine travelling ten miles would require six 1cwt (50kg) bags of coal, and about 200 gallons of water. The Clayton & Shuttleworth engine in the painting would weigh about 10 tons with fuel, and could develop the power of six horses.

This particular traction engine, registration number HK 9836 was built in 1899, and, when bought by a Mr C. Philp in 1957 was no longer in use and becoming derelict. It was not until 1977 that restoration was put in hand by a

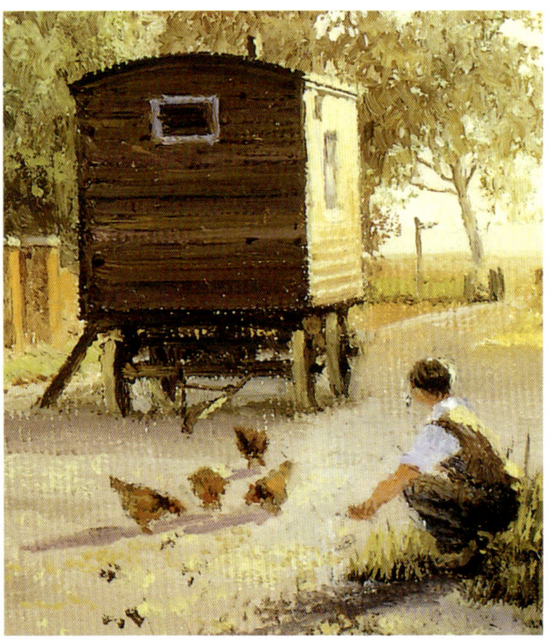

Mr J. Garwood, and by 1980 it was again in working order, and one of the oldest surviving engines by this maker. The engine continues to be owned by the Philp family of Castle Hedingham in Essex. Clayton & Shuttleworth were founded in 1842 and made pipes, branching into the making of traction engines at the end of the 1800s. The main factory was the Stamp End Works, in Lincoln, where this engine was built. In the First World War the company switched production to howitzers and aircraft.

This very atmospheric painting reminds us of another disadvantage of the traction engine, which enabled the petrol tractor to eclipse them in such a short time. Raising steam could take a couple of hours before the engine was ready for work, and though in this picture one member of the team is using his time fruitfully for the benefit of some appreciative chickens, it was not a good start to the working day, especially in cold, wet weather.

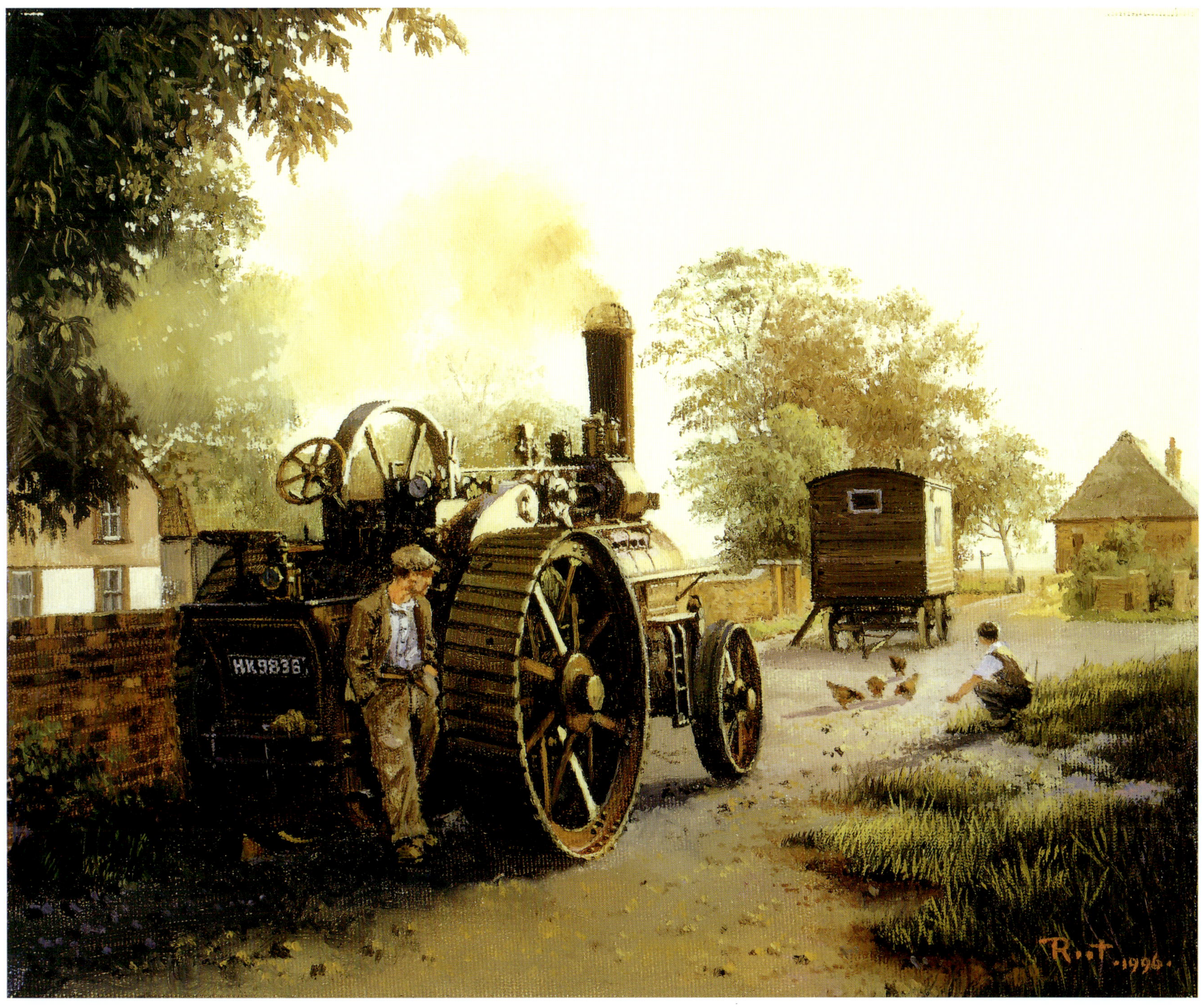

Pulham Leviathan

Painted 1997

Man's preoccupation with flight can be seen in the drawings of Leonardo da Vinci, but it was not until 21 November 1783 that the Montgolfier brothers achieved the first manned flight over Paris, in a hot air balloon made of cotton and paper fuelled by wood. Development was slow, and at the mercy of weather conditions, until in 1900 Count Von Zeppelin flew his first powered airship. Airships were then developed quite rapidly, being seen as weapons of war, and were so used during the First World War. They had both advantages and disadvantages compared with aircraft.

As early as 1912 the Royal Navy made a secret purchase of land at Pulham in South Norfolk with the intention of setting up an airship base there. By 1915 about 100 people worked at the base, and the rotund airships had become so familiar that they were nicknamed 'Pulham Pigs'. In September 1916 a German Zeppelin airship was brought down intact in Essex, a rare occurrence. The commanding officer at Pulham, Colonel Maitland, went down to inspect it, measured all its dimensions and learned as much as he could about its construction. The result of this was the construction of Britain's first rigid airship, the R33. Her sister ship, the R34, is shown at the mast at Pulham in Malcolm's painting. The base has long since closed down and most of the land has been restored for farming. One of the large hangars was moved to the base at Cardington, near Bedford, and a few foundations still remain. A small industrial site occupies a part of the base area today.

The lorry shown in the foreground is an AEC 'Y' Type, rated at 30 hp. By 1919 ten thousand of these lorries had been supplied to the War Department. After the First World War many were bought for civilian use. It is unloading bags of coal to fuel the traction engine standing behind it. The traction engine would have been used to winch the airship down to ground level if necessary, and also to move it around on the base.

During the 1920s airship development was carried on apace, with engineers like Barnes Wallis and Nevil Shute Norway much involved in the UK. A competition developed between Vickers, building the R100, and the government-sponsored R101. This culminated in the disastrous crash of the R101 in autumn 1930 and, when the great German airship *Hindenburg* also perished in a much publicized crash in the USA, the world airship programme came to an abrupt halt, and the aeroplane triumphed. However, airships are once again being seen in our skies, and with new, safer gases, and more efficient propulsion units, who knows what the future may hold?

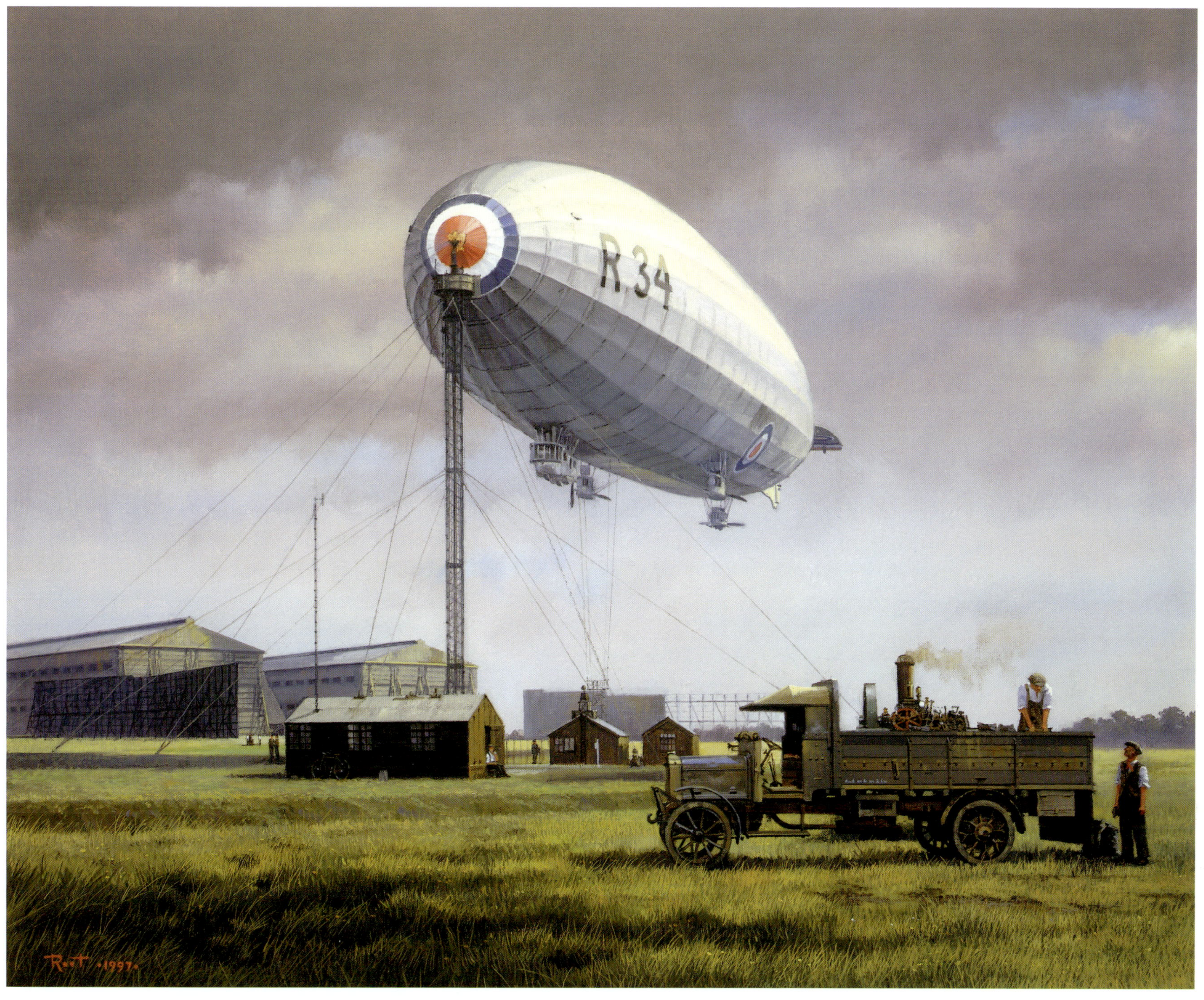
R.34

Sussex Spectacle
Painted 2005

East of Lewes, in Sussex, the rolling chalk ridges of the South Downs run parallel to the sea on their way to Beachy Head, and the coastal railway and road follow them from Brighton to Eastbourne. In this lovely painting the occupants of a Bentley 3-litre Tourer have pulled off the road up a track to stretch their legs and perhaps open up the picnic basket, and are just in time to watch a magnificent Pullman express on the London, Brighton & South Coast Railway.

W.O. Bentley began production of Bentley cars in late 1919, and although the company only produced 3000 cars in its ten year independent history, its fame is firmly established. The power, size and robustness of the later Bentleys prompted Ettore Bugatti, a leading competitor, to remark 'Mr Bentley produces the worlds fastest lorries!' The first 3-litre Bentleys appeared on the roads in late 1921, so the following year would seem a good date for this picture. The car had a four-cylinder long stroke engine with four valves per cylinder, twin magneto ignition and a separate four-speed gearbox. Later 3-litre models were capable of over 100mph.

Hauling the express, and resplendent in umber livery, is a Marsh H2 Atlantic, number 424, built in 1911. D. Earle Marsh had only six years as Chief Engineer on the LBSCR, retiring early in 1911 due to ill health. As chief draughtsman of the Great Northern Railway, Marsh had been much involved with the production of the most successful Ivatt Atlantics, and he quickly produced five 'HI' Atlantics for his new company. The Atlantics not only looked good, but

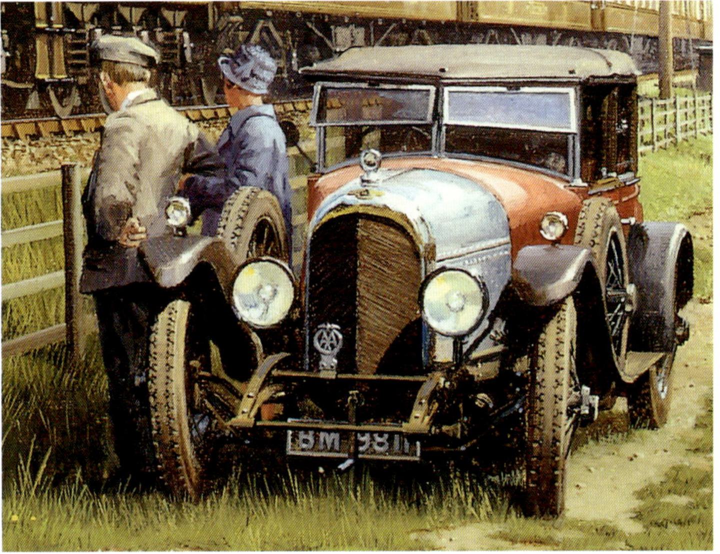

performed very well on the surprisingly taxing routes they travelled, and some were still in service in the 1950s. The locomotive is pulling an equally handsome rake of Pullman carriages.

The 1920s were a very important decade for the motor car. My mother took delivery of her first Model T Ford in 1919, - without any driving test- and this replaced the pony and trap and the donkey cart. For the first time cars began to replace trains on longer-distance journeys on a regular basis. Meanwhile in 1923 the many smaller railway companies were merged into the 'Big Four' and a great period of railway development also began which would last through the 1920s and 1930s.

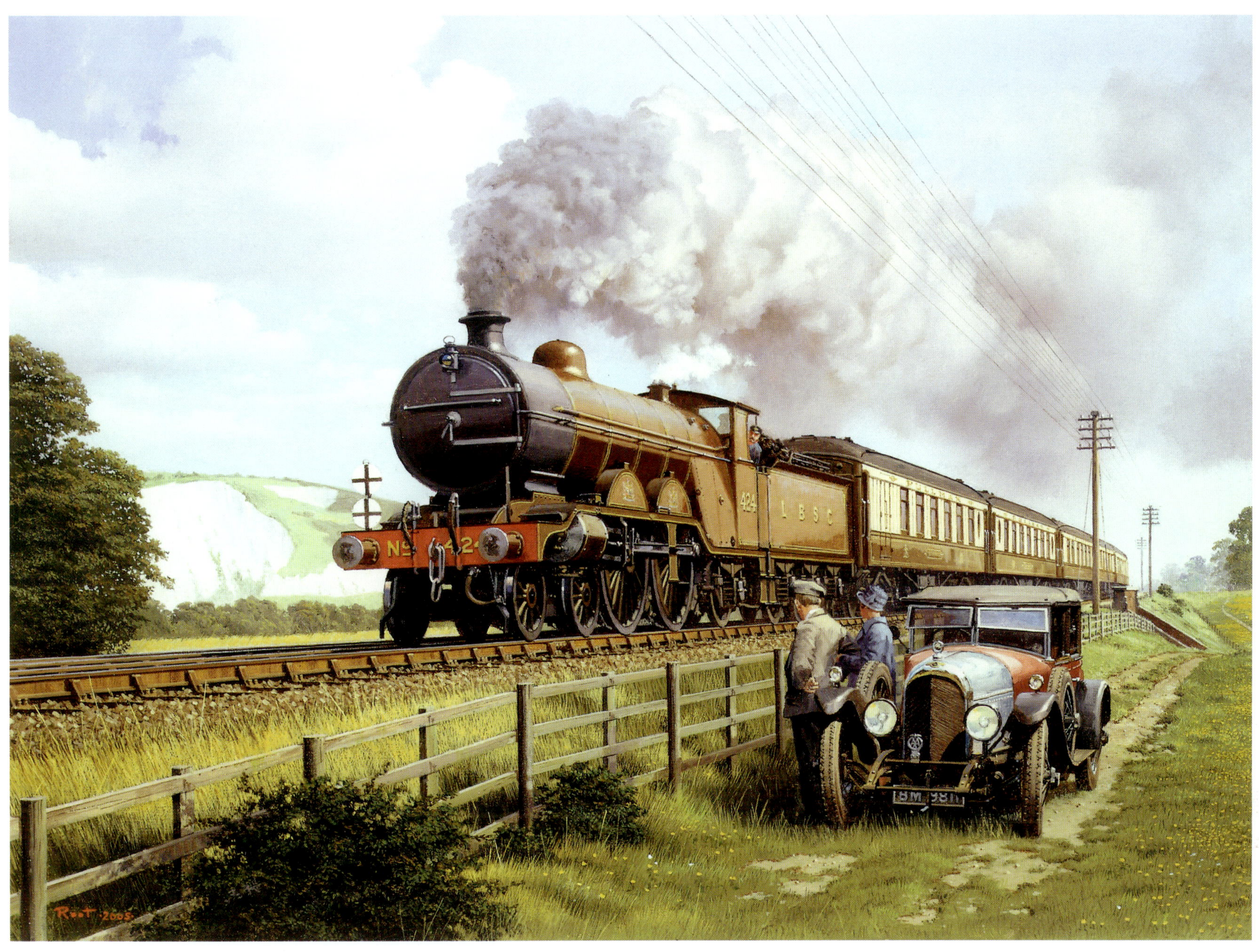

N° 424
424 L B S C
BM 98
Root 2005

Burrell and Boiler

Painted 1997

It is a fair distance from Preston in Lancashire to Halstead in Essex, and rather a cross country route in the early years of the twentieth century, with no motorways to help. Transporting large and heavy objects such as the boiler shown in this painting was a real challenge. Some items could do the bulk of the journey by rail on a low loader bogie wagon, provided they could squeeze through tunnels and bridges. Some might do the bulk of the journey by sea, from the Mersey to Harwich maybe. In this instance we know the huge boiler was brought by rail to Halstead Station, and after being put on a trailer was towed by Mark Gentry's traction engine to its final destination. We have photographs taken on that day in 1904 showing what a challenging operation it was, with a right angle turn off the High Street and a very narrow lane down to the factory.

This Burrell traction engine was bought new by Mr Mark Gentry of Sible Hedingham in Essex, and it spent its working life in that area. Malcolm has shown the engine delivering the boiler, made by J. Foster & Sons of Preston, to the Courtaulds factory in his home town. The narrow streets and road surface are typical of the period, and driving a traction engine with a load like this demanded a great deal of skill and experience. Halstead and the surrounding district are far from flat, and the traction engine had inadequate braking power, and also pretty primitive steering as well. Fortunately it could not go very fast, so the whole operation took place in slow motion. The traction engine shown is a Burrell 7 nominal hp single crank compound machine, built around 1899 at Thetford in Norfolk.

In spite of the slow motion, the assembled crowd, which includes a policeman and a rather scruffy dog, are all hoping for some catastrophe which will cause excitement and provide a story to tell in the pub that evening, heavily embroidered for the benefit of those poor folk who missed out on the spectacle! In fact the whole operation took two full days, and showers of rain did not for a moment dampen the spirits of the many onlookers along the route. In the days before television you had to take your entertainment where you could find it!

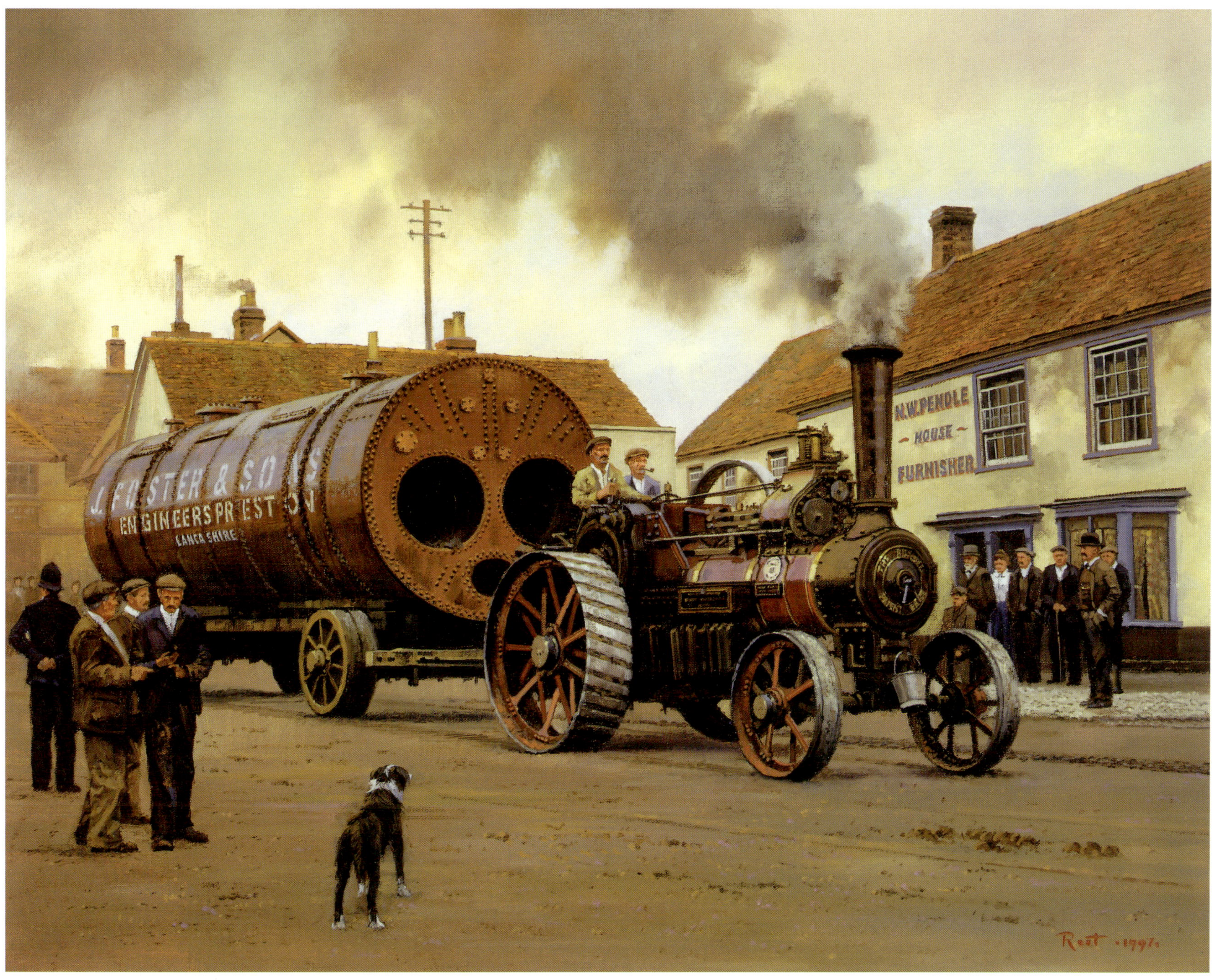
J. FOSTER & SONS
ENGINEERS PRESTON
LANCASHIRE
M.W.PENDLE
~ HOUSE ~
FURNISHER
Root 1997

Char-a-banc

Painted 2006

The setting for this detailed painting is again Malcolm's home town of Halstead in Essex, and he has portrayed the High Street as it would have appeared in the 1920s. Although there are several cars to be seen in the background, and the famous Austin Seven had come into being, this was still very much a period when few people had cars of their own, and the great majority depended on either trains or buses. The latter were just beginning to become widespread, following the experience of their use in the First World War, but there was also a lot of scope for private enterprise and for individuals with a talent for invention.

In the painting we see a char-a-banc conversion on a Model T Ford one-ton chassis. This vehicle was acquired in 1920, and used by Chaplin & Keeble to transport fourteen passengers. The side windows, with opening louvres above, together with the circular cab windows make it a distinctive vehicle, even if its performance was not notable. Luckily it did not have to cope with the sort of hills found in the western parts of the country. The seats were all removable, and so the char-a-banc could be converted into a van and used to carry cargoes on behalf of Courtaulds, the local manufacturing firm.

The char-a-banc is just departing from the shop of Chaplin & Keeble, which is described as a 'Motor and Cycle Works' and agent for BSA, Humber and Enfield Cycles, as well as selling gramophone records. They also sold Shell petrol, and the pump is an interesting one, as it has the necessary extension hose which swings across above the pavement, to allow vehicles to be refuelled in the road without inconvenience to pedestrians. Electricity is available in Halstead, so the pump is an electric one, whereas out in the countryside it is quite likely to have had a handle on the front, and something which resembles a goldfish bowl on top, with a 'plimsoll line' to measure a gallon, which then passes by gravity down the hose and into the fuel tank. The proud owner of the shop is checking that all is well. Behind the vehicle are to be seen three splendid hats!

When at school we are taught the basics of perspective, and I am sure many people are familiar with the disappearing railway lines and telegraph poles vanishing to a point somewhere on the horizon. This is perspective in its simplest form. However, this picture presents many problems as the scene is set on a hill, and also on a bend, and the vanishing point for the buildings is somewhat lower than that of the vehicle and the road. As the road moves round to the right, so does the vanishing point. These technicalities may not always be apparent with the first glance at a picture.

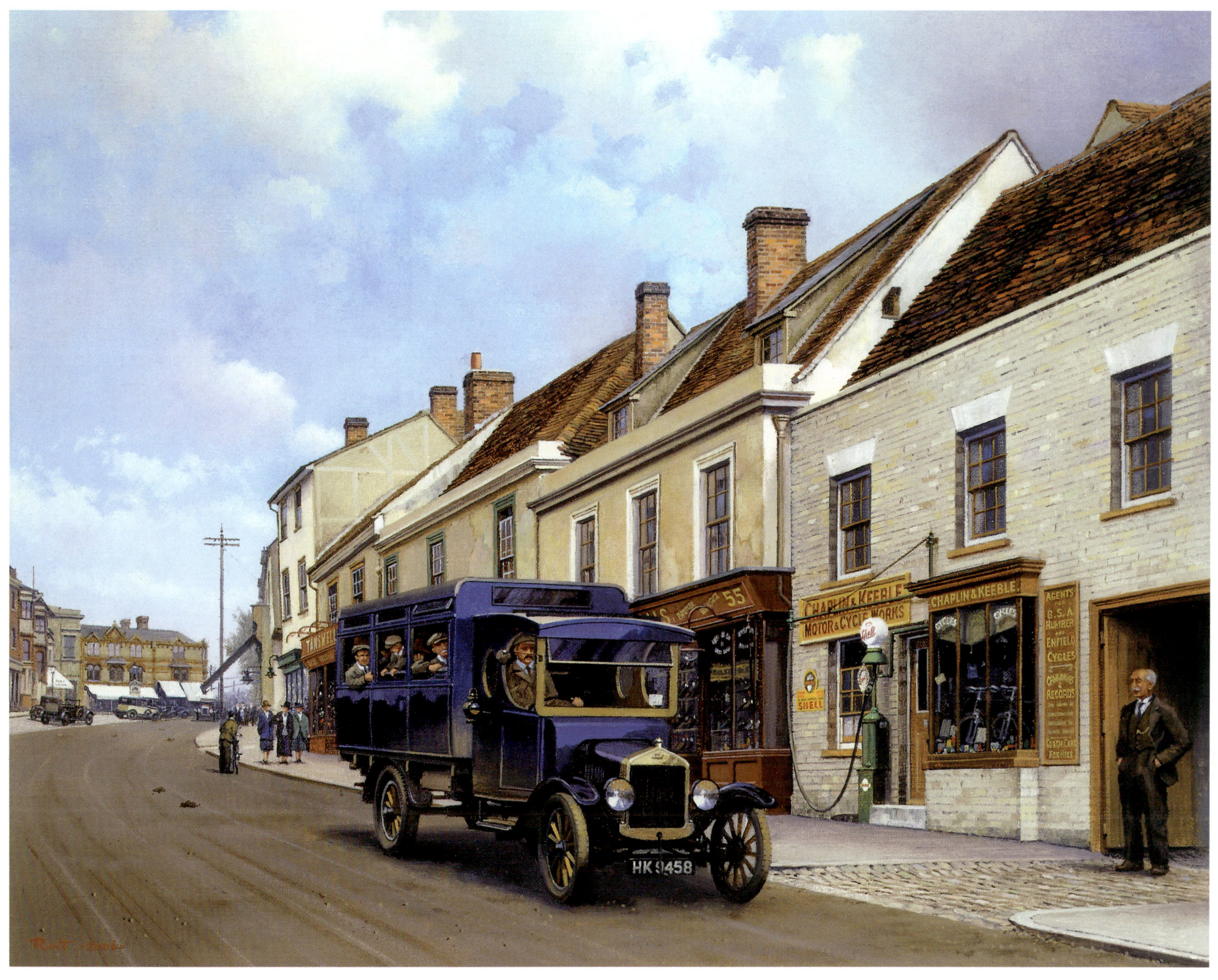
CHAPLIN & KEEBLE
MOTOR & CYCLE WORKS
CHAPLIN & KEEBLE
SHELL
AGENTS
B.S.A
HUMBER
ENFIELD
CYCLES
RECORDS
55
HK 9458

Halstead's Own
Painted 1982

This is a beautiful portrait of a Colne Valley & Halstead Railway class F9 2-4-2 tank engine. By 1887 the railway, situated in north Essex, was in need of new locomotives, with a delicate balance required between the weight of the locomotive, and its performance. Here we see the first of the three locomotives provided by Hawthorn Leslie & Co Ltd, of Newcastle upon Tyne, who specialized in producing small numbers of locomotives required for specific conditions. A long-established company, they also produced a lot of locomotives for industrial use. It is very appropriate to have this locomotive depicted at this stage of our pageant of transport, as it underlines two features of locomotive design throughout the twentieth century. The basic principles of the steam locomotive did not change, despite a brief experiment with a steam turbine, and Bulleid's unsuccessful 'Leader' locomotive. Coal and water were carried in a bunker or tender, or in 'saddle' water tanks. Drivers cab with controls, and firebox door were also situated at the back. The boiler was mounted on a chassis, which contained the cylinders, whether internal, external or both. Finally the chassis was mounted on wheels, some or all of which were driving wheels connected to the cylinders. Smoke from the firebox and steam from the cylinders would be exhausted through the smoke box and out of the chimney.

Given these basic principles, there was scope for amazing development of design, resulting in locomotives that were many times more powerful than the tank engine shown, and capable of hauling heavy express passenger and freight trains up hill and down dale at remarkable average speeds. Within forty years of the building of the locomotive *Halstead*, just as it was being withdrawn from service, Kings, together with Gresley Pacifics and Princesses were transforming the main railways of the realm. However, much of the success of our railways was due to the thousands of tank engines going quietly about their business on branchlines and sidings, and giving invaluable service over amazingly long periods of time. The class F9 2-4-2 shown weighed about 44 tons, and with a modest boiler pressure of 140lbs produced a tractive effort of about 12 000lbs. Only three of the class were built.

The Colne Valley Railway left the Stour Valley line at Chappel to wind through north Essex before rejoining it at Haverhill. This is Malcolm's home territory, and is an appropriate setting for one of his earlier paintings.

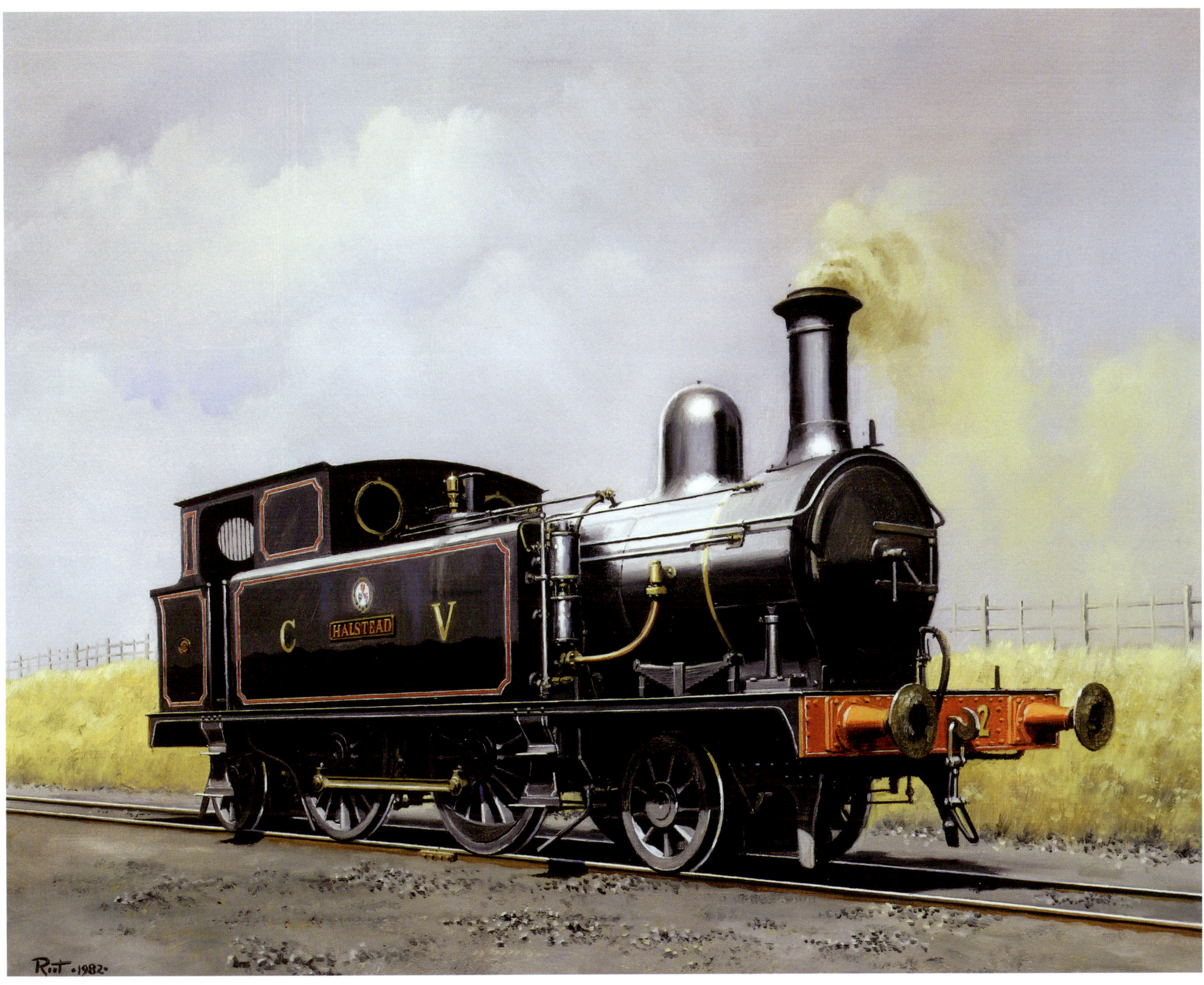
C HALSTEAD V

History in the Making
Painted 1998

Since the days of Christopher Columbus the crossing of the Atlantic Ocean had provided one of the greatest challenges and in the first two decades of the twentieth century huge efforts were made to speed the crossing. A number of nations, including Britain, France, Germany and the USA vied with one another, and liners like the *Deutschland*, *Mauretania*, *La Savoie*, *Aquitania* and *Titanic* added epic and sometimes tragic chapters to the great story. But what about a crossing by air? The *Daily Mail* newspaper offered a prize of £10 000 for the first person to achieve this feat.

During the First World War huge advances in aircraft design and performance had been made. During the war Vickers had produced the twin-engined Vimy bomber, named after one of the great battles of the war to date. For the transatlantic flight the Mk 4 version was used. It was fitted with Rolls-Royce Eagle III engines capable of 98mph at 5000 feet. Vickers modified the Vimy further, adding extra fuel tanks in place of bombs for the pioneering flight. They chose as pilot Captain John Alcock, born in 1892 near Manchester, who had flown during the recent war, been shot down and held as a prisoner of war in Turkey. As navigator they chose Lt. Arthur Brown, born in Glasgow in 1896, who had also flown in the war and been shot down over Germany. One has to remember that most First World War flyers were either shot down and taken prisoner, or killed.

Alcock and Brown took off in the Vimy from Lesters Field, St Johns, Newfoundland, on 14 June 1919, and they landed after a flight of 16 hours 27 minutes at Clifden, Ireland, on the following day. Alcock remarked 'Yesterday I was in America, and I am the first man in Europe to say that.' They had averaged nearly 120mph so must have had a good tail wind on the trip. The flight was not without hazards, with low cloud and fog making navigation very difficult. Malcolm's painting shows the moment when the two flyers descended to sea level when they became disorientated, and were saved by a sudden break in the cloud cover enabling them to see where they were in relation to the sea. Later the same type of aircraft was used for the first flight from England to Australia, in 1919, and from England to Cape Town in 1920. Truly the world was getting smaller very quickly as aircraft showed what they could do.

The account of Alcock and Brown's historic and near disastrous flight in 1919 is well documented by text, but not prolifically covered by illustrations. The challenge for this picture was then set, but with only three elements involved (sky, sea and the aircraft), drama and spirit would need to be introduced to complete the spectacle. I hope I have captured the moment when they became disorientated and descended through a break in the clouds to find themselves a few feet above the inhospitable Atlantic. A visit to the Science Museum to see the Vickers Vimy not only provided reference material but also a feeling for the machine that was the vehicle for that historic flight.

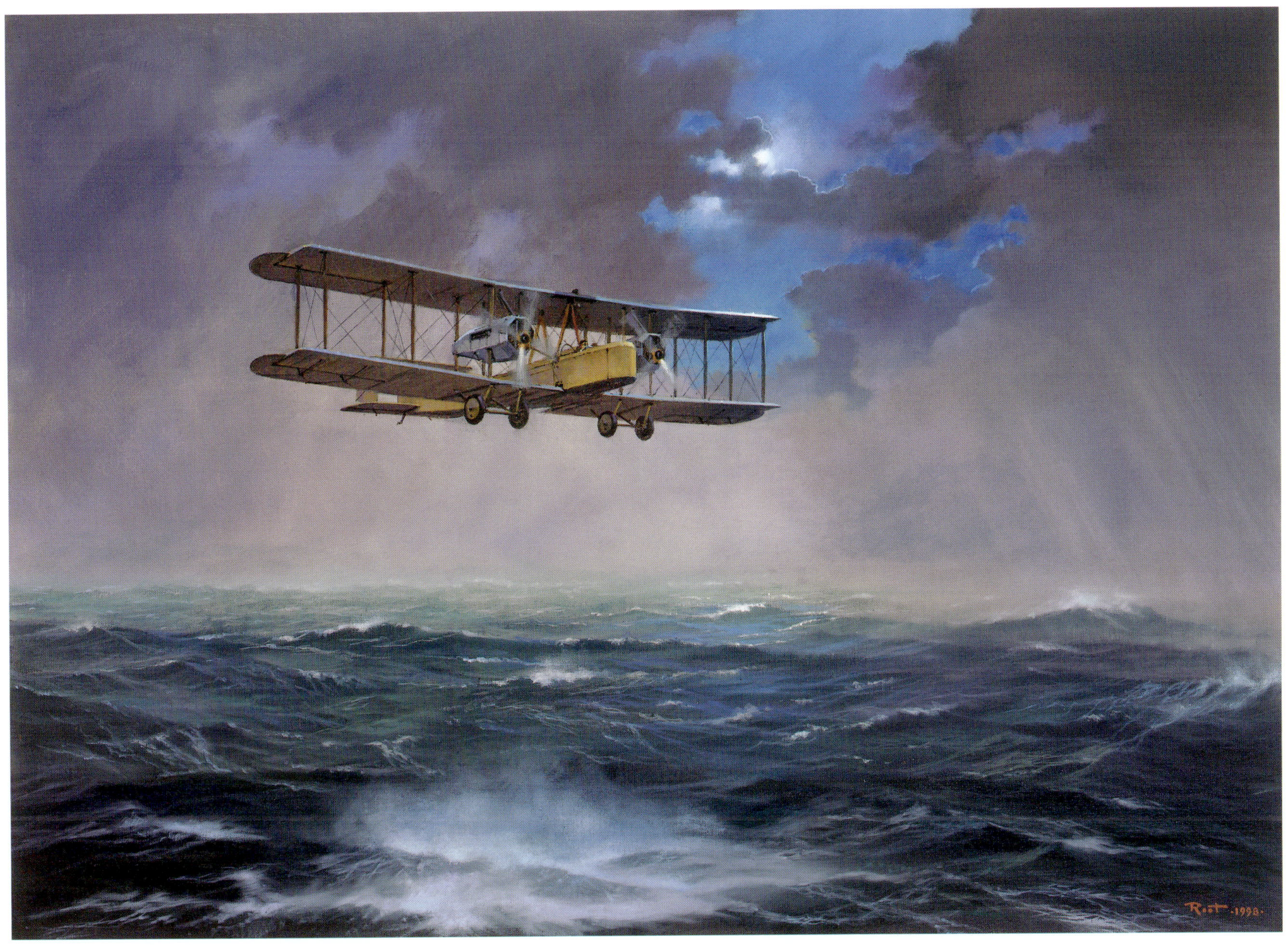

Ploughing by Steam

Painted 2002

During the 1800s great advances were made in farming techniques, and in particular the two most important operations, ploughing and harvesting. As early as 1811 a 'Roundabout' system was patented by Major Pratt, using cables and pulleys, with motive power supplied by a portable steam engine and winch. This worked quite well, but was cumbersome to move around. In 1854 John Fowler came on the scene, and he was to do more to revolutionize ploughing than any person since the plough was invented. As has been suggested (page 10) the traction engine was not ideal as a towing vehicle on wet or shifting ground. John Fowler developed the winch and cable system, but simplified it by having two engines which could move forward under their own power along the headland of the field, pulling the plough to and fro between them. The ploughman travelled on the plough itself and steered it across the field.

A full ploughing team could include five men, and machinery costing as much as £2500, in 1900 a considerable sum. This would include two ploughing engines, one right-handed and one left-handed according to the side of the engine the cable was paid out, looking forward. As can be seen in the picture, the massive winch was positioned as low down as possible and just forward of the rear wheels, to minimize the possibility of the engine pulling itself over when working. The foreman would drive the left-handed engine, and tow the plough on the road. The second driver would drive the other engine, towing cultivator, living caravan and water cart. A third driver was part of the team, together with the ploughman and cook boy. The latter would hope one day to work his way up to being a foreman, but in the meantime had to produce the day's meals – bacon and egg for breakfast, and scrumped vegetables with perhaps a poached rabbit or pheasant for supper, or even a hedgehog baked in clay.

Shown in the painting is a pair of Fowler 'BB' ploughing engines, which were introduced in 1913 and were rated at either 14 or 16 horsepower. They weighed in at about 20 tons. The engines could pull the six-sheared plough at up to 6mph and could be as much as 600 yards apart across a field. The drivers signalled to one another using their single note whistles, seen perched on top of the cylinder block. Except when close to the engines, the ploughman worked in almost total silence with only the swishing of soil passing the blades beneath him. A team could plough up to 30 acres in a day, but it was a very long day, often 4am to 10pm or so. Teams only went home between Saturday lunchtime and Sunday night, yet they enjoyed the work. However, a still, sunny autumn day, as shown in this lovely painting, must have been best of all. At the 'Power from the Past' show near Woodbridge in Suffolk beautiful engines still demonstrate how steam ploughing was done in days gone by.

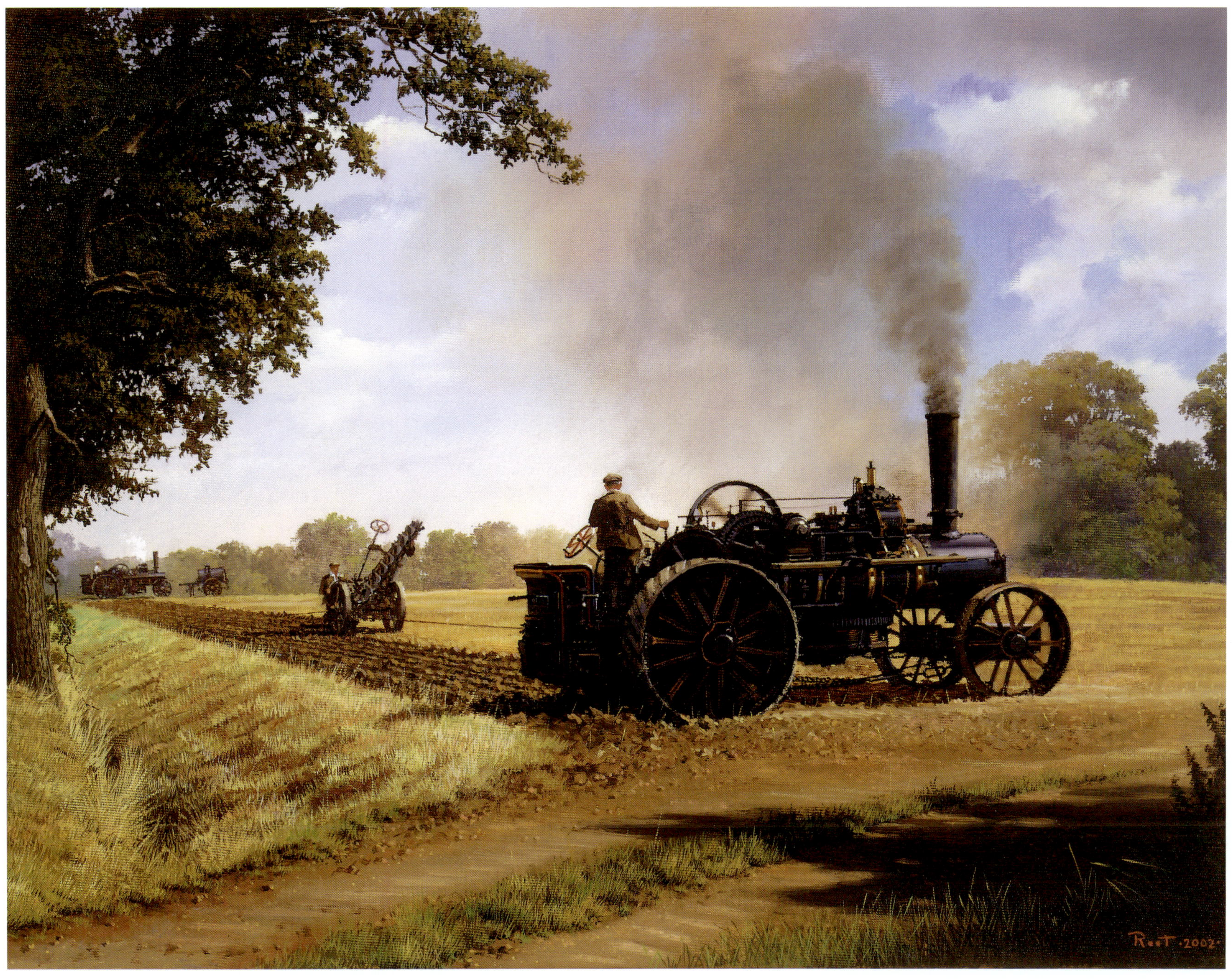

The Flying Scotsman
Painted 2005

At the Empire Exhibition at Wembley in 1924 two new and impressive railway locomotives stole the show. One was *Caerphilly Castle* from the Great Western Railway, the other was the A1 Pacific *Flying Scotsman* from the London & North Eastern Railway. The A1 appeared much the larger locomotive, but the GWR claimed their new Castle was the more powerful of the two, and in exchange trials later that year they achieved a total victory to prove their point.

Nigel Gresley, the Chief Mechanical Engineer of the newly formed London & North Eastern Railway, returned to base at Doncaster to ponder why. Gresley, as Chief Engineer on the Great Northern Railway after the First World War had already showed an unusually open mind by investigating the merits of American locomotives. It seemed that the difference lay in valve settings and boiler pressures. Gresley improved both on his A1, raising the boiler pressure from 180lbs to 220lbs, to nearly equal that of the Castles. New valve settings also made a big difference to performance. A1 number 1472 was built at Doncaster in 1923, but the following year was re-numbered 4472, and given the name *Flying Scotsman* ready for its appearance at the Empire Exhibition. Perhaps because of its distinctive name, the loco-motive always caught the eye as it thundered from London to Scotland, and this despite the competition from the more glamorous A4 introduced by Gresley in the 1930s. *Flying Scotsman* was rebuilt as an A3 in 1947 and continued in service with British Railways until withdrawn in January 1963.

This iconic engine was immediately saved for preservation by Alan Pegler. It must be almost every man's dream to own a great locomotive, and Alan was often pictured with it. It was not all plain sailing however. A ship has the freedom of the seas, and an aircraft the air. Old vehicles can travel free wherever there are roads. The preserved loco-motive must have rails however, and unless limited to a short preserved railway, must fit in with the many modern trains earning a living for the railway network. Also, supplies of water and suitable coal may be hard to come by when required. *Flying Scotsman* actually pulled two tenders some of the time, to provide enough coal and water for the longest non-stop journeys. These were corridor tenders so that crew changes could take place while travelling. In addition, old locomotives need constant attention and costly refitting

Flying Scotsman is now in the safe hands of the National Railway Museum and continues to pull the crowds, as one hopes she will for many years to come.

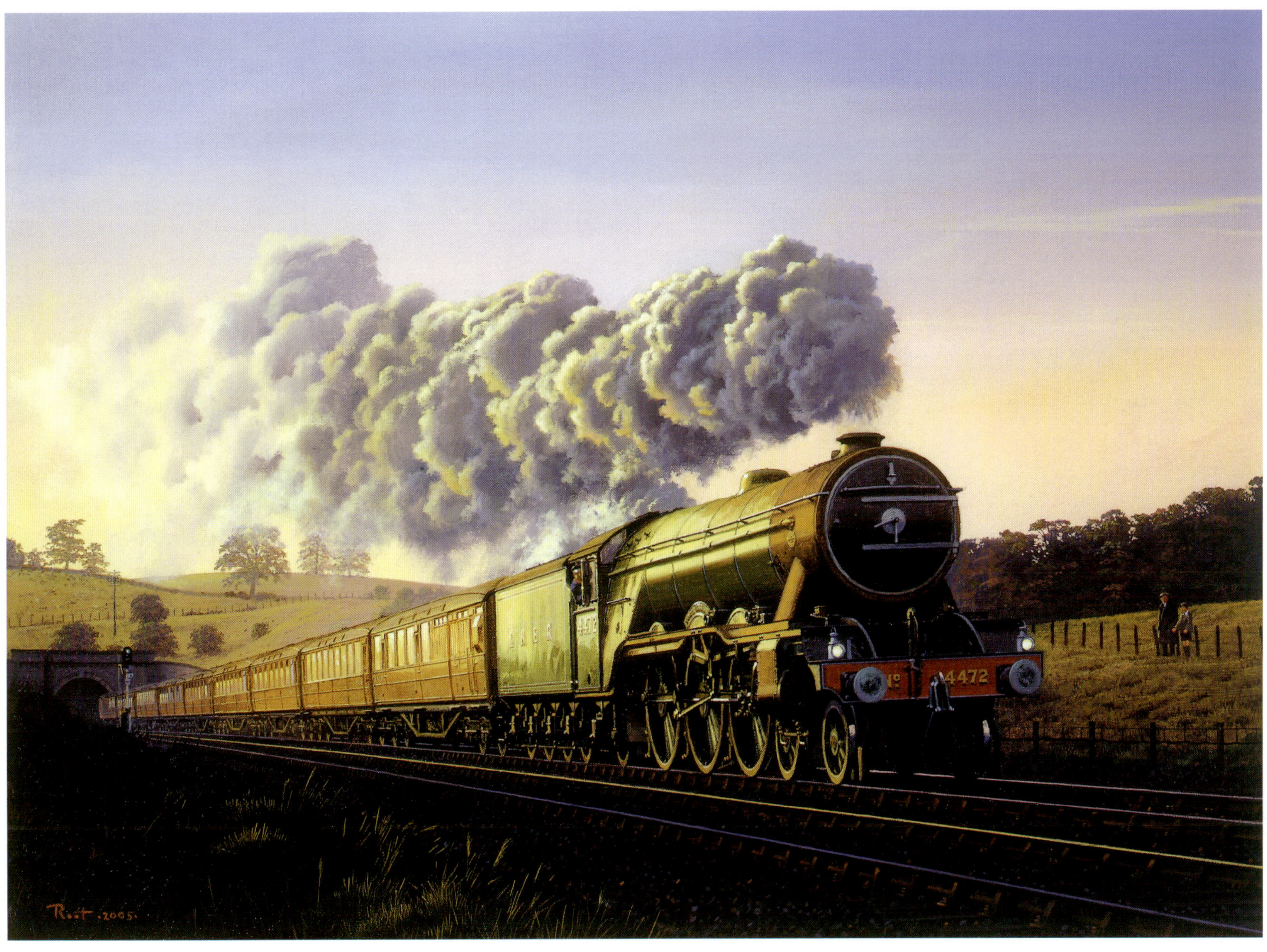

Cutting Edge of Steam

Painted 2003

This interesting picture shows a typical scene from the 1920s when wood was a vitally important commodity for all manner of building and manufacturing, and the harvesting of trees was an important part of the rural economy, and one which was treated with great care. Stewardship and respect were needed for such a valuable resource. Manually-operated cross-cut saws would be used to fell the trees. The metallic whine of the saw and the muted clanking of the traction engine driving it would disturb the wildlife in the area. In this picture the team operating the saw consists of five men. Three are positioning the timber to be cut, one drives the traction engine, and one is spare – perhaps the foreman. All are quite neatly dressed, and no attempt is made to wear close fitting clothing despite the quantity of unguarded machinery. The scene is something of a Health and Safety nightmare, with a large unguarded saw blade, and a lengthy belt driving it. There certainly were accidents, but on the whole common sense and care prevailed.

Details of the saw can be seen, with the rails let into the ground on which the logs were pushed to and fro. The traction engine is a 1924 7nhp model, built by William Foster & Co Ltd of Lincoln, who were well known makers. The caravan can be seen in detail, and perhaps there is a cook boy inside preparing an evening meal, for the team's routine

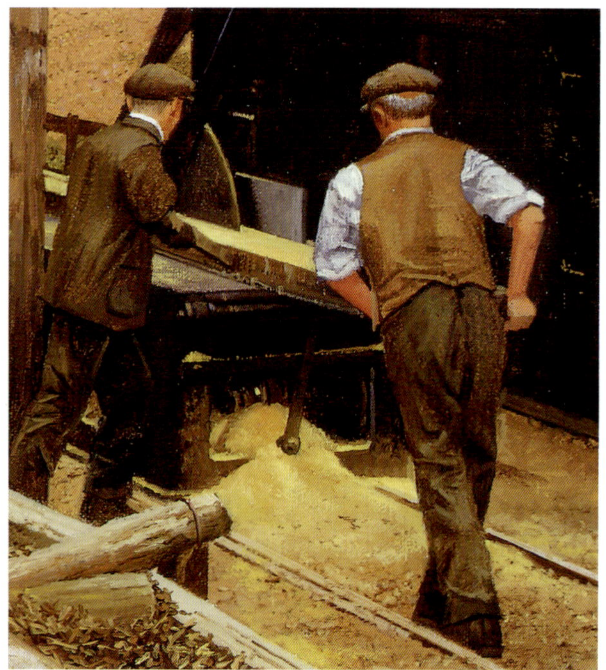

would probably be the same as that for the ploughing team (page 24). The smoke issuing from the stove chimney indicates that something is cooking! The other vehicle behind the saw shed is the necessary water cart, without which no traction engine could run for long. A hand pump was used to transfer water from the cart to the engine, and to fill the cart, often from a handy pond or stream.

Once again, as in all Malcolm's paintings, the detail is remarkable. Look at the bark on the tree trunks in the foreground, and the wooden trough full of wood chippings beside them. The trees in the wood are just beginning to put on their best autumn colours, and you feel you could run your hands through the pile of sawdust beneath the saw bench. There will be birds singing in the background, audible when the saw isn't cutting, and even if you are half a mile downwind of the traction engine the smell of its smoke will be quite unmistakable. I remember it well!

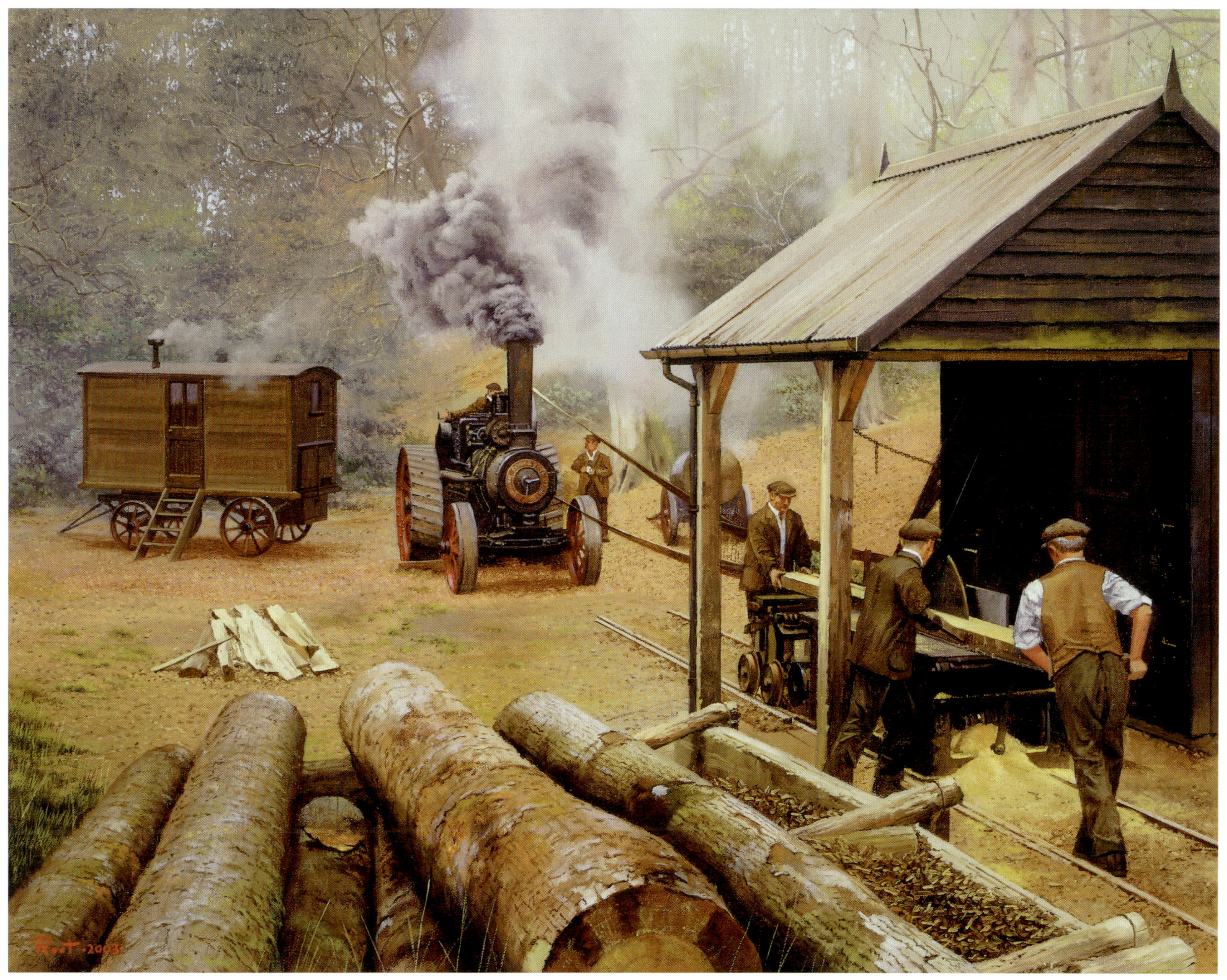

Lynton Evening
Painted 1995

This striking scene not only depicts what was one of the most beautiful railways in the country, but the Lynton & Barnstaple Railway could also claim to be the most significant narrow gauge railway in Britain. The line was opened in 1898, to link the two towns of Lynton and Barnstaple in North Devon. The distance was about 20 miles, and the gauge chosen was 1ft 11½ inches. The railway shared Barnstaple Town station with the London & South Western Railway, and then followed the valley of the river Yeo past Chelfham and Bratton Fleming, before climbing to Blackmoor Gate and following the higher ground to the terminus at Lynton. Passengers for Lynmouth could descend using the cliff railway, and thus return to sea level. The three places mentioned all had stations on the line, as did Wooda (now Woody) Bay, and later halts were added at Snapper, Paracombe and Caffyns. The railway passed through unspoilt wooded and hilly North Devon countryside, and the impressive viaduct at Chelfham, where the railway crosses a valley, still stands today and is the largest structure on any narrow gauge railway in the country. Pilton Yard, just outside Barnstaple, was the location of the locomotive and carriage depot, and there was also a signal box sited there. In 1923 this railway became part of the Southern Railway, and was in use until closure in 1935. I suppose that by then cars were powerful enough to climb Porlock Hill!

When the line was first opened, the directors had bought three Manning Wardle 2-6-2 tank engines, which were named *Yeo, Exe* and *Taw* after local rivers. When a fourth engine was needed, there were delivery problems from the original supplier, and the locomotive was built by Baldwins, of North America, and named *Lyn*. After the Southern Railway assumed control, a fourth Manning Wardle Tank was added, and named *Lew*. (Presumably after the river not the impresario!). Passenger and goods stock were built by the Bristol Wagon & Carriage Works Co.

Now exciting developments are taking place. A lively preservation society is in existence, and already stations have been bought back, and the viaduct at Chelfham repaired. Fortunately most of the route of the railway remains intact, and some rolling stock is being restored. It seems likely that through the efforts of devoted and hard working enthusiasts trains may again run on this notable narrow gauge line. The website for the association gives a great deal of interesting information.

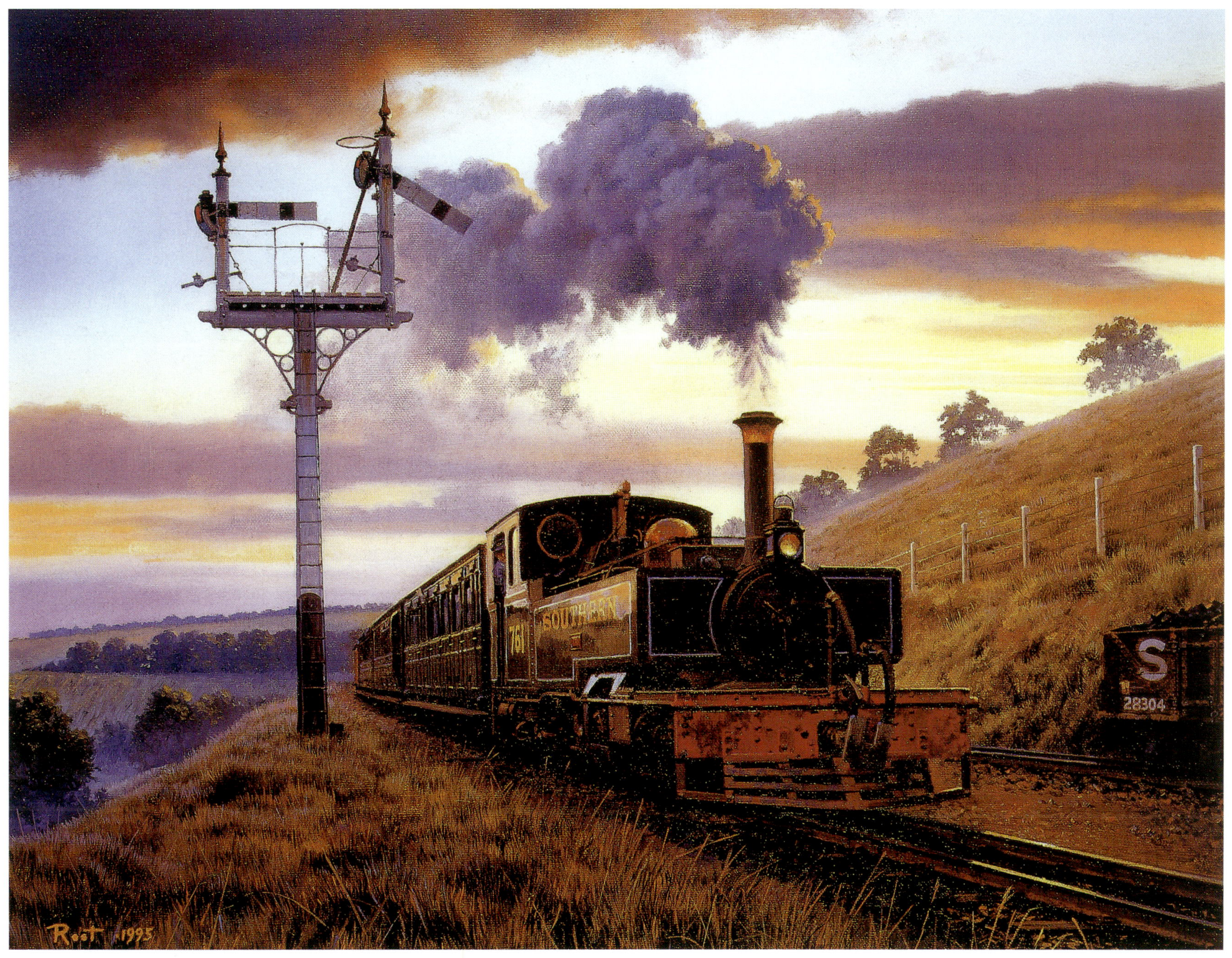
SOUTHERN
761
S
28304

Rigid Six

Painted 2003

This painting tells a story which is very relevant to our pageant of transport. The company Fisher Renwick was founded in 1874, but in those days land transport was mainly by rail. They operated a fleet of coastal steamers based first in Newcastle and then Manchester, with regular services to London. This was quite satisfactory except that goods still had to be delivered from the docks to their final destination, and the company was quick to appreciate that with the development of goods transport, and improvements to roads, there was another way. As the twentieth century unfolded, Fisher Renwick began to invest in a fleet of lorries to run in parallel to their steamers. At times the two could operate as a team, the lorries delivering the ships' cargoes to the eventual customer. This development was taking place all over the country, and a variation is beautifully chronicled in R. Delderfield's *Swann Saga*. It was a very important period for the whole transport network, and in the end road transport came out as the main solution to the carriage of goods.

The Scammell Rigid 6 was the ideal vehicle to tackle such work. The company G. Scammell & Nephew had been established as coachbuilders and repairers at Spitalfields in London in 1837, the year that Victoria became queen. The company flourished during her reign, but after the First World War they began experimenting with lorries, and in 1921 exhibited their first 7½ ton articulated lorry at the Olympia Motor Show in that year. It was received with much interest and orders followed, so a new company, Scammell Lorries Ltd, was set up and moved to new premises at Tolpits Lane, Watford, to provide more space. The first 6-wheel tractor was produced in 1922, and from the beginning the company specialized in heavy haulage vehicles.

Scammell Lorries produced the Rigid 6 shown in the painting in the early 1930s, and it proved to be a strong and reliable vehicle, able to carry heavy loads almost anywhere. Meanwhile Scammell also produced a range of rugged military vehicles, including a tank transporter, artillery tractor and recovery truck. The odd one out was the very successful 'Mechanical Horse' with its three-wheel tractor and amazing manoeuvrability, which could be found in almost every station yard. Two of my favourite Dinky Toys were the recovery tractor and the Mechanical Horse with its detachable trailer. Scammell Lorries was eventually swallowed by British Leyland, although it survived longer than many other companies, while Fisher Renwick became part of the mighty British Road Services.

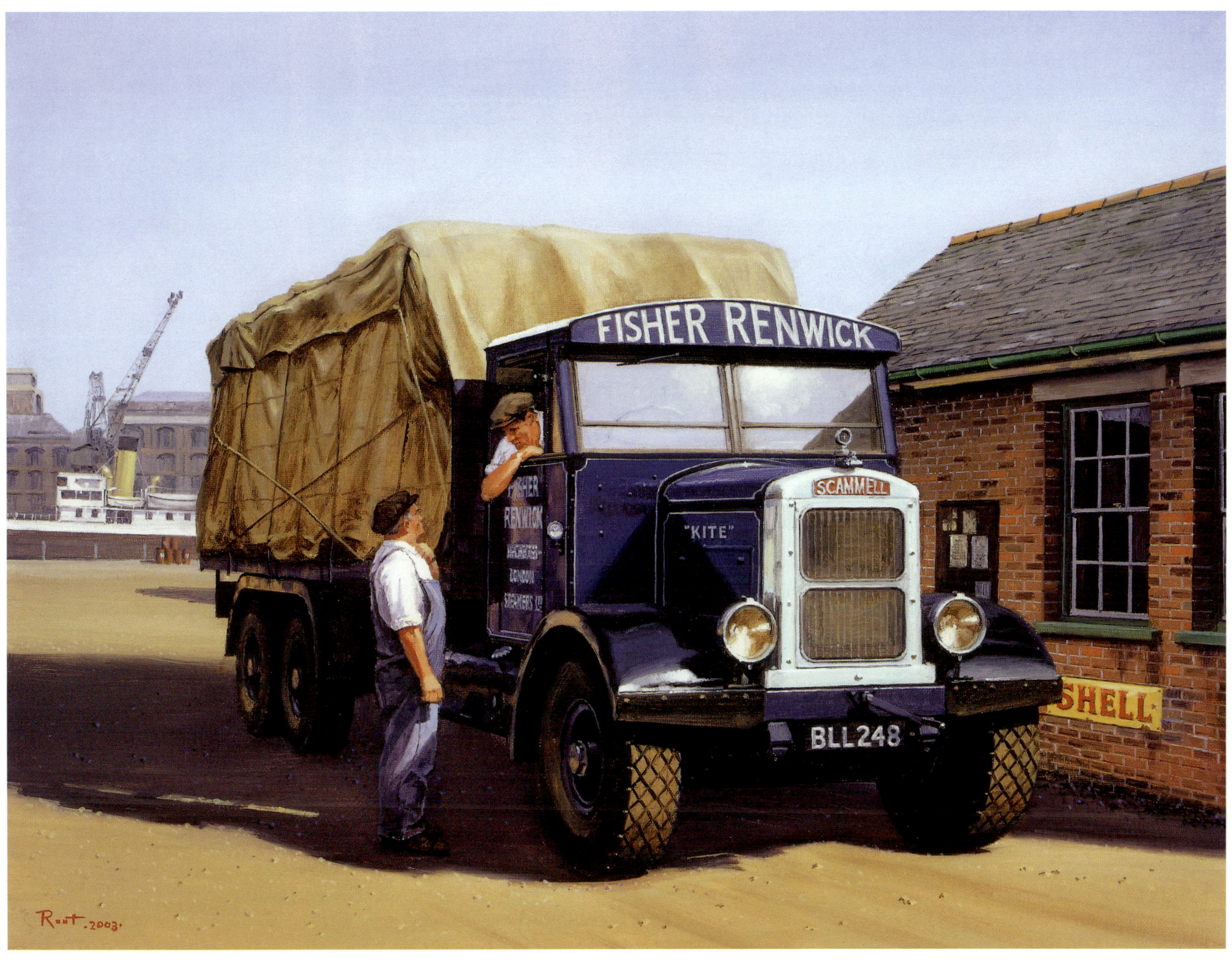
FISHER RENWICK
SCAMMELL
"KITE"
FISHER
RENWICK
LONDON
BLL 248
SHELL
Root. 2003.

Flushing Continental

Painted 1986

This is a typical scene from the great days of the London & North Eastern Railway, as a boat train arrives at the imposing station at Parkeston Quay, Harwich, around the year 1938. War has not yet engulfed Europe, and the passengers here will be going to or coming from the Continent. The train shown in the painting is the 'Flushing Continental' boat train, and the steamers they connected with were owned by the Dutch Zeeland Steamship Company. This steamship line had transferred from Folkestone to Harwich as their English home port at the beginning of 1927 to provide a daytime service only. The LNER provided the boat trains to take the passengers on to London Liverpool Street. The locomotive headboard and carriage roof boards were of simple design, but the train did include Pullman restaurant cars. The down train left London at 9.30am to connect with the ferry, and the up train left Parkeston Quay at 6.55pm and reached Liverpool Street at 8.38pm. The service was, of necessity, discontinued during the war, and when it was reinstated in June 1947 it was renamed 'The Day Continental' because the steamers used the Hook of Holland as their Dutch port, and not Flushing.

In the picture the train is hauled by B12 class locomotive number 8572. This class was originally designed by S.D. Holden for the Great Eastern Railway, and called the 1500 class. Because of the severe size and weight restrictions on the Harwich route a 4-6-0 design was settled upon. The class was notable for having two inside cylinders, and being of modest power due to the size of the boiler. They weighed a total of 101 tons. A distinguishing characteristic was the placing of the rear driving wheel almost underneath the cab. Many of the B12 class were rebuilt by Gresley in the early 1930s, and they continued in service for many years, despite the competition from much newer locomotives, thus demonstrating what a good basic design had been achieved originally. This particular locomotive is now preserved on the North Norfolk Railway, and can be seen in perfect condition going about her daily duties as a reminder of the great days of steam.

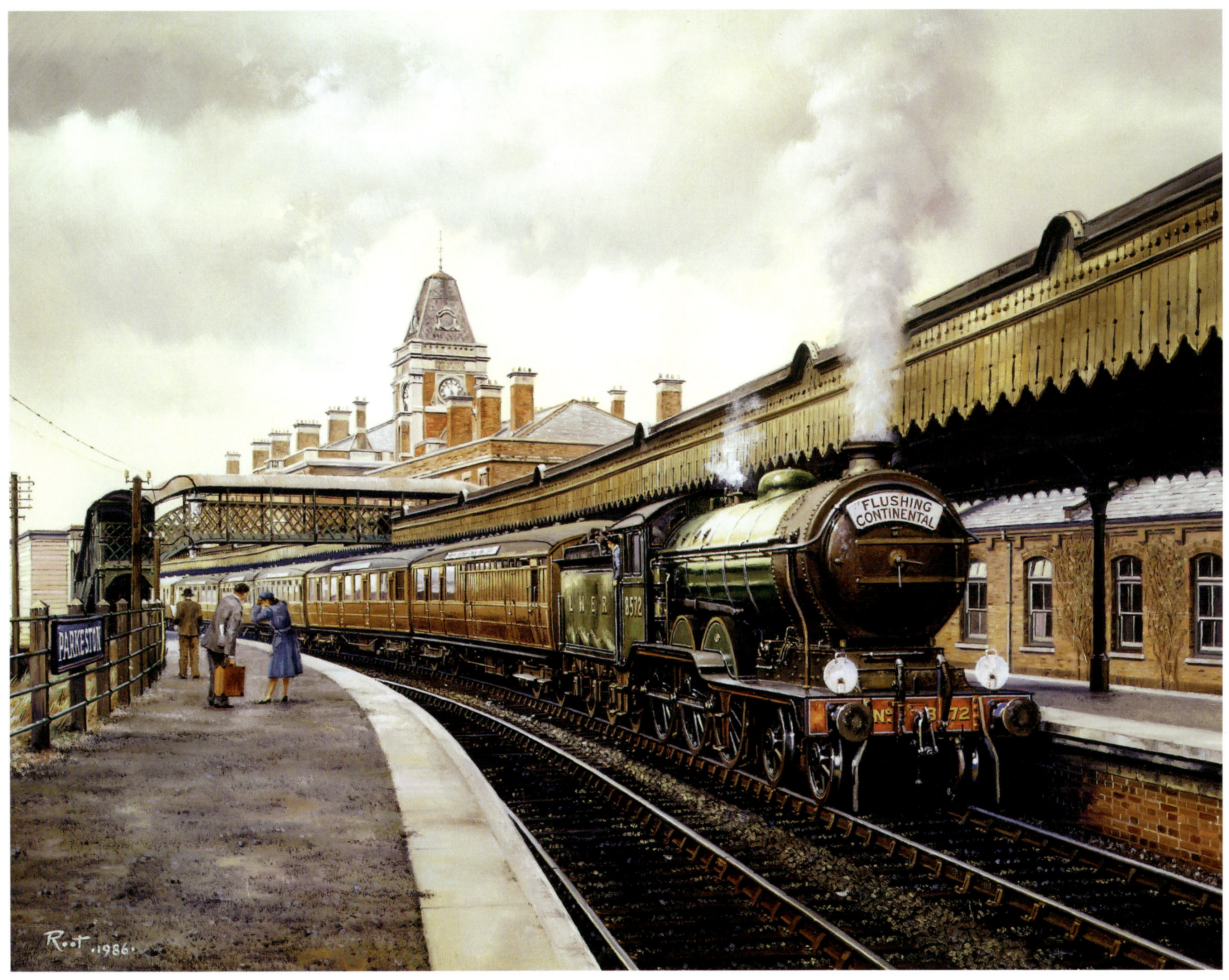
PARKESTON
FLUSHING
CONTINENTAL
L N E R 8572
No 8572
Root .1986.

Sunderland Trams
Painted 2004

The lowest crossing point on the River Wear in County Durham was always an important place, and in the Middle Ages the monastery of Monkwearmouth was built on the north side of the river. The land to the south of the river, ('sundered' by the river), became 'Sunderedland', and in due course Sunderland. In 1719 Sunderland became a separate parish, and eventually it expanded and swallowed up Wearmouth in the north. In 1796 a cast iron bridge, with the longest span in the world at 236 feet, was built to carry the coast road across the river, and this was replaced in 1929 with the steel girder bridge which dominates the scene in Malcolm's painting. Today this bridge still carries all the road traffic from the south up to South Shields and Tynemouth.

Sunderland established its first trams in 1900. This was the period when steam, petrol, diesel and electricity all vied with each other to be the means of power for road vehicles. Electricity boasted a number of advantages: cheapness, lack of noise, cleaner emissions, and easier maintenance of motors. Providing the power was the drawback however, and both overhead wires and electrified centre rails had their problems. Further, as seen in the picture, the tram rails took up a good deal of space in the road, and as other motor traffic grew in volume space became very important. In Sunderland motor buses appeared before the end of the 1920s, and the trams were finally withdrawn in 1954. Here, in a scene from the early 1950s, trams number 24 and 97 pass one another.

Sharing the magnificent bridge are two other vehicles. Seen on the left is the ubiquitous Morris 8, of pre-war design, which we shall meet in the next painting. Beyond Tram 97 is a Commer truck I think, but I am open to correction. In the 1950s a lot of people still had satisfactorily functioning legs, which accounts for the large number of pedestrians on the bridge, and the small amount of road traffic. There was also a wonderful view to be enjoyed on a sunny day!

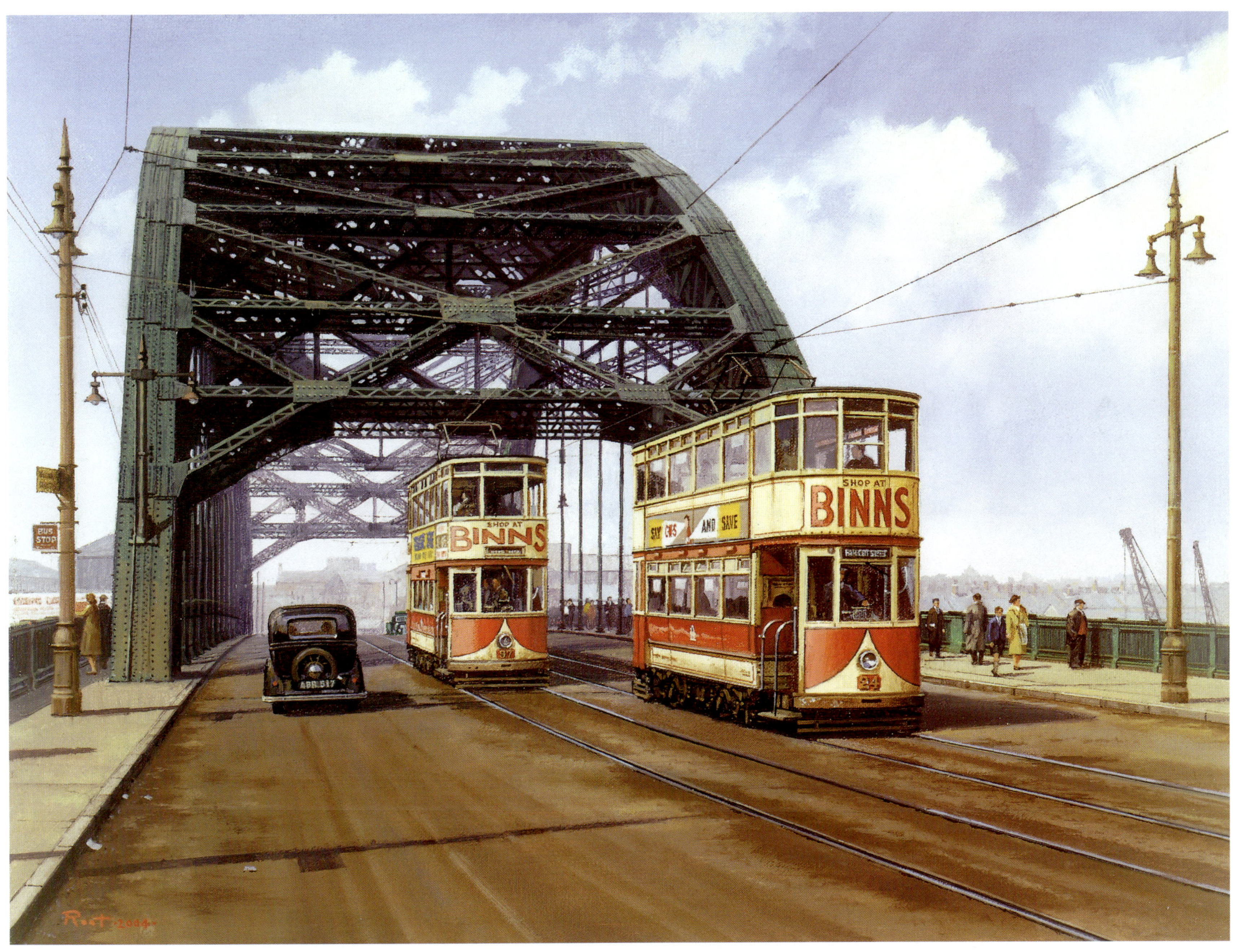

BUS
STOP
SHOP AT
BINNS
SHOP AT
BINNS
SAY CWS AND SAVE
FALCON STREET
Root 2004

North Essex Winter

Painted 1995

This is about as chilly as it gets, and writing in September it sends shivers down the spine! Halstead is a picturesque old town in north Essex, and happens also to be Malcolm's home town, so he is familiar with every view. Here brightly-lit and snow-covered shops stand in front of the church, and the traffic has been heavy enough for the snow on the actual carriageway to melt, while the pavements remain pretty treacherous. We have all experienced just such a day, and the artist has caught the onset of evening to perfection.

Only one car is about, and that is a series I Morris 8, in the usual black livery. The series I dated from 1935, and was the Morris answer to the Ford Model Y, providing affordable family motoring to a wide public. It was a comfortable four-seater, or you could cram a number of children in the back if necessary. As it was a 2-door saloon they couldn't escape! It was powered by a 22.5bhp 918cc sidevalve engine, driving through a 3-speed very non-synchromesh gearbox. My own 1935 tourer had to be cosseted a great deal on a day such as this, or it remained dead to the world. Blankets and muffs, under-engine heaters and kettles full of boiling water were all necessary to encourage it to start!

During the dread winter of 1962–63 a student friend in Cambridge had just such a Morris 8 as depicted here, and one cold icy morning the poor thing, which sat out in the street in all weathers, refused to start. The owner, who was not mechanically minded, recognized that there were no available hills, and no one to tow-start it, so a push-start was the only option. He rounded up three large friends, all members of the college rugby team, and bade them scrum down behind the car. They then proceeded down the street, and every so often the driver let in the clutch, the car shuddered to a halt, and the rugby players sprawled in the icy road. The players were fit and tough, and after a few of these episodes, gave it all they had got. Suddenly the little car shot off down the street, and they sprawled for the last time. I thought they had achieved success, but the car gradually came to a stop, and eventually we discovered that the problem was that the driver had been trying to start it in first gear, and as a result the differential gear wheel had been stripped of all its teeth! Man had triumphed over machine, and I think the poor little Morris was sold for scrap by a disillusioned owner.

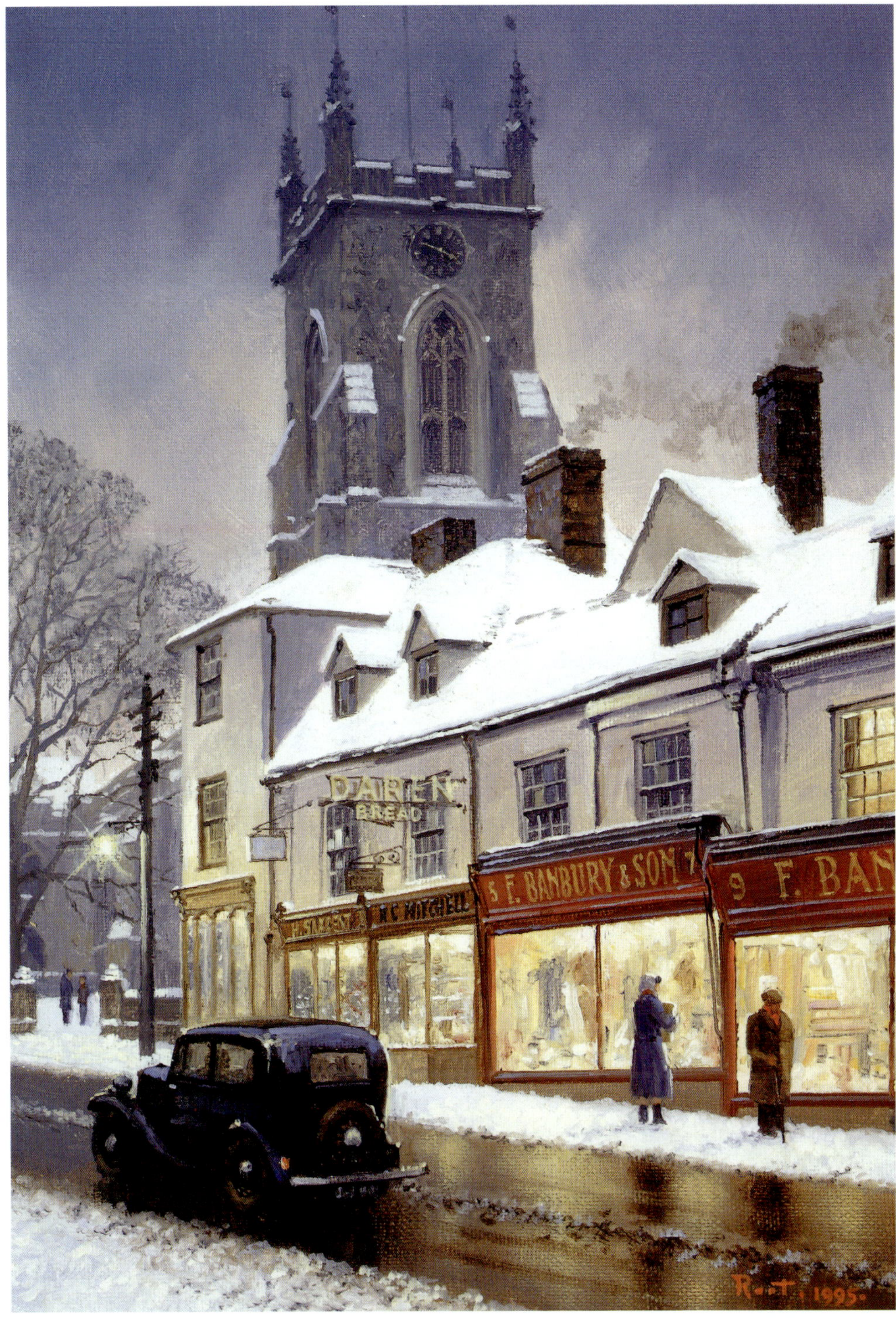
DAIREN
BREAD
W.C. MITCHELL
E. BANBURY & SON
9 F. BAN
Root 1995.

Sir Douglas

Painted 2004

This beautiful painting shows a late summer country scene, with the corn ready for harvest and a hint of autumn showing in the leaves on the trees. Centre stage is a splendid Fowler road locomotive, which was built in 1920, and was the A9 type rated at 7nhp. Its rear wheels are shod for road as well as cross-country work, and it has a large cab roof to give its crew protection in bad weather, something which must at times have been very welcome. It carries a hosepipe to enable it to pump its tank full of water from a convenient stream or pond. The hosepipe would have a filter on the end to prevent passing fish being sucked in!

This picture is the precursor to 'Cutting Edge of Steam' on page 28, and again reminds us how important wood was in the pre-plastic days. As early as the seventeenth century laws on forestry were passed, requiring anyone felling woodland to leave at least twelve large trees per acre to continue growing and maturing, so that sufficient timber would in the future be available for shipbuilding and roof beams.

Moving large heavy tree trunks was a real challenge before the arrival of the heavy machinery we have today. In this instance it looks as though the wood has been dragged to the side of the track from the spot where it was felled, either using a traction engine, with winch if necessary, or else horses. Then came the tricky operation of loading the trailer. Heavy baulks of timber would be used to make a ramp, and the logs rolled using chains, either pulled by the engine or using a winch if fitted. It was a case of 'stand well clear' for if something slipped some very heavy and lively trunks would roll a long way! Getting the upper trunk, usually a lighter one, into position was especially challenging, but the crews were very skillful. Once the side bars were in place, and the trunks secured with chains, the load was a very safe one and could be towed off to the sawmill. Unloading was a lot easier, and could be left to gravity, provided a long stop was in position!

I watched a giant machine in a Welsh forest some years back. It gripped the upright tree, sawed through its base, stripped the side branches and the top off, and placed the clean trunk flat on a nearby trailer ready to be towed away. Each tree took about a minute to process, a far cry from our scene here.

I hope it will not be misconstrued when I say that I know Sir Douglas intimately! I do however know this road locomotive very well as I helped in a small way with the restoration. My job, along with others, was to paint and line the engine. It was no surprise then that sooner or later brush would be put to canvas to show the engine in a natural setting doing what it was designed to do. Reference for the engine was no problem at all, but the wagon and logs were fabricated.

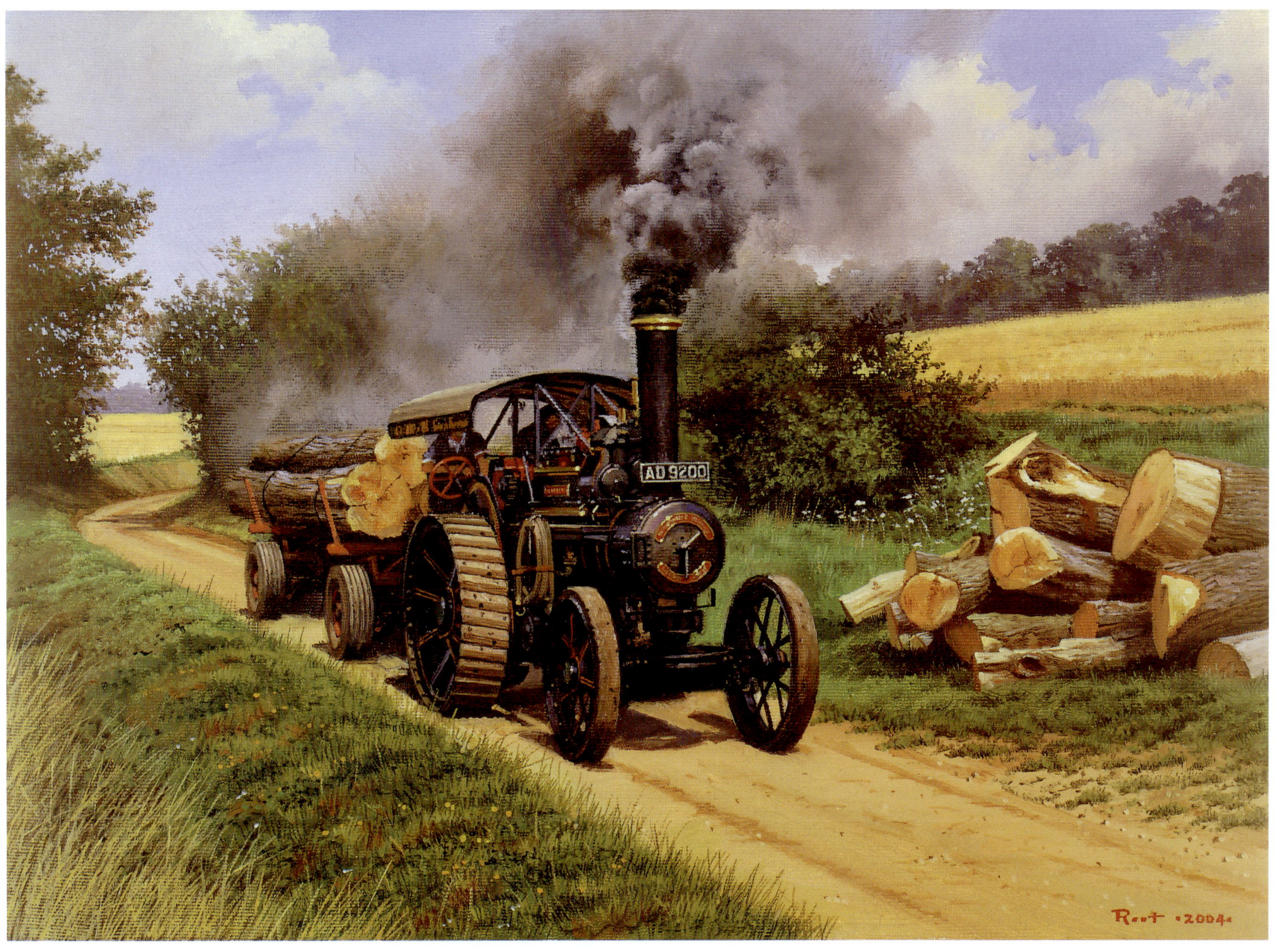

Station Yard

Painted 1988

A very evocative picture which reminds us of the importance of the town station yard in the past, even if the scene is not one of frenzied activity! A local train on the Colne Valley Railway has made its usual stop at Halstead Station on a calm and sunny day. The locomotive letting off steam is one of the J15 0-6-0 tender locomotives which worked this line for many years. They were designed by T.W. Worsdell as far back as 1883, and as they weighed only 68 tons were ideal for a railway with weight restrictions on many bridges. The tender also helped to spread the weight of the locomotive, though having to run 'tender first' due to lack of turntables was very cold in winter. Spraying the coal with water helped prevent the crew getting dust in their eyes when running tender first.

Waiting for whatever the train may bring are two people and three vehicles. The bicycle is a true 'sit up and beg' model. I had a Hercules which looked exactly like it. It reminds us what an important means of transport the bicycle was for many people. G.E. Cook & Sons of Halstead, who were brewers and wine and spirit merchants, have sent their van to collect an expected consignment. Cooks had a very thriving business with their fine ales, and in the mid 1920s had to replace their horse-drawn drays with a fleet of motor vehicles, of which two were Dennis vans. The type shown was probably a 30cwt van powered by a four-cylinder 18 hp engine which continued in production until 1933. It had rather old-fashioned spoked wheels, and solid tyres, so the liquid cargo must have arrived pretty shaken up! Its brakes also left a good deal to be desired, but at least it didn't get punctures.

The most interesting vehicle in the picture is also probably the newest. It is an Austin 7 Box saloon, long wheelbase model, and was introduced in 1932. Herbert Austin was already well established as a car manufacturer at Longbridge when he produced his first Austin 7 in 1922, largely thanks to the genius of a young designer called Stanley Edge. Before this small cars tended to be made of bits and pieces often including motorcycle engines. Herbert Austin was determined to produce a properly designed small car, and this was achieved with a small four-cylinder engine. For the next 19 years the car was successfully developed, beating off competition from Morris and Ford. The 1932 Box saloon, shown here, was one of the most successful, and was able to compete with many larger cars. Brakes and clutch took a bit of getting used to, and being overtaken by huge lorries in the 1990s has left an indelible mark on my memory! I was eventually persuaded to part with my own Austin 7 named 'Delilah' (because she tempted me), when one day we were overtaken by a very sedate funeral procession. My wife insisted on something that would go a little faster! The Austin 7, and the rivals it inspired, brought family motoring within the reach of thousands of people, and caused a revolution in the history of motoring.

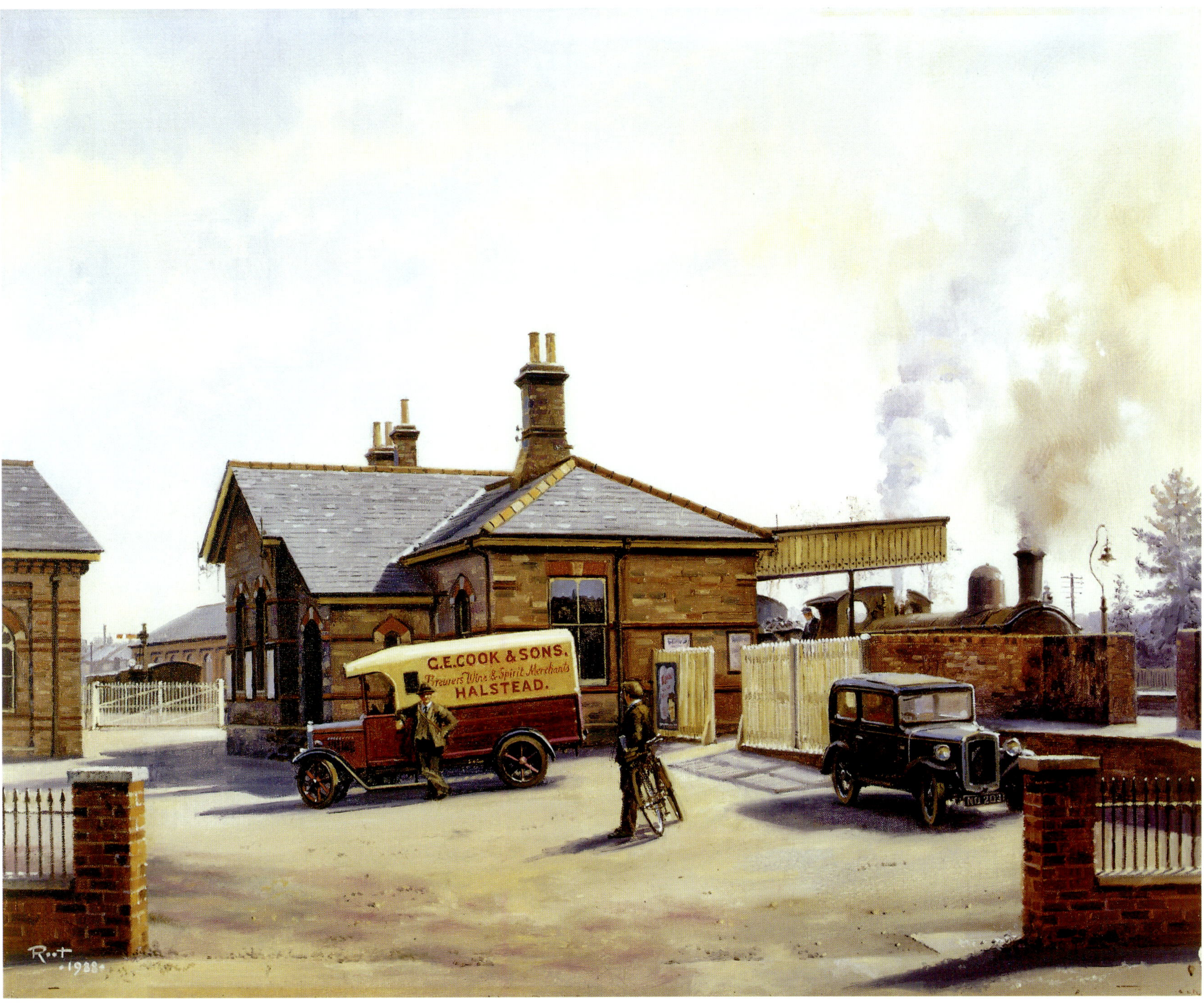
G.E. COOK & SONS.
Brewers Wine & Spirit Merchants
HALSTEAD.

Dunkirk Evacuation

Painted 1997

The British defeat which culminated in the evacuation from Dunkirk between 26 May and 4 June 1940 was the result of an almost total misreading of both German intentions and their overwhelming military power. Fortunately for the British, the Germans were also amazed by the speed and success of their advance, and they sat down to wait for the surrender of the British army which they had penned against the channel coast, and for the expected decision by the British to sue for peace as a result of their defeat in the field.

The British have never been very good at surrendering, or allowing their island to be invaded. Also, being an Island Race, they saw the sea at Dunkirk not as the ultimate disaster, but as an opportunity for escape. During the following days an incredible flotilla of small ships, manned by a cross section of the population with a common experience of boating in its many forms, crossed and re-crossed the channel to bring back nearly 340 000 exhausted and often wounded soldiers. About 850 vessels took part, from destroyers down to cabin cruisers and fishing boats, and about 100 ships were lost, 30 of them Royal Navy ships which were pivotal to the operation. They ran the gauntlet of the Luftwaffe in the air, artillery from the shore, and mines and E-boats at sea. It was a staggering operation, and seen as a miracle at the time. It did much to stiffen the morale of the British nation and prepare them for what was to come.

The paddle steamer *Sandown* was built by William Denny of Dumbarton and went into service in 1934. She was 216 feet long and about 29 feet beam, with a gross tonnage of 684, and was powered by triple expansion diagonal steam engines. She was owned, together with several other steamers, by the Southern Railway and employed for the ferry crossing from Portsmouth to Ryde on the Isle of Wight. At the outbreak of war in 1939 *Sandown* was requisitioned by

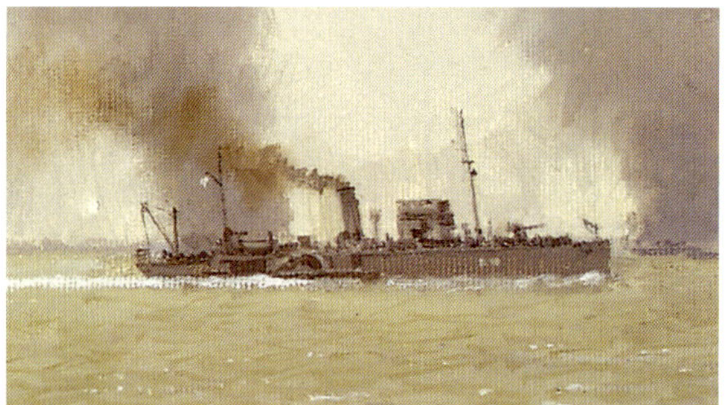

the Admiralty and assigned to the 10th Minesweeping Flotilla, based at Dover. She was fitted with a forward gun, as shown in the painting, and proudly flew the White Ensign. The ship behind her is the paddle steamer *Medway Queen*. After the invasion of Normandy four years later, the *Sandown* was moved to duties on the river Scheldt, returning to her peacetime duties in the Solent when the war ended. She was finally withdrawn from service and broken up for scrap in the mid 1960s. A sad ending to over 30 years of service.

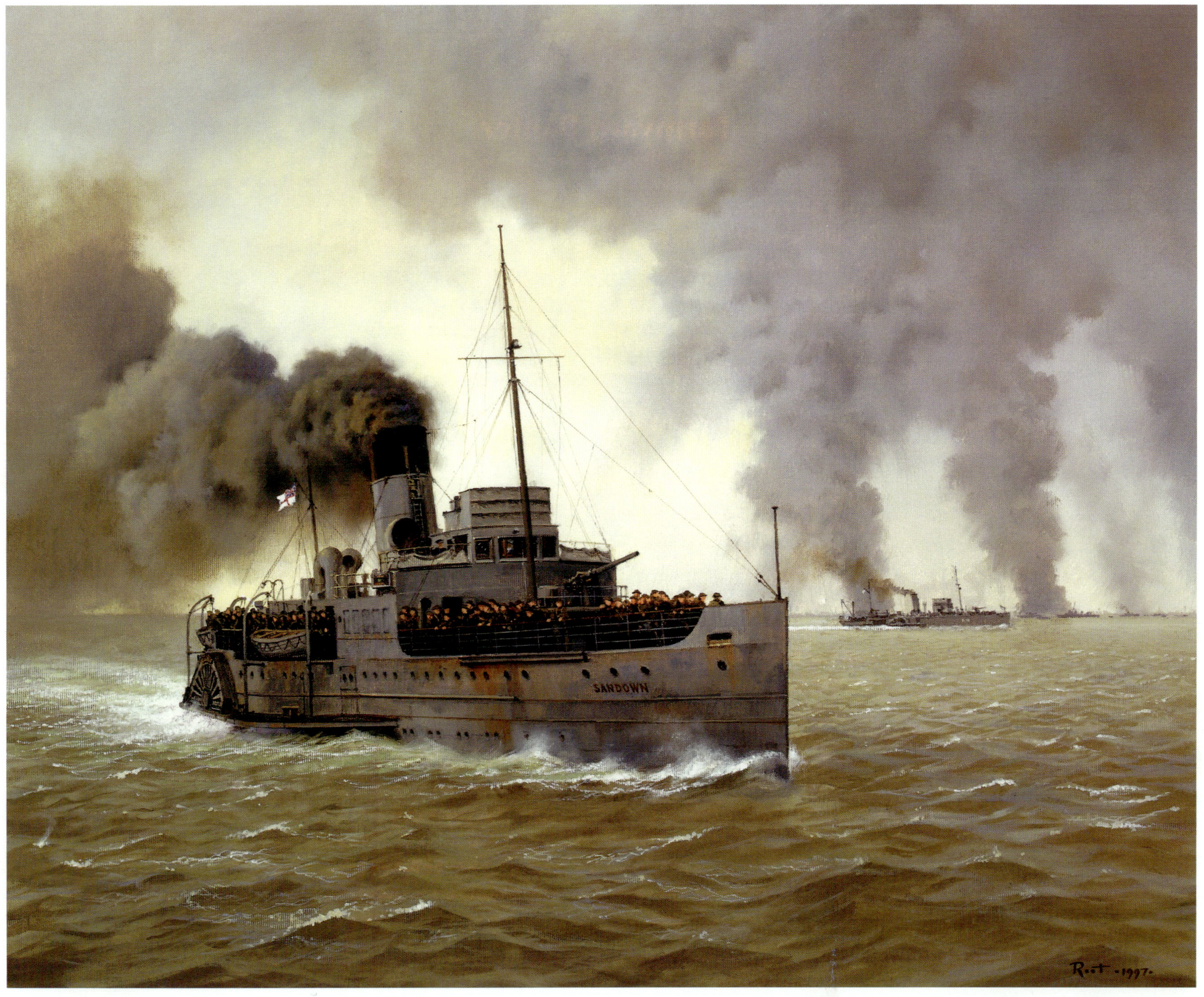
SANDOWN
Root ·1997·

Farmyard Banter
Painted 2006

Farm transport has always divided into two categories, that which is used for the actual work on the land, and that used to link the farms to the outside world. In the past it has been usual for the farmer to supply the former machinery, sometimes sharing larger items such as combine harvesters with neighbours. The road vehicles used to bring in supplies to the farm, and take away farm produce were often supplied by outside contractors, as in this case. The Great Western Railway employed a large fleet of vehicles to link up with their stations, including the Mechanical Horse (page 92), other lorries in many shapes and sizes, and also char-a-bancs in places. Here we see a specialist cattle lorry, which will be loaded at the farmyard and then driven to the nearest station, where special loading facilities are provided to transfer the animals to a cattle truck with the minimum possibility of escape on the way. I do remember it happening at least once; several bullocks charging down a station platform certainly keeps human passengers on their toes, or confined to the waiting room!

The cattle lorry in Malcolm's painting is a Thornycroft built vehicle, probably adapted from the well known 'Sturdy' model. Thornycroft built a comprehensive range of lorries, and they ranged from the Nippy, which appeared in many different forms, to the Mighty Antar Tank Transporter used by the army. They were very straightforward and dependable vehicles, with a loyal following of owners, though the company never rivalled the large concerns like Austin, Bedford and Leyland. The GWR monogram roundel on the lorry was the last such emblem in use before nationalization, so we can date the scene about 1947. Behind the lorry can be seen two very traditional types of farm buildings: the stone built barn and the newer Dutch barn, which is more of a shelter for stacked hay or straw. I would guess that the farmer and his staff have paused to have a drink of something before the hot work of loading the cattle begins.

Whilst waiting, the lorry driver has stopped work for a few minutes to pass the time of day with a local who has been down to the further end of the farm with his dog. The Sunbeam Talbot 10 Tourer, which had a very good cross country ability, was first introduced in 1936, and is a typical pre-war design. This particular car, which is now my own, was first registered in East Sussex in 1946. It has the disc wheels of the post-war models, where the pre-war cars had wire wheels. Beneath the quite imposing bonnet is concealed the Rootes Group Hillman Minx 10hp sidevalve engine, which gives the 1 ton car very slow acceleration! The car is, however, a relatively comfortable four seater, and as much of the body is made of aluminium, it does not suffer the rust problems of many sixty-year-old cars. I much enjoy driving her round the quiet Suffolk lanes.

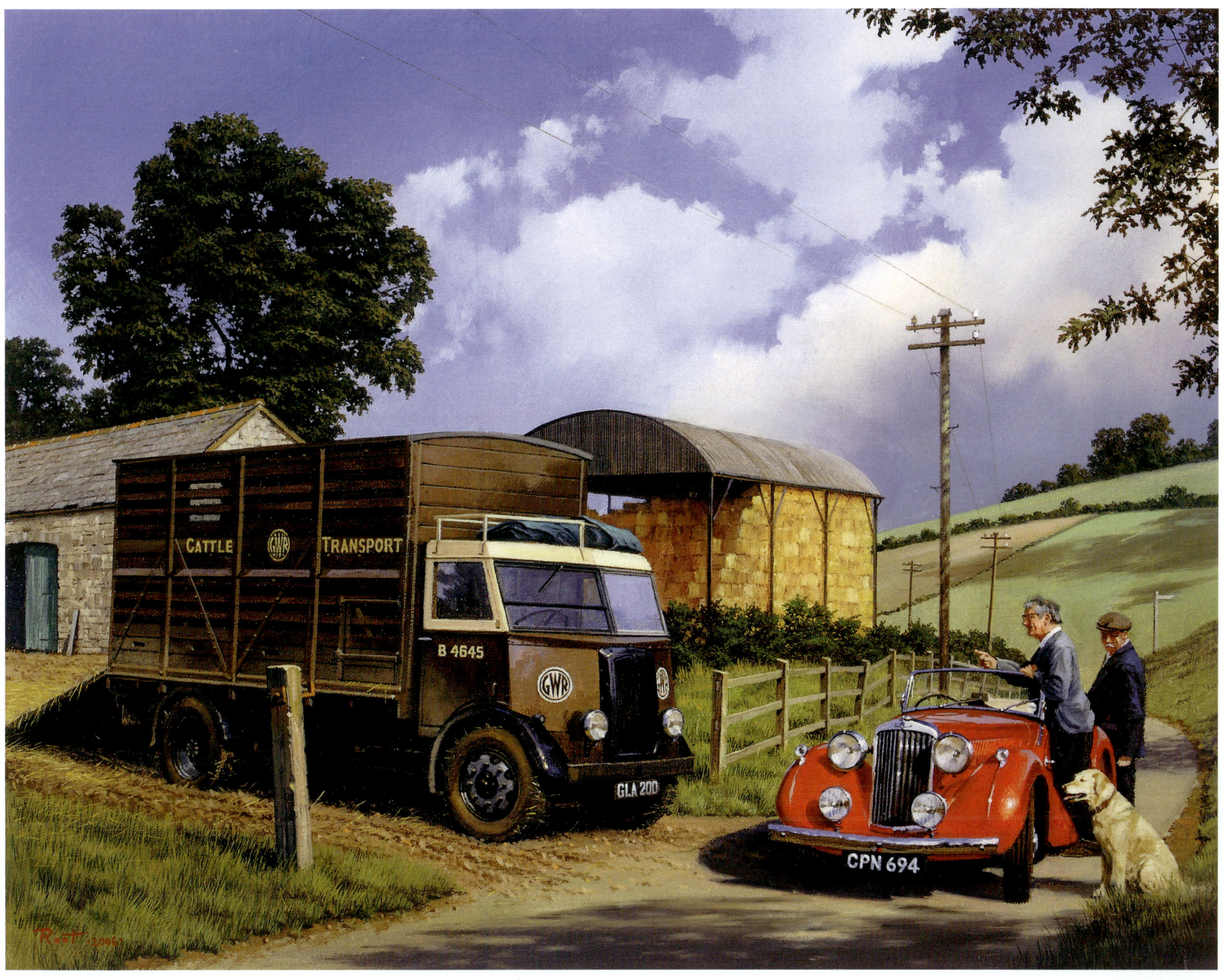

CATTLE GWR TRANSPORT
B 4645
GWR
GLA 200
CPN 694

Road Versus Rail

Painted 2003

Chelmsford is the county town of Essex, and is well placed geographically as a centre of communications for the county. The main A12 road passes through it, or did until a bypass was built, and so does the main railway line from London to Norwich . Roads also fan out to the north and north-west.

We have three main types of transport shown here. The char-a-banc (page 18) has been developed in time with a demand for increased public transport, and the Eastern National Dennis Ace bus is a result. This twenty-seater was first produced in 1936, and is a typical pre-war design, though this scene is set in the later 1940s, and the bus continued in service until replaced by a model with a larger passenger capacity in 1949. Such buses plied between Chelmsford and many surrounding villages, bringing people in for shopping, to market, and to catch the train to travel further afield.

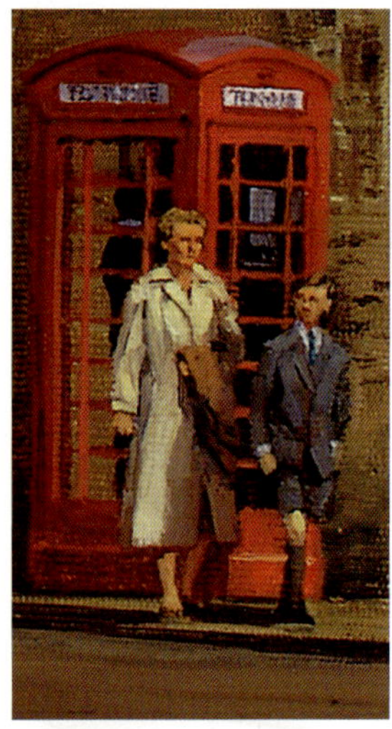

While the bus has an Essex registration number, the lorry originally came from Manchester. This vehicle is a Leyland TSC Beaver, dating from 1934. In 1907 Leyland Motors Ltd offered both steam and petrol powered lorries, all over 3½ tons. Their real success came with the 'RAF Type' produced during the First World War, of which over 6000 vehicles were sold up to 1926. Badger, Buffalo, Bison, and Bull were names given to a range introduced in 1929 by Leyland. The Beaver, shown here, first hit the roads in 1934. In the world of transport these became household names. From 1933 diesel engines were also offered as an alternative, and it is likely that this Beaver had a 32.4hp diesel engine fitted.

A boat train hurries through Chelmsford station on its way to Harwich. Chelmsford station would be a regular stop for most of the express passenger trains on this route, however, as it still is. It is headed by a London & North Eastern Railway Gresley designed B17 (see page 86). This one is called *Naworth Castle* although the nameplate is obscured by the bridge.

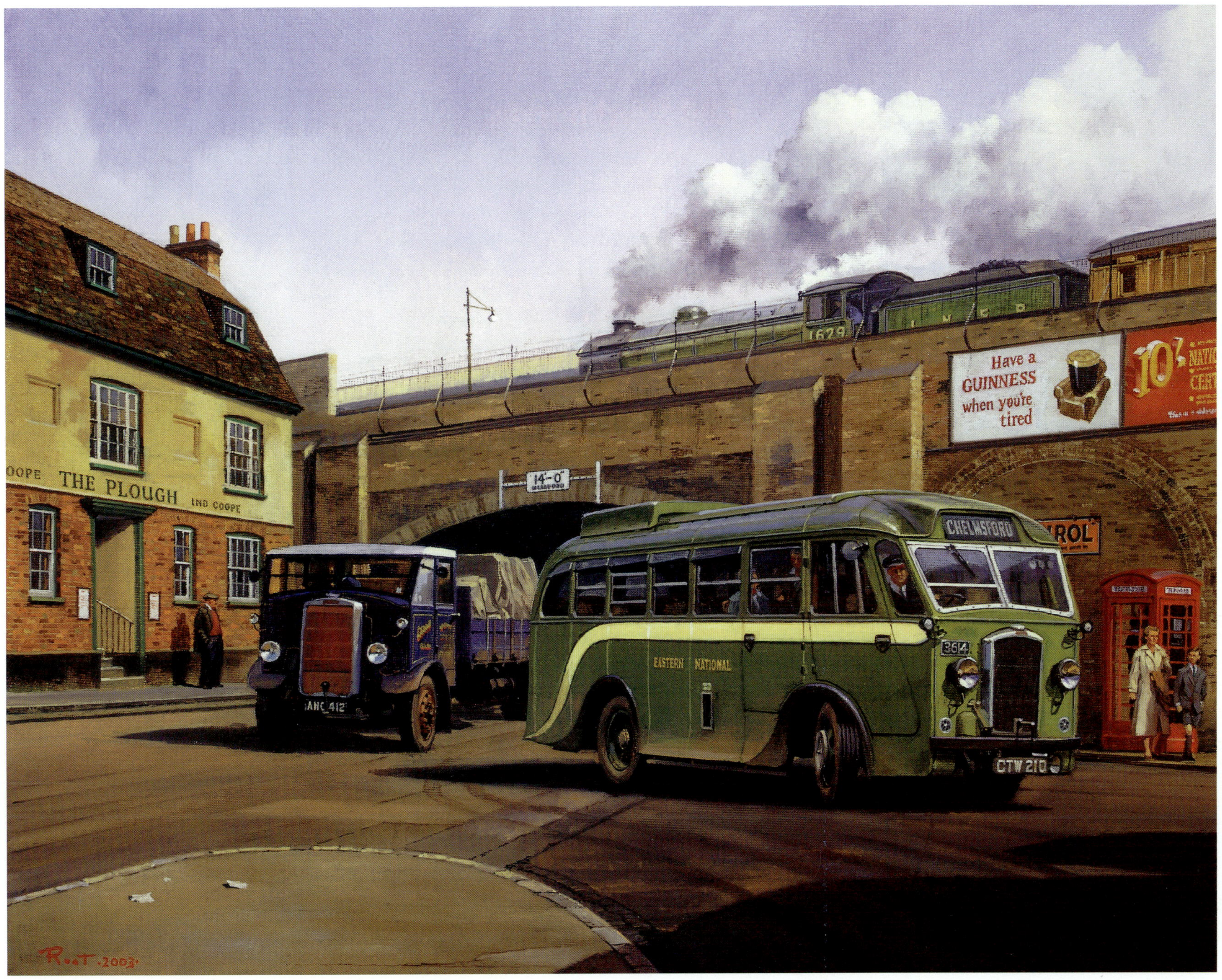
THE PLOUGH
IND COOPE
Have a
GUINNESS
when you're
tired
14'-0"
CHELMSFORD
EASTERN NATIONAL
364
GTW 210
Root 2003

Old Workhorses

Painted 2004

This striking painting marks another important transitional point in our pageant of transport. We will shortly see the ubiquitous tractor (page 54) which will challenge the role of the working horse which had reigned supreme for several centuries since the days of oxen. Now, at the end of the 1940s, with the after effects of the Second World War still being felt, the working horse is bowing out, retained already more for sentimental reasons on a scattering of farms. The recent war has produced a rapid development in all types of vehicles, and many are suitable for use in the countryside, as seen by the number of ex US Army Jeeps now with farmers at the wheel, which in turn would inspire the invention of the Land Rover. A new generation of tractors sounded the death knell of horse-drawn implements.

No one can deny that the horses were magnificent animals, as demonstrated by this quartet of Clydesdales. This breed can be dated from the middle of the eighteenth century, and they naturally originated in Clydesdale, or present-day Lanarkshire. It has been a very popular and successful breed, with many horses being registered with the Clydesdale Society down the years. The white faces, and white lower legs with 'feathers', are typical of the breed. It is interesting to remember that many breeds of working horses derived from the war horses which carried knights of old into battle. They were bred to carry heavy loads, and that wasn't just the armour!

The other 'old workhorse' is nearly 40 years old, and is overtaking the plough team along the adjacent embankment. This ex Great Eastern Railway F5 class tank engine was designed by S.D. Holden, and first introduced in 1911. It has served all the days of the London & North Eastern Railway, and is now in the first British Railways livery, before the logo was added to brighten things up a bit. The tall chimney and forward-placed dome were distinctive features. This locomotive no 67211 and its counterparts were a welcome and familiar sight in the London suburbs and rural East Anglia.

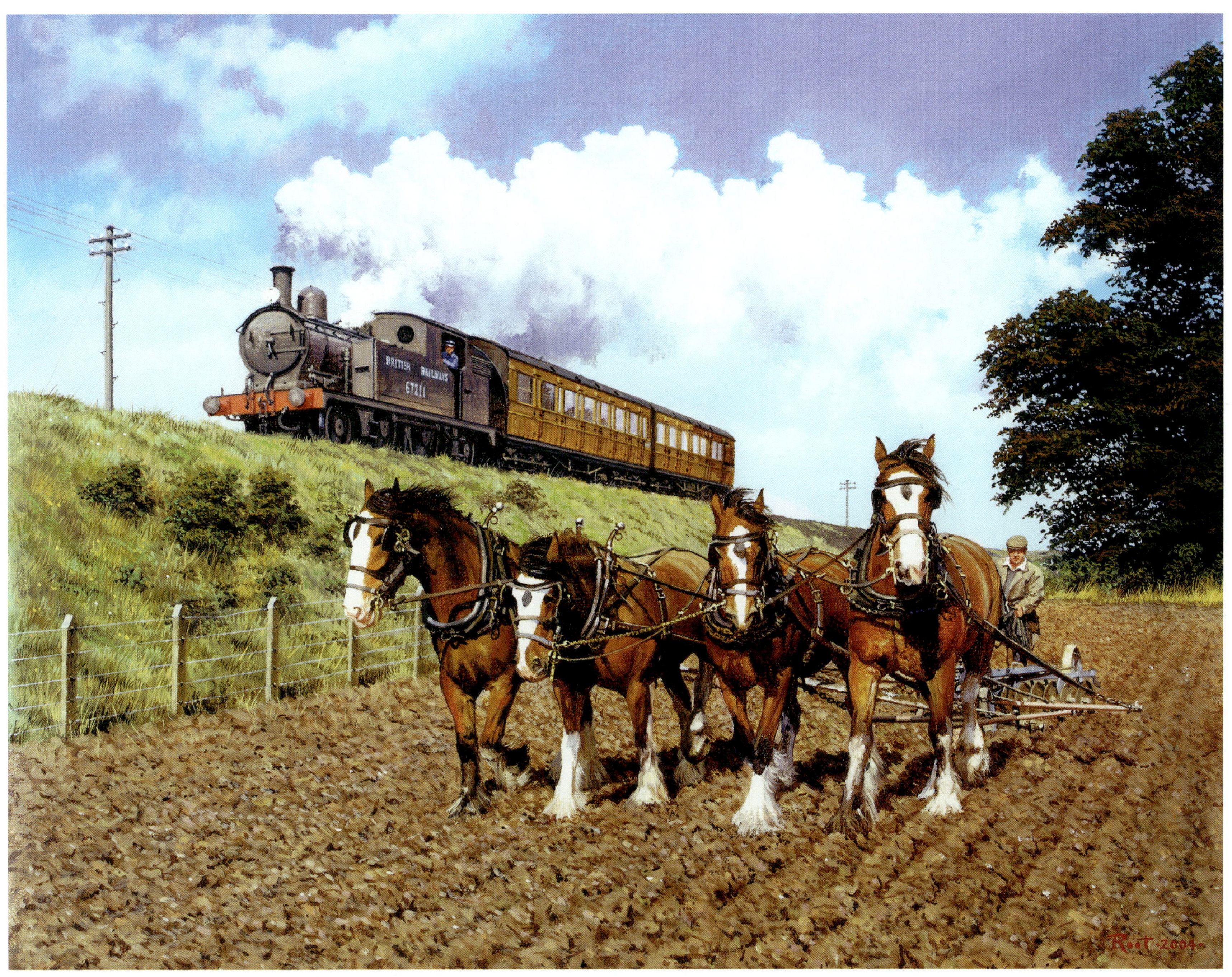

Caronia
Painted 1998

Caronia was one of the provinces of the Roman Empire, and thus the name was used for a famous Cunard two-funnel liner launched in 1904. She was soon outclassed by the *Mauretania* and *Aquitania*, but still had a long and distinguished career, often working as a relief liner for transatlantic crossings. After World War II Cunard took the brave decision to build a new liner, which would be designed essentially for cruising to all parts of the world. This liner, the 'new' *Caronia*, was built by John Brown's shipyard on the Clyde, and was launched by Princess Elizabeth in 1947. She was 715 feet long, with a tonnage of 34 274 tons. She was a lovely ship, built on traditional lines, but she did have the largest funnel of any ship in the world, including the *Queen Elizabeth*, and at times this acted as an unwanted sail and caused minor mishaps to the ship in a high wind! After the *Caronia* was fitted out she did her speed trials off the Isle of Arran, as shown in this lovely painting, before sailing in late 1948 for Southampton.

In a time of post-war austerity the *Caronia* received great publicity, and was nicknamed Cunard's 'Green Goddess' because of the colour of her hull. A glimpse of her career is seen in the details of her first Great African Cruise in early 1950. Starting from New York, she carried a crew of 682 to look after around 560 passengers, who paid between $2400 and $20 000 each for the 73 day cruise. Total earnings for the ship on this one cruise were reckoned to be $7 million. She visited four continents and called at 27 ports. At Cape Town 120 cars were assembled to transport the passengers on sightseeing tours, and passengers visited places like Cairo and Luxor. The *Caronia* offered a level of luxury not known on any liner before, and in a life which spanned nearly 20 years she was a great investment and dollar earner for Cunard and Britain. She was eventually retired by Cunard in 1967.

Those twenty years were to witness a huge change in the pattern of overseas travel, with the arrival of the package holiday, and soon after the *Caronia*'s retirement the appearance of the Jumbo jet, carrying over 400 passengers (page 114). By 1967 few people could afford either the time or money for a ten week cruise, and though cruising remains popular today, cruise liners have become more like floating hotels as they try to compete within the holiday industry by keeping prices down. In 1999 the Cunard Company renamed the Vistafjord liner *Caronia*, but she is now known as *Saga Ruby*.

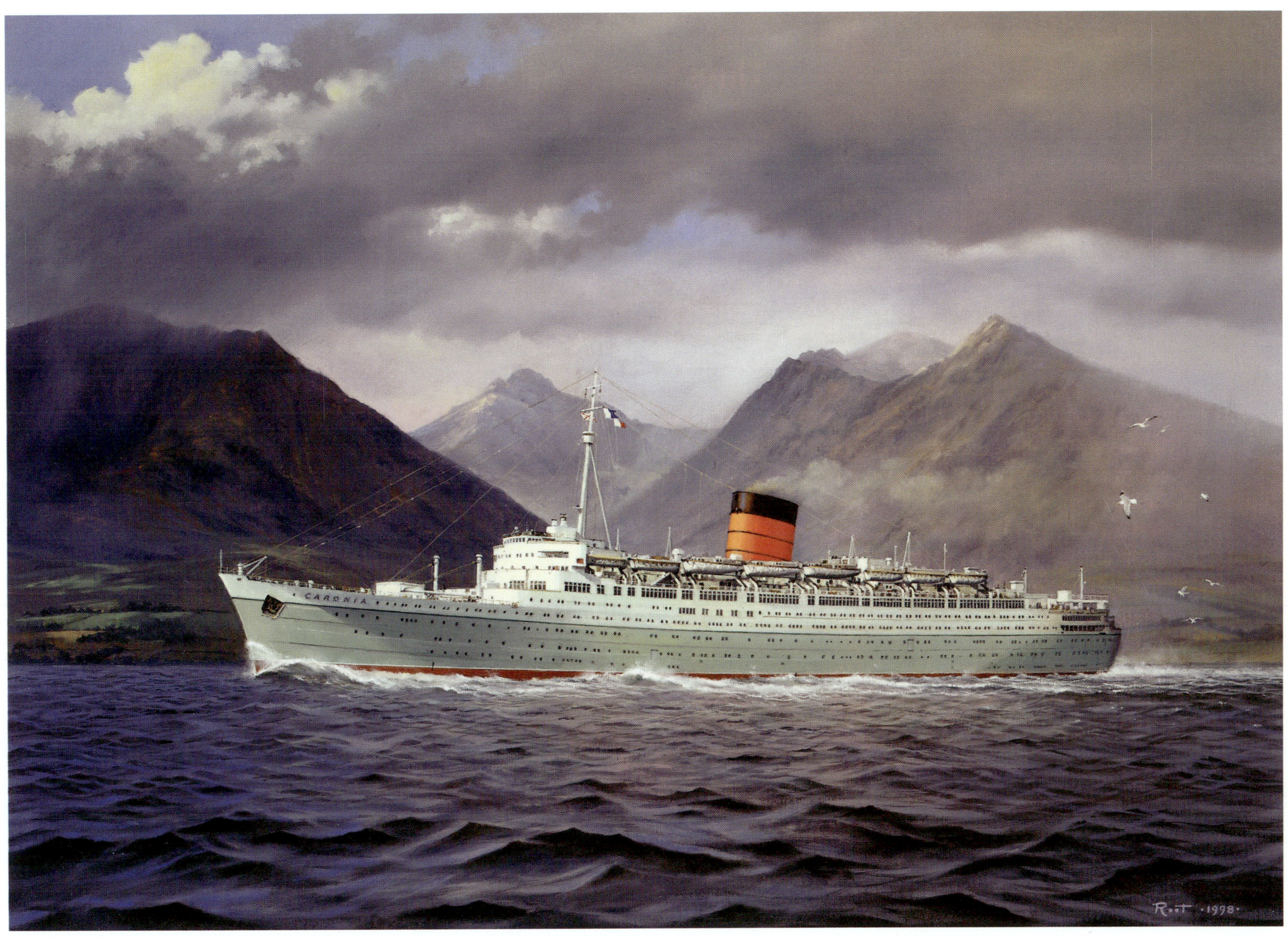

Time for a Rest
Painted 1994

This rural scene is set in a neglected corner of a farmyard. The farm buildings are in need of repair, the cart has not been connected to a horse for some long time, and it does not look as though the Fordson tractor has moved very recently either. This Fordson Major tractor was the post-war development of the first Fordson tractor introduced in the early 1930s, which established Ford's reputation for making farm tractors. This was a bigger tractor, with higher ground clearance, with the designation E27N, and it was introduced in 1945 and powered by a four-cylinder engine which would run on both petrol and TVO (paraffin) once the engine was warm. A later model was fitted with a six-cylinder Perkins diesel engine. The tractor was a very versatile machine, giving the driver good visibility and manoeuvreability, and a significant number of them have been preserved in good working order today.

The rather abandoned appearance of this tractor reminds me of Uncle Ted. He was able to sell his cooperage, which included 8 acres on the Tottenham High Road, and move to North Devon to be a farmer, something he had secretly wanted to do all his life. He had a passion for machinery, but no one had explained to him that it was possible to unhitch an implement from a tractor and substitute another. We counted eleven tractors, all different, on his farm, and each one with its implement was left in the middle of a job where Uncle had got bored and moved on to something else. He bought a new muck loader which took his fancy, then found some muck to load. He then got a spreader and debated which field to spread it over. Finally he had to decide which crop to sow! In the end he was not a very successful farmer, but he was a great blessing to the local agricultural machinery salesman!

Today a restored Fordson Major of this vintage can be bought for up to £3000, and many will be seen at agricultural shows and vintage farm vehicle rallies. Ford continued to develop this relatively simple design of tractor for many years with great success.

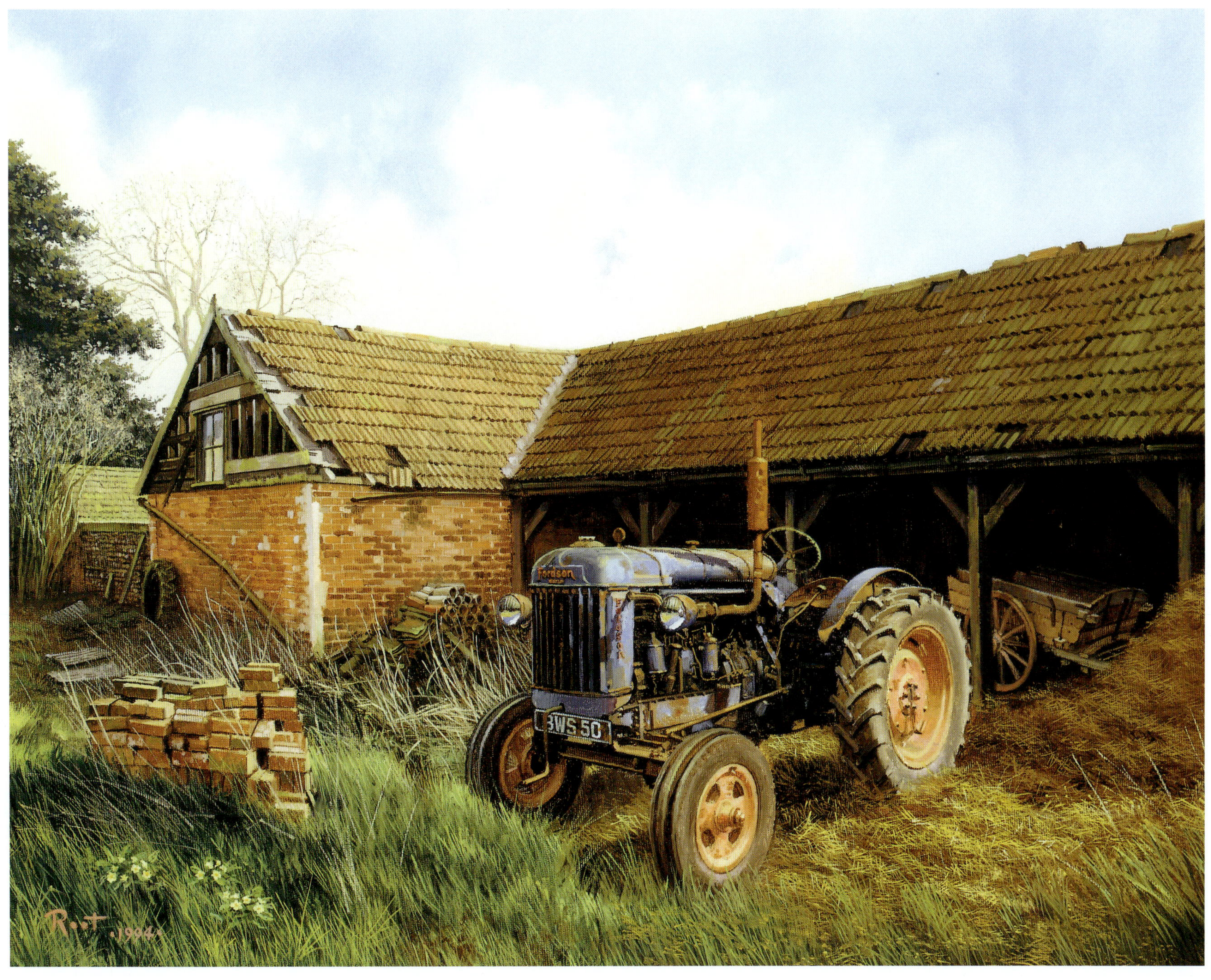

York Roundhouse
Painted 2003

The important and ancient city of York lies almost midway between the capitals of London and Edinburgh, and thus naturally became a very significant place for the railways as they linked the two cities. Not only did York boast a magnificent station (page 94), but also carriage works, marshalling yards, and the locomotive depot with its splendid Roundhouse. This painting perfectly captures the atmosphere where locomotives could pause to rest between duties or be serviced. Three locomotives stand facing the turntable pit, and between them they encompass a lot of LNER history.

The amalgamation of museums at York, Clapham, Swindon and Glasgow during the 1960s meant that larger premises were needed. The obvious place would have been the Science Museum, but they hadn't the space. York was chosen because it had a suitable sight and buildings with rail access, as well as an already thriving tourist industry. The National Railway Museum has been using this splendid building, complete with turntables, since 1975, exactly 150 years since the inauguration of the Stockton & Darlington Railway.

On the left is *Cock o' the North,* but this time the name is on an A2/2 locomotive designed by Edward Thompson, being a rebuild of the distinctive 2-8-2 'Mikado' engine designed by his predecessor, Nigel Gresley. The Thompson Pacifics were easily recognizable as their outside cylinders were set further back than on the Gresley Pacifics. These engines were designed for express passenger traffic and they worked through to the end of steam traction.

In the middle of the group stands a B16, designed by Vincent Raven, and first introduced in 1920. These 4-6-0 locomotives, with a tractive effort of about 30 000lbs, were designed as mixed traffic engines, and 70 of the class were built. Some of the class were rebuilt by Gresley in 1937, and again by Thompson in 1944, thus giving them a long life in service. These two locomotives are a reminder of the way in which steam engines could be updated and given a new lease of life as locomotive design progressed, and the railways produced new power requirements.

The third locomotive is a 2-6-2 V2 class designed by Nigel Gresley and first introduced in 1936. This versatile engine was used for both express passenger and fast freight traffic. It is significant that a total of 184 of the class were built, of which only a few carried names; *Green Arrow* being the first. This impressive group is very representative of LNER motive power over the whole period of that company, and beyond into the British Railways era.

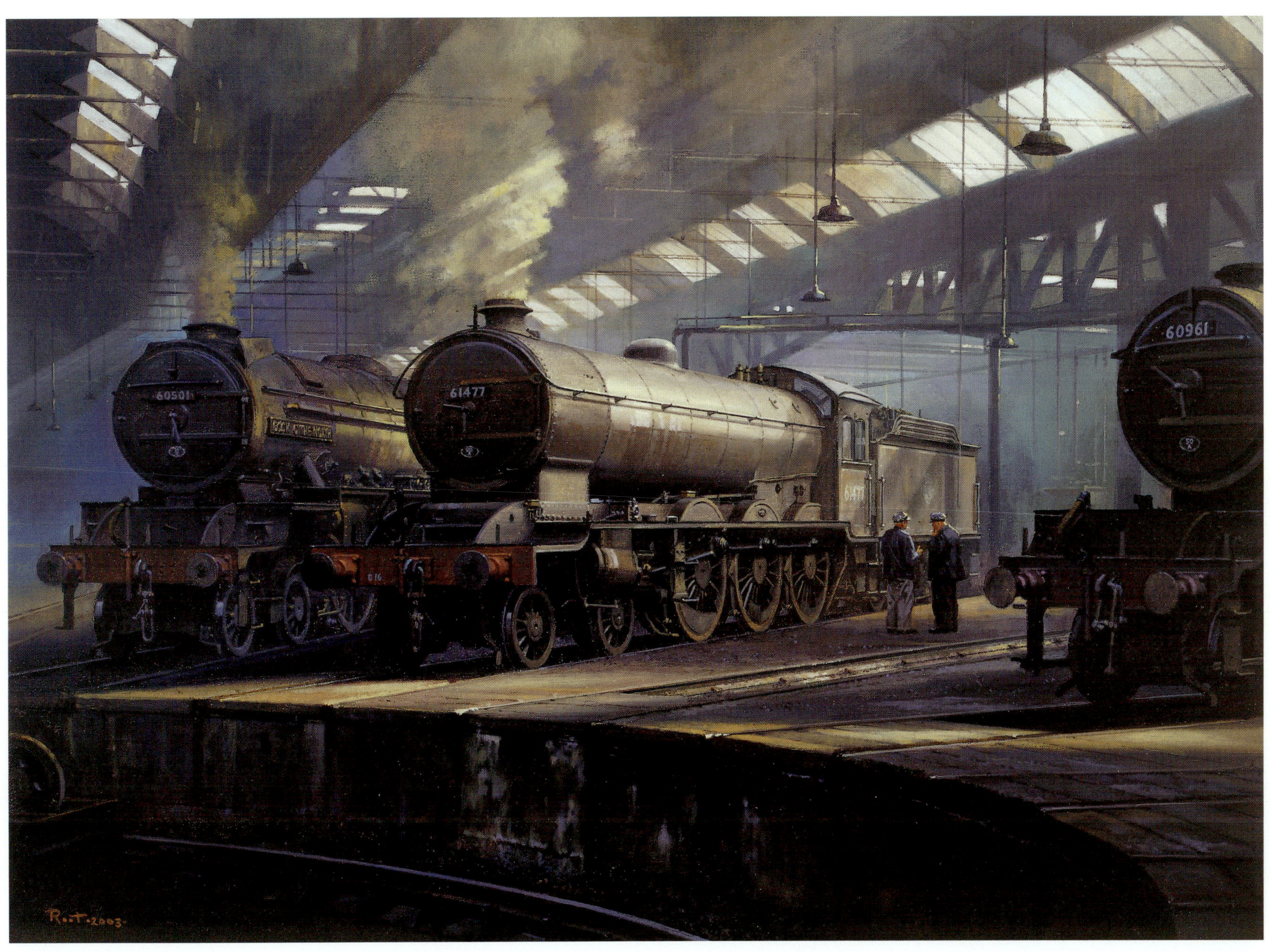

60501
61477
60961

The Quarry
Painted 2002

Once our ancestors discovered the advantages of building with stone, quarrying became a most important industry, and brought with it attendant problems, such as how to transport heavy blocks of stone. However the builders of Stonehenge may have managed, horse-drawn carts, and preferably ships, were the chosen method, and especially the latter until roads were much improved. It was not really until the twentieth century that lorries were powerful and robust enough to tackle this heavy work, and the Bedford S Type, introduced in the 1950s is a good example of the sort of vehicle capable of carrying out these gruelling duties.

The main feature of this lorry is its reinforced cargo carrying space, and in particular the canopy which protects the cab roof. However gently it was loaded it was always going to be subjected to heavy rocks falling from a height of several feet. Bedford lorries were built by Vauxhall Motors at their plant in Luton, and they in turn were a subsidiary of General Motors of the USA. The S Type was a 'no frills' lorry, driving on its four rear wheels, and available with either a petrol or diesel engine. Malcolm has set this scene in Cumberland – modern day Cumbria, and the lorry's registration number is a local one.

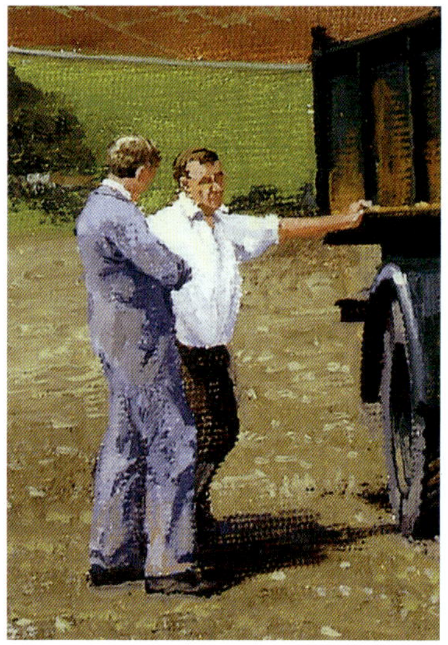

The mechanical shovel in the picture is also an interesting vehicle. It was made by Ruston Bucyrus, and is one of the smallest in their range. The Bucyrus Foundry was established in Ohio in 1880 and produced steam shovels and dredges soon after. By 1894 they had sold 171, and their shovels were used for the construction of the Panama Canal. In 1922 Ruston Bucyrus was formed and they were the leading manufacturers of excavating machinery in Britain. Their largest machines were gigantic 'walking' dragline excavators capable of filling several lorries with one shovelful. The machine shown is much more mobile on its caterpillar tracks, and the shovel empties by slipping the catch at the back, and allowing the contents to fall through into the waiting lorry. The driver, who is doubtless grateful for a breather, had a lot of controls to manipulate in order to do the job smoothly.

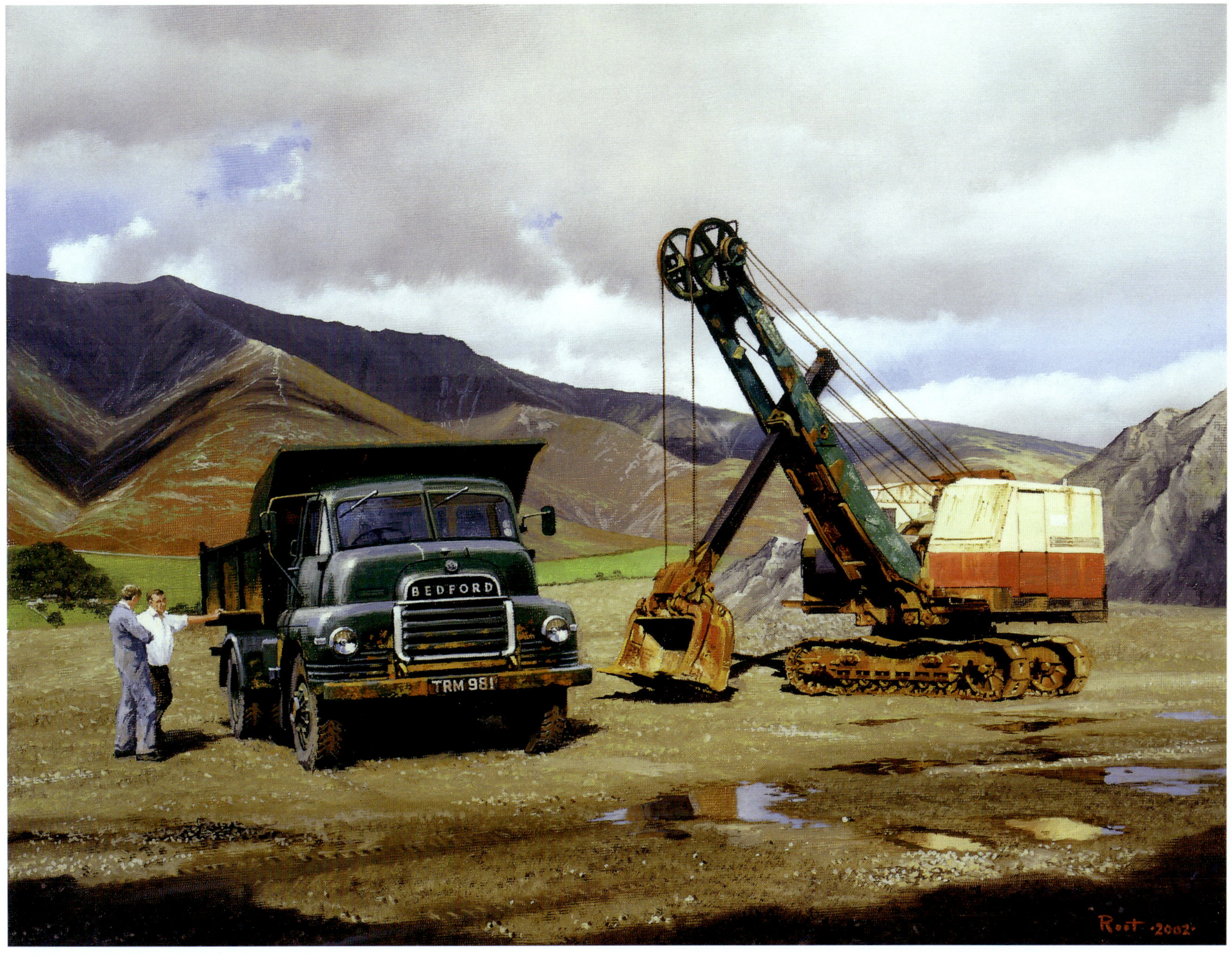
BEDFORD
TRM 981
Root ·2002·

Country Delivery
Painted 2004

What a contrast, moving from an austere Cumberland quarry to a beautiful Suffolk village in high summer! For those who do not know the village of Kersey, the milkman from Country Dairies seems to have stopped his Trojan van just in time. In fact at this point the village street fords the stream at the bottom of the valley, so the ducks are going to have to move out of the way to let the milk pass. Meanwhile two schoolchildren are waved off to school, a housewife in the background takes her newly delivered milk in, and a cat eyes the ducks hopefully and schemes their capture without getting wet feet! There is a small anomaly in the picture which you may be able to detect.

The Trojan van being used for the milk round is an interesting vehicle. Although Trojan was founded in 1913, they did not really get underway until 1923, because of the war, and then the 5cwt van they produced was built by Leyland. It was not until 1929 that they had their own premises at Croydon, and during the period up to the Second World War they produced a range of increasingly large but pretty basic vans. In 1947 Trojan introduced an entirely new design, pictured here, which looked smart and efficient, and was a 15 cwt model. However, it still had the two-stroke petrol engine of the pre-war vans, though a Perkins diesel could be an alternative. The petrol engine made a distinctive 'tonk tonk' sound when idling, which I remember well. Dinky Toys made a model of this van in the 1950s, in six different liveries, which is very collectable today. Once upon a time I had several of them, but they seem to have driven off over the years.

The two other cars in the village are typical for the early 1950s. On the hill up to the church is a pre-war Morris 8 (see page 36) reminding us that it was very difficult to purchase any new car until well into the 1950s. My father got a Land Rover in 1952 because he had ordered a Rover 16 in 1939! In late 1947 the Austin Motor Company produced their first striking post-war design, the A40 Devon. This most successful car was superseded in February 1952 by the Austin Somerset, shown on the right in this scene. Costing £727 when new, and with a 1200cc engine rated at 42 bhp, this attractive saloon could reach 70mph with the wind and tide! Their life was rather short, however, as they were replaced in October 1954 by the very different Cambridge model.

Somewhere not far from this village scene there is a country lane with a similar ford, where I baptized two of my early cars, 'Sally' and 'Jezebel', a Land Rover and Hillman Husky. I even managed to avoid getting my feet wet, to my then girlfriend's disappointment!

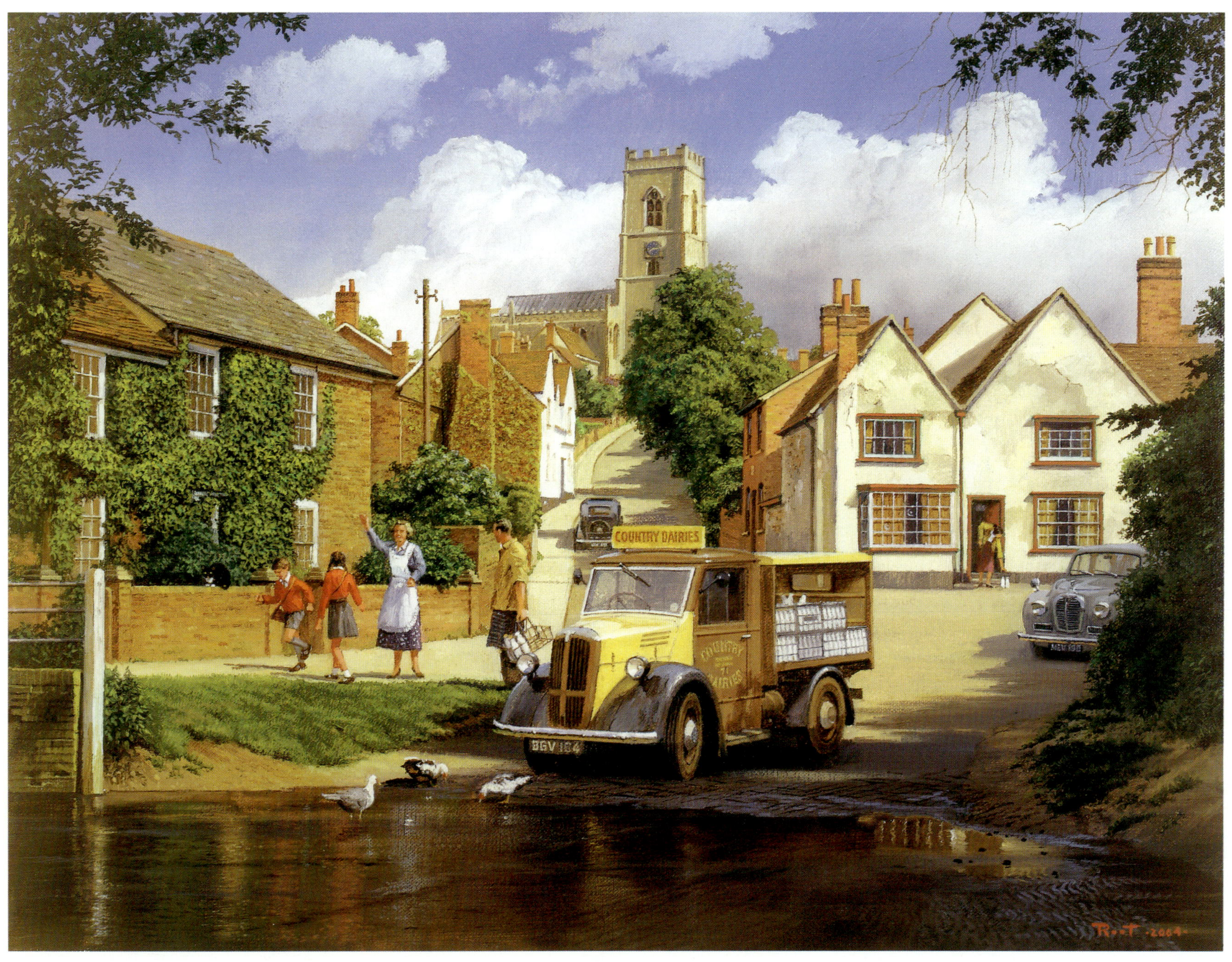
COUNTRY DAIRIES
COUNTRY
DAIRIES
DGV 134

Attacking Shap
Painted 2003

One of the bleakest spots in England, and especially in deepest winter, serves to emphasize the power and majesty of the passing locomotive. The wind, which has piled the snow up in drifts in places, seems to have kept the track clear, but it is a very cold scene, and it is no surprise that there is no smoke coming out of the chimney of the platelayer's hut which is obviously unoccupied. It would be a very cold place to be hiding away! This is a typical British Railways express of the early 1950s, with the green liveried locomotive displaying the earlier 'Lion and Wheel' emblem. In the model railway world we used to refer to these coaches as 'blood and custard' and in my opinion they never looked as smart as the all maroon LMS livery which they replaced.

The gradient which is being tackled is at Greenholme in Cumbria, and leads up to the summit at Shap, 916 feet above sea level. This is one of the most testing climbs in the British Isles, given the weight of the London Euston to Glasgow expresses. Before the later 1930s most trains had to be double headed to tackle the climb. Sir William Stanier, the CME of the London, Midland & Scottish Railway in the 1930s had the challenge of designing locomotives powerful enough to climb the gradients at Shap and Beattock single handed, and the result was the Princess Coronation Class of 4-6-2 Pacifics, with a tractive effort of about 40 000 lbs.

Seen in this lovely painting is one of that famous class, number 46233 *Duchess of Sutherland*. The first locomotives of the Princess Coronation class were streamlined with blue livery and silver stripes, and later ones red, but the casing proved a hindrance to maintenance, and in fact the streamlining made no difference to the engine's performance below speeds of 90mph. so later examples were of conventional design, and these included the *Duchess of Sutherland* built in 1938. This handsome locomotive would regularly head a London to Glasgow express taking only 6½ hours for the journey, and she worked to the end of the steam era. When steam was phased out, *Duchess of Sutherland* was fortunately saved from the scrapyard by Billy Butlin, and put on display at one of the Butlin's Holiday Camps. From there she moved to the Alan Bloom collection at Bressingham Hall in Norfolk, where I made her acquaintance, and travelled on her footplate. In 1998 she was transferred to the Princess Royal Class Locomotive Trust, and given a refit lasting three years and costing half a million pounds. She was ready for service in 2001, and was given the honour of pulling the Royal Train in North Wales for the Golden Jubilee celebrations in 2002. She is in fine health, and can still occasionally be seen storming up Shap as in days of yore!

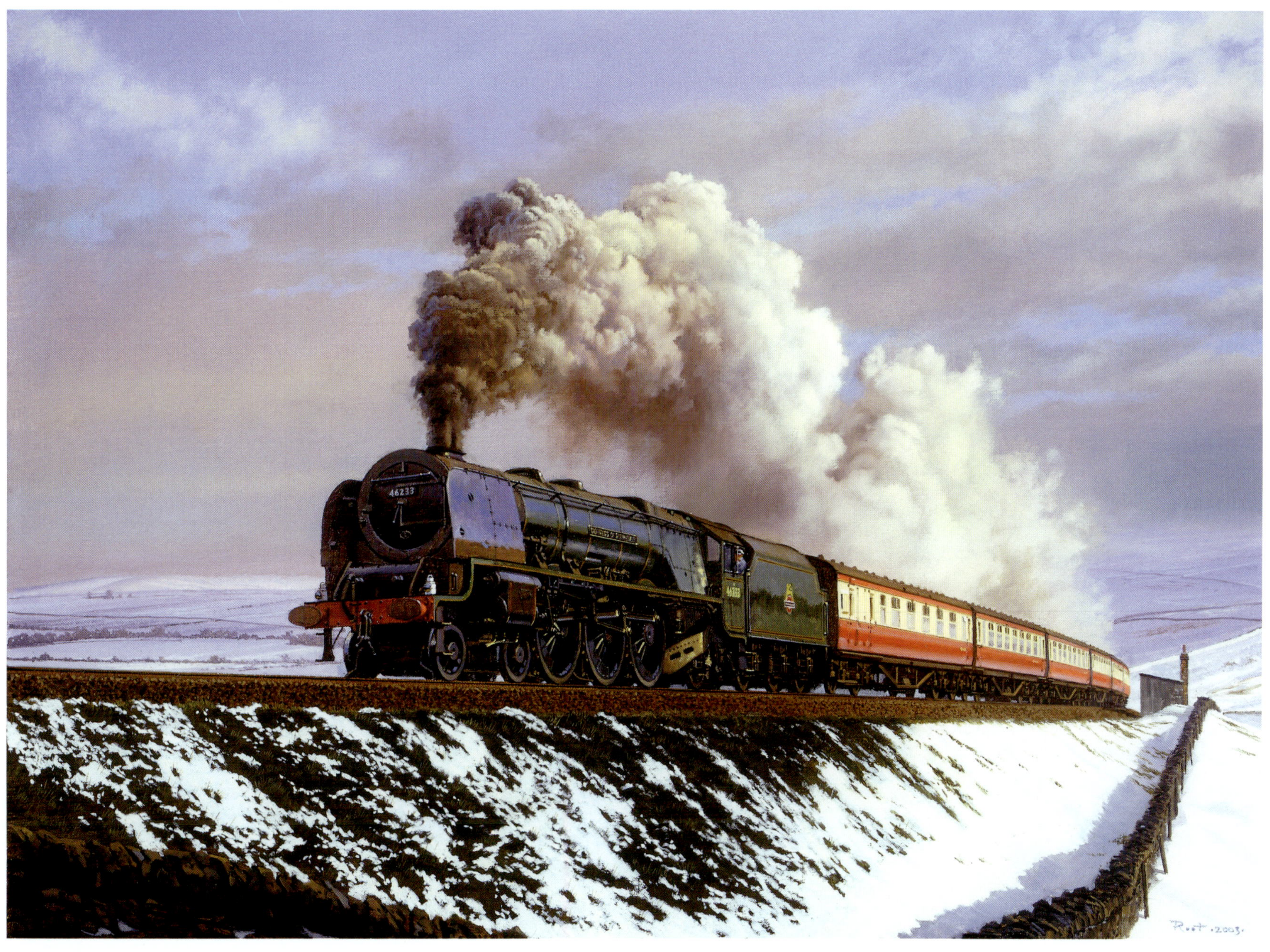

Bournemouth Tower Wagon
Painted 2005

We move to Bournemouth, on the south coast, which is an interesting town from the transport point of view. In 1800 there were very few dwellings of any sort between Christchurch to the east, and Poole with its impressive harbour to the west. Halfway between these two towns the Bourne stream flowed down Bourne Bottom and into the sea at Bourne Mouth, flanked by attractive sandy beaches on which a few fishing boats were pulled up. The rough road linking Christchurch to Poole passed a small distance to the north. In the ensuing years of the nineteenth century the Victorian passion for sea air and bathing, combined with the coming of the railways and better roads, transformed Bournemouth, which boasted some of the best beaches within reach of London. The Southern Railway provided the 'Bournemouth Belle' express, and Bournemouth became a noted seaside resort.

Within the town the usual progression of transport took place, with the horse-drawn omnibus being replaced by trams and in due course by trolley buses in 1934. Two cliff lifts were provided for those who found toiling up the steep cliff paths too much for them. Later in the twentieth century motor buses eclipsed the trams and trolley buses, as they did everywhere else, the railway station was further developed, and cars spread everywhere. Bournemouth became a noted place for party political and other conferences. It developed a notable pier, as well (page 126).

The trams and trolley buses drew their power from overhead cables, via roof-mounted trolley poles. In the case of single-deck vehicles these had to be very long to reach the power supply, and were spring-loaded to keep contact with the wires. They could be pulled down and secured when a vehicle was being turned on the turntable or at other times. The high wires and poles required regular maintenance work, and Bournemouth Corporation Transport bought an old AEC Regent double-decker bus from Huddersfield Corporation in 1945, and got their workshop department to convert it into a tower wagon to assist with this work. The bus made a good stable platform, and the tower could be raised as required. Inside the bus was ideal space for the maintenance crew and their equipment, which doubtless included a kettle! This important vehicle has been preserved and is the property of the Bournemouth Passenger Transport Association.

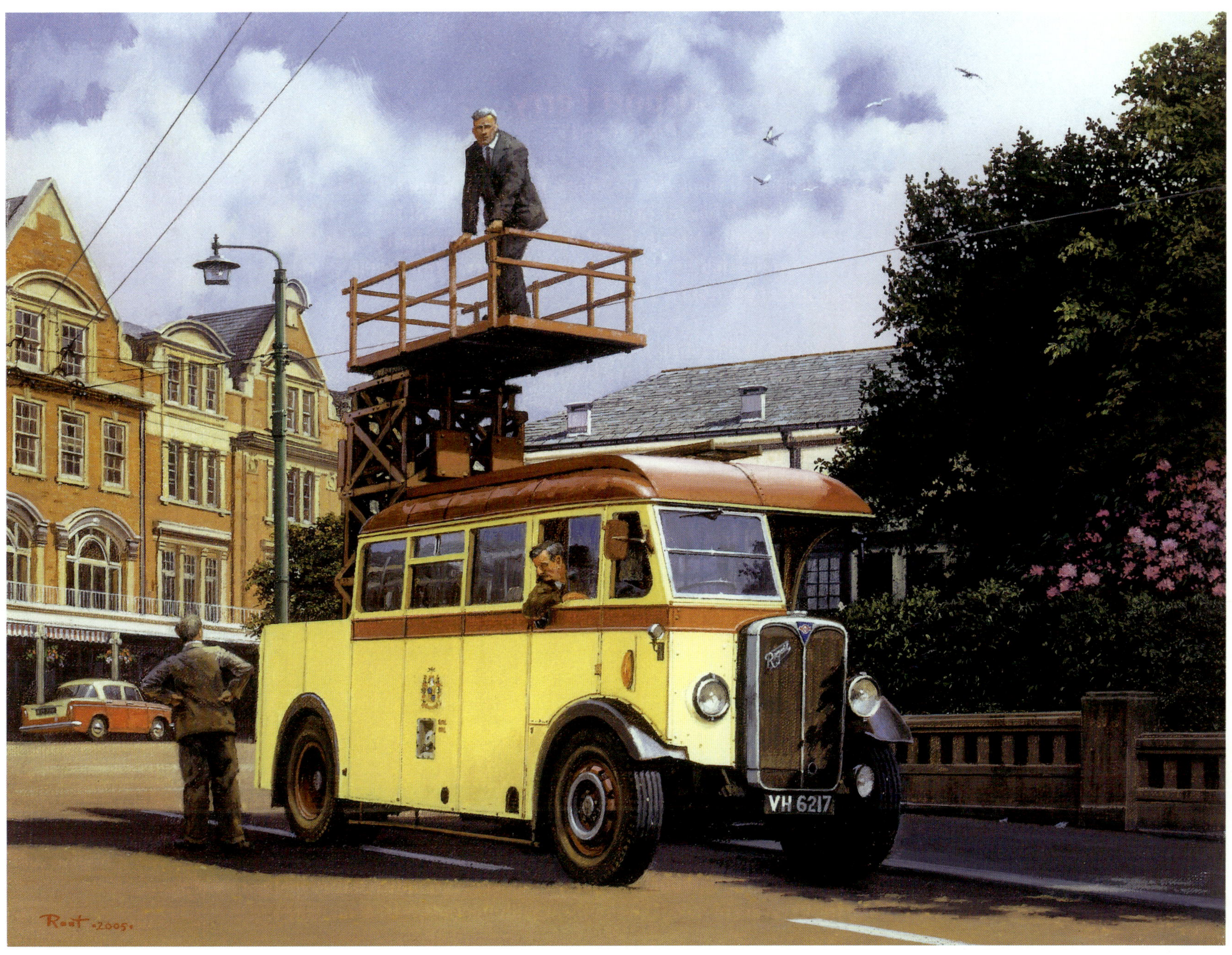

Gosport Ferry
Painted 2005

The south coast of England is endowed with many fine harbours, but those around the Isle of Wight are among the best, and include Portsmouth harbour which has for centuries been a great naval base. The harbour has a narrow outlet to the sea, making it sheltered and easily defended, and the city of Portsmouth proper is on the east side, with Gosport on the west. The two were connected by a steam powered ferry. This lovely painting shows the scene looking east at Gosport Ferry, with lots of interesting activity.

Four double-decker buses are drawn up in the parking bays, some of which might be waiting for the ferry to dock and provide a flock of passengers to replace those who have been brought down to catch the boat, which can be seen departing beyond the building. The four buses all belong to the Provincial Bus Company and the first three from the left are AEC Regents, with Park Royal bodies. Their fleet numbers were 35, 53 and 45. The fourth, fleet no 57, is a Guy Arab. Buses 35 and 57 have both been preserved. The bus behind is a Bristol K5G, waiting in reserve.

Moving very slowly down the centre of the channel, under her own power, is the last of the British battleships, HMS *Vanguard*. She was conceived during the dark days of the Second World War, and her keel was laid down on 2 October 1941 at John Brown's shipyard on the Clyde. It was not until 9 August 1946 that she passed her acceptance trials for the Navy, having been launched by Princess Elizabeth. At 45 000 tons she was the largest warship ever built in Britain, and she was 814 feet long. Her main armaments were 15-inch guns taken from the reserve of guns used on other ships including the Royal Sovereign class of battleships, so that extra work was not placed on armament suppliers during the war. She cost about £9 million to build.

Vanguard's career began with a trip taking Princess Elizabeth and the Duke of Edinburgh on their tour of South Africa, and I went aboard the ship at Plymouth and saw several of the cabins prepared for the royal couple. But by the 1950s the day of the battleship was over, as aircraft and submarines became increasingly powerful and sophisticated. In 1956 *Vanguard* was placed in reserve and on 4 August 1960 was towed away to be scrapped. But she had the last laugh. Watched by thousands, she became erratic while the tugs tried to manage her. She nearly rammed a pier, threatened a public house, and went aground on the ebb tide! After desperate efforts by more tugs she was re-floated before her stern swung round and blocked the harbour. The many onlookers certainly felt they had got their money's worth! It is interesting to compare 400 years of naval development with the *Golden Hind* on page 7.

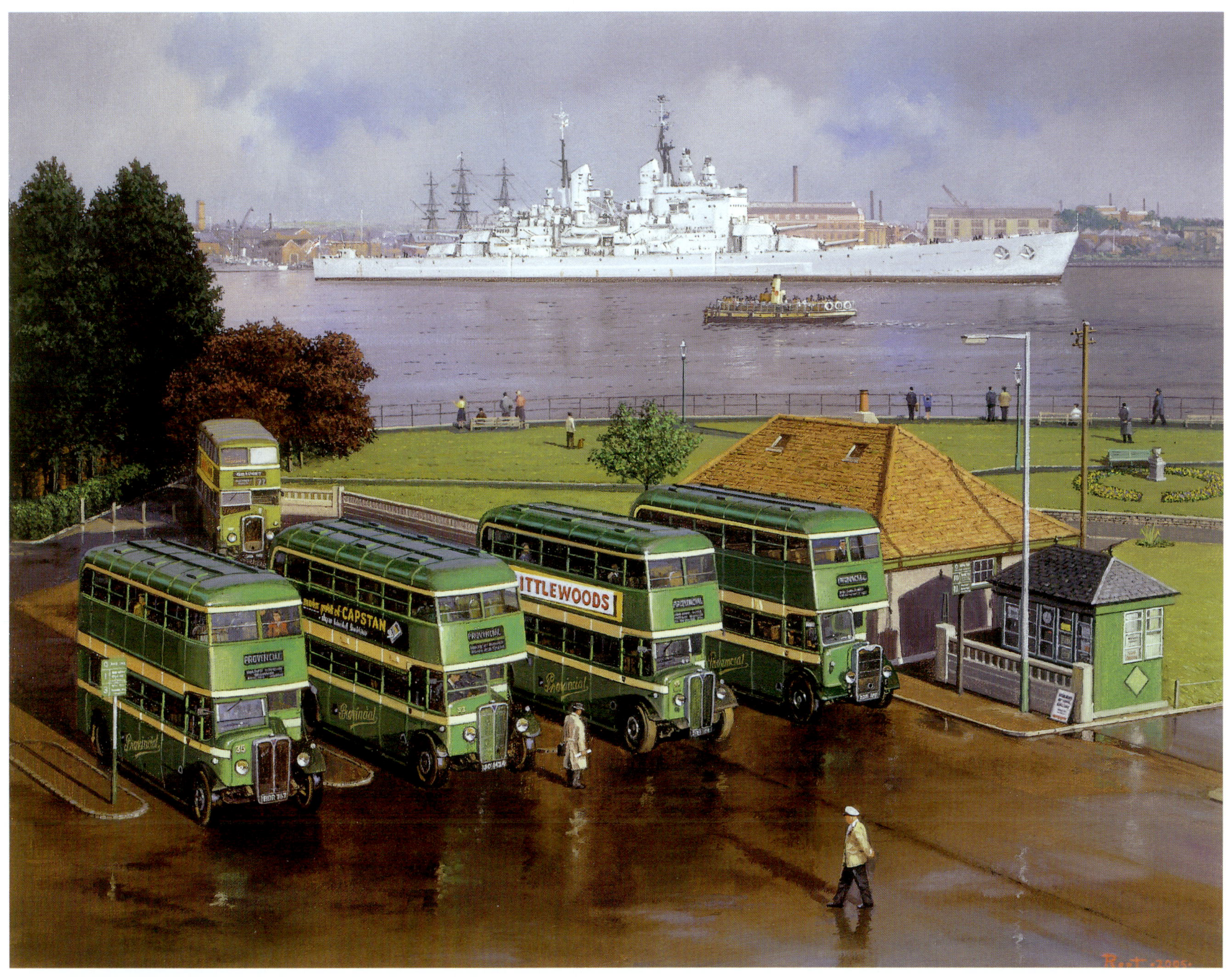
CAPSTAN
ITTLEWOODS
PROVINCIAL

Playing to the Whistle

Painted 2006

My literary skills are not in the same class as Tom Tyler's, but he has allowed me to write a description for this picture. In previous books I have said that I am very lucky inasmuch as I can recreate scenes that no longer exist, and such is the case here.

If ever there was a picture that recaptured the many facets of my youth, then this is it! In 1958 the family moved to a semi just out of view on the right of the picture. The close proximity of the branchline and the football pitch, as well as the meadows that lay beyond was a real bonus. There was a cinema opposite the football ground for Saturday matinées, and as if that wasn't enough there were tennis courts to the left of the bowling green and in front of the gas holder. In a pre-computer, pre-game station era, what more could an eight year old want?

The branchline is of course the Colne Valley line, with Halstead being the largest centre of population on the line. Portways Foundry, maker of the world famous Tortoise stove, can be seen to the right background, the waste products from which formed much of the ballast on the railway track bed. The old white coach body by the bowling green was used to store rollers, mowers and other gardening paraphernalia. I remember having a nose inside on many occasions, but know not the origin of the vehicle. The Colchester-based J15 on the Saturday afternoon freight is about to cross the unofficial footpath, a short-cut created by locals who either wanted a cheap view of the football, or a walk across the fields. The fence at this point seems to have suffered a strategic failure!

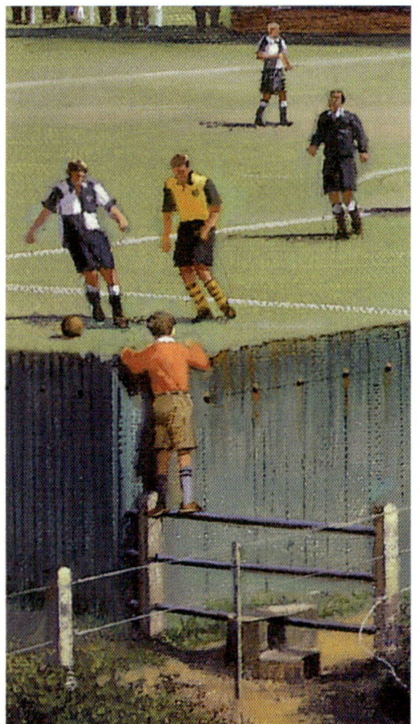

Although I had in mind what I wanted the picture to show, it was a very difficult picture to plan and paint. The football ground remains largely unchanged, as do the churches and town in the left background. The rough trackway in the foreground also remains, but the gas holder, Portways, the bowling green and tennis courts, and of course the railway have long gone. Aerial photographs and an Ordnance Survey map were used to verify what could and could not be seen, together with photographs of individual buildings which were pieced together like a jigsaw. In order to show the football match in progress an imaginary elevated viewpoint was essential, thus adding to the complexity of the perspective.

I am pleased with the picture and hope it gives pleasure to other people who may have had an equally happy childhood.

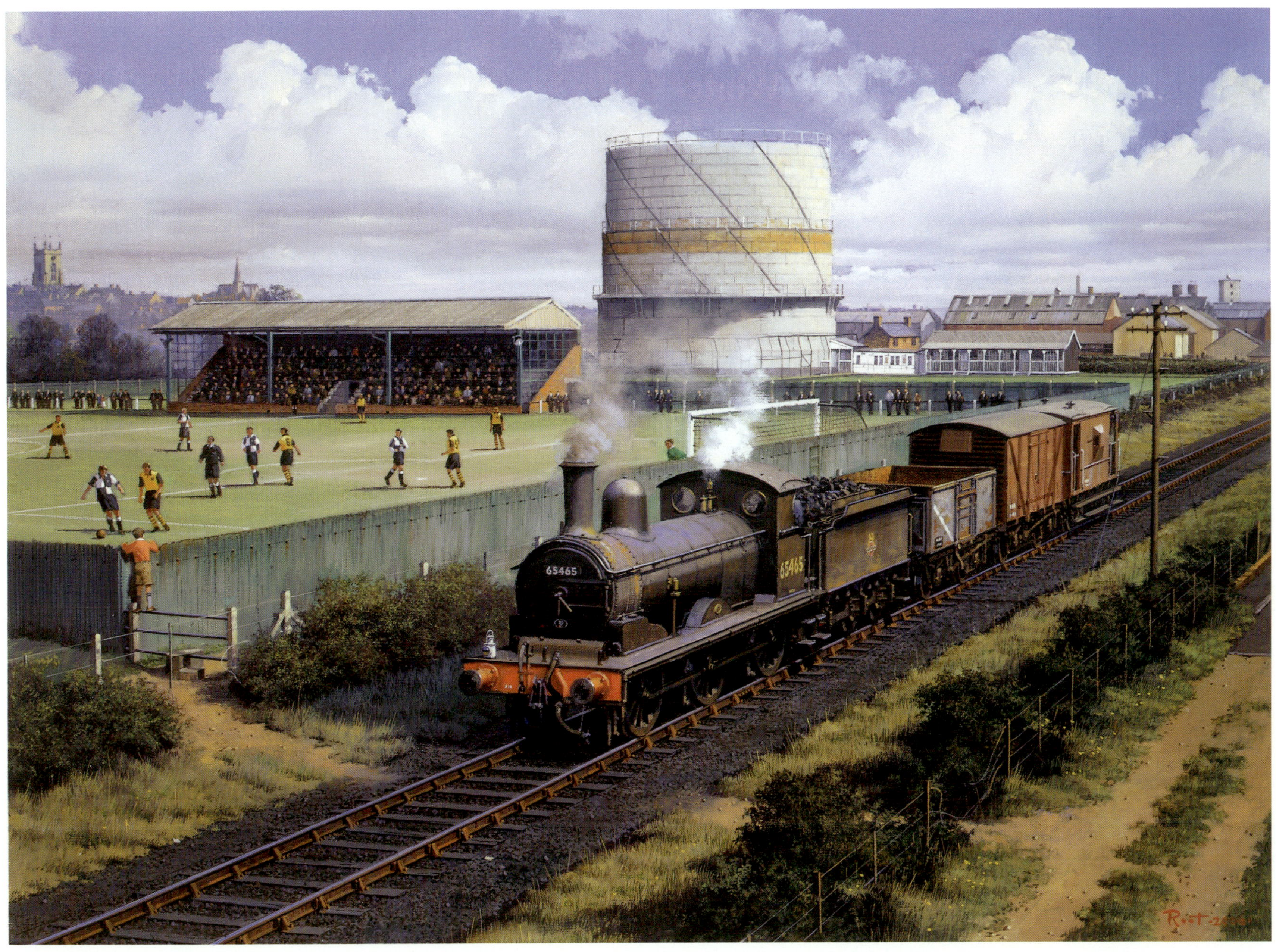

65465
65465

Winter Collection
Painted 1994

It's the sort of winter's day one dreams about, with bright sunshine, no wind, and the newly-fallen snow crisp and sparkling, giving the trees a fairytale quality. Then there is the fun of tracking, seeing who has been where. The fox has done his rounds in the night, different birds have been up early, and another dog with its owner has been for an early morning walk. As was often the case, however, the postman in his van is the first vehicle out and about in this corner of rural Essex. Luckily he does not have to encounter the hills of, say, the West Country, so he has not had to resort to chains on his wheels. He has just made the collection from the postbox, but has time for a chat with another dog owner, to the disappointment of the collie who is patiently waiting for master to throw his stick for him in the usual fashion.

In the 1950s the Royal Mail was still the main means of communication, together with the Post Office Telephones, and the authorities took a great pride in their service. It is true that this was the era before junk mail had been invented, and thus the volume of mail was probably half what it is today, thank goodness, but even so in the rural area where I lived we had two deliveries and two collections every weekday. Further, the service seemed to be 100 per cent reliable, with very few letters lost in the post, or arriving in a thoroughly mangled state. There was no first or second class, as I remember, and stamps cost 2½d for a long period – about one pence in today's currency (of course a loaf of bread only cost 8d!). The combination of vans and mail trains ensured an amazingly speedy service to every part of the British Isles.

At this point in time Morris supplied all the vans for the Post Office, and the example in this painting is a Morris Y Type van first introduced in 1939. The position of headlights and sidelights is typical of pre-war designs. The fact that this van does not have a radiator muff, even on a very cold day, enables us to see that it was designed for the use of that very excellent aid to cold operation, the starting handle! By 1945 the fleet had grown from two vans to two thousand vans, and this in spite of the war. The vans continued to give good service for about a further ten years. Rated as a half ton van, it was originally powered by a four-cylinder 1547cc sidevalve petrol engine. Fuel economy was poor, but given lots of stopping and starting that would be the case anyway. The postbox set in the churchyard wall is of unusual design, and the village church also seems to have an unusual yet attractive little spire as its crowning glory!

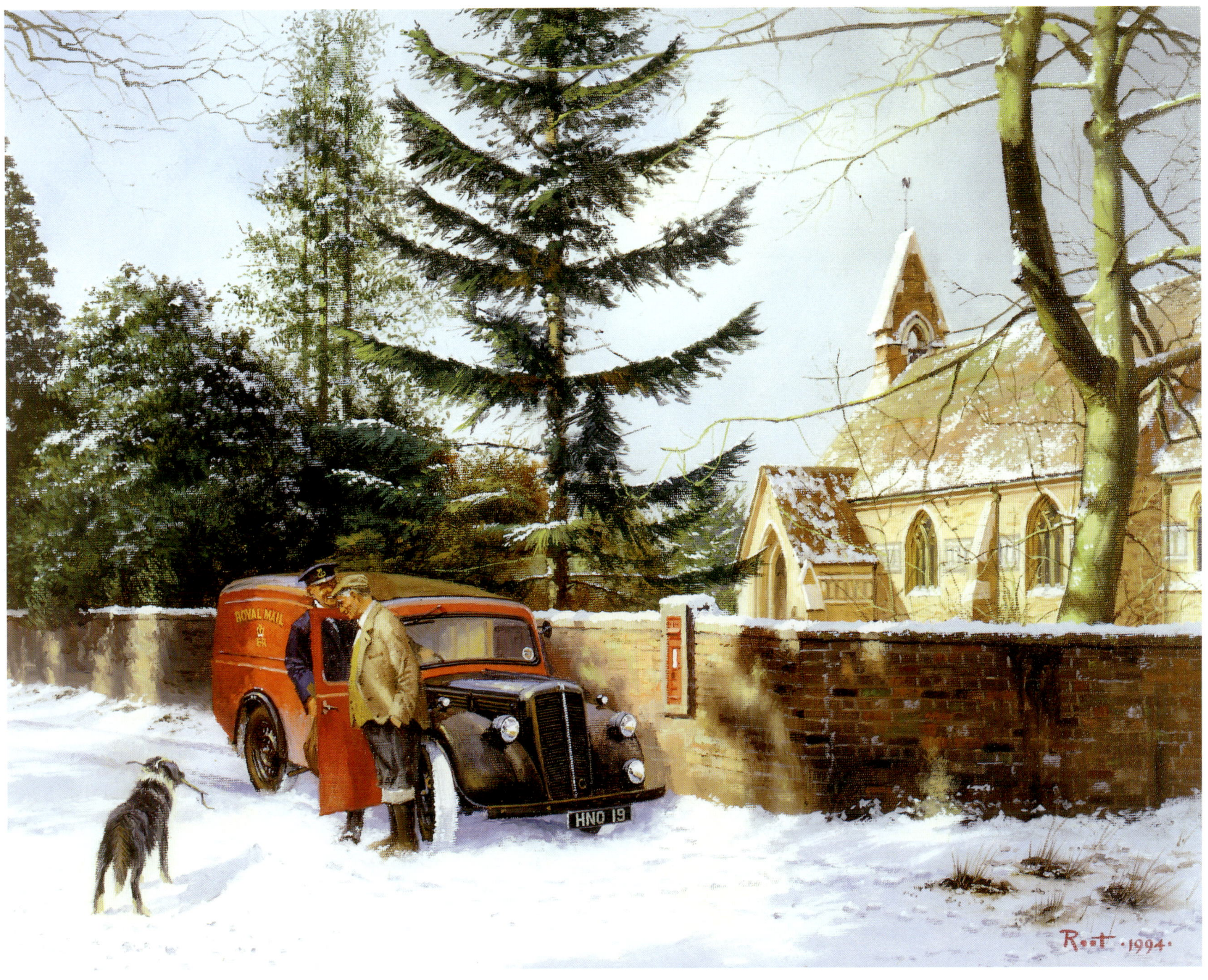
ROYAL MAIL
HNO 19
Root ·1994·

Princess Mary

Painted 1985

We move from a crisp winter's day to a balmy summer one, and to a vehicle which will always hold a pride of place in any history of transport. Travelling fairs developed over the centuries, but as they became more elaborate and much heavier in the nineteenth century, so a more powerful means of motive power was required. In 1859 the first traction engine used by a showman was produced by Bray's Traction Engine Co. of Folkestone for the use of fairground proprietor James Washington Myers. The first Burrell Showman's Engine was produced in 1887. Progress was very slow in these early years because of the punitive Road Traffic Acts which favoured horse-drawn vehicles and almost drove steam off the roads. On the Liverpool road the toll charge for a horse-drawn vehicle was 4 shillings, and for a steam vehicle 48 shillings! Fortunately the Locomotive Act of 1878 removed this injustice, and progress with steam vehicles became rapid.

The great manufacturers of the period were Burrell of Thetford, Garrett of Leiston, Aveling & Porter in Rochester and Ransomes, Sims & Jefferies of Ipswich. With few exceptions, notably Fowler of Leeds, the bulk of major manufacturers were located in the flatter eastern side of the country. I suspect that far more traction engines worked here than in the much more hilly west, and I for one would not fancy driving a traction engine over Dartmoor, though I am sure it has been done! Burrells began as a foundry in Thetford, Norfolk, in 1770, and Charles Burrell, a lad of 19, and grandson of the founder, took over in 1836. He and his three sons were largely responsible for the success of the business, and his son, another Charles, was chairman until the mid 1920s. The *Princess Mary* shown in this lovely painting was built in 1923.

By the late 1800s, electric lighting had been developed, and the showmen were quick to see the advantage of lighting up their travelling fairs with it. The steam-powered road locomotives used to pull the fair trains were ideal to power generators, which could be connected up for use on arrival at the new site for the fair. They also had the advantage of being remarkably quiet, unlike internal combustion engines, even if they did produce rather more smoke! And what a presence they possessed, as this picture shows! The *Princess Mary* is an 8nhp Scenic Road Locomotive double crank compound with works number 3949. She was delivered new to William Nichols, of Forest Gate, London, in 1923, and in 1943 was sold to her final working owner, Charles Presland. In 1958 she was bought for preservation by Dr T.R. Green. *Princess Mary* is believed to have been the last Burrell Showman's Engine in use whilst still in the ownership of a professional showman, and Malcolm remembers seeing her in Halstead during the 1950s.

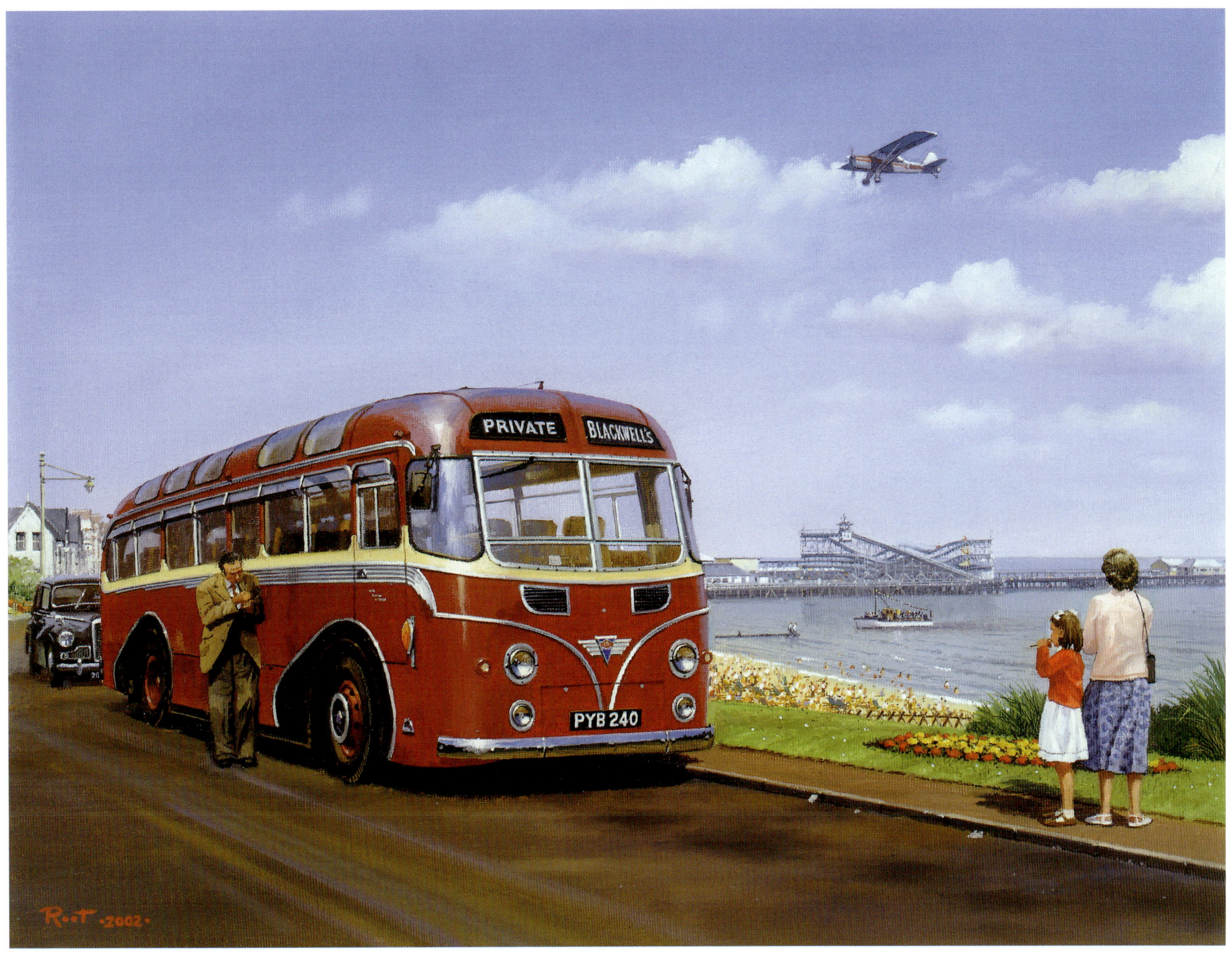
PRIVATE BLACKWELL'S
PYB 240

Wynns Pacific

Painted 2004

The transport firm of Robert Wynn and Sons of Newport had a fascinating history spanning 120 years from 1863 to 1983, and the photographs taken of their operations over this period tell the whole story of heavy haulage development. The firm began with Thomas Wynn doing local deliveries with a horse and cart, and by 1900 was pulling a tank locomotive on a four-wheel trailer pulled by six horses! In 1906 the company registered its first road locomotive. These provided motive power until the arrival of petrol lorries. From an early date timber extraction and haulage formed a large and important part of the company's business.

After the Second World War loads became ever bigger, and thus tractors and trailers had to increase in size to do the tasks required. Locomotives, transformers, boilers, steel converters and girders, both concrete and steel, all required heavy haulage and very careful handling, as one notable accident outside Pontypool in July 1969 demonstrated, when a huge 35 ton tank became detached from its tractor. A number of ex WD vehicles were acquired by Wynns, including tank transporter tractors. When they needed larger vehicles they purchased several US manufactured Pacifics, which were substantially rebuilt by Wynns own workshop, and given names. In this painting we see a Pacific Drawbar M26 tractor GDW 277, which carried Wynns fleet number 192 and was named *Dreadnought,* hauling a 100 ton transformer round a very tight corner. The shop doesn't help the situation! Loads like this progressed very slowly, with extra crew members able to help the driver navigate in tight situations. Some large trailers had a rear driver and rear wheel steering to help. It was also common practice to attach a second tractor to the rear of the trailer for power or braking purposes. On narrow roads and streets, the skill of drivers and crew was very remarkable.

Behind the Wynns tractor is an industrial locomotive busily going about its business. The locomotive is an 0-6-0 tank produced by Peckett. Thomas Peckett established his locomotive works in Bristol in 1880, modifying the designs of his predecessor Fox-Walker. Supplying locomotives solely for industrial and light railways they gained a reputation for reliability, and gave long and faithful service hauling millions of trucks over the years.

A painting in my opinion should be convincing, and this can be a problem when, as in this case, only the vehicle is based on reality. The giant cooling towers and little railway locomotive provide an industrial setting, possibly somewhere in Wales, as might be suggested by the distant hills. The action of figures adds to the conviction that we are watching a scene, in this case the progress of a huge lorry being hampered by the newsagents on the right, causing concern to the man giving instructions.

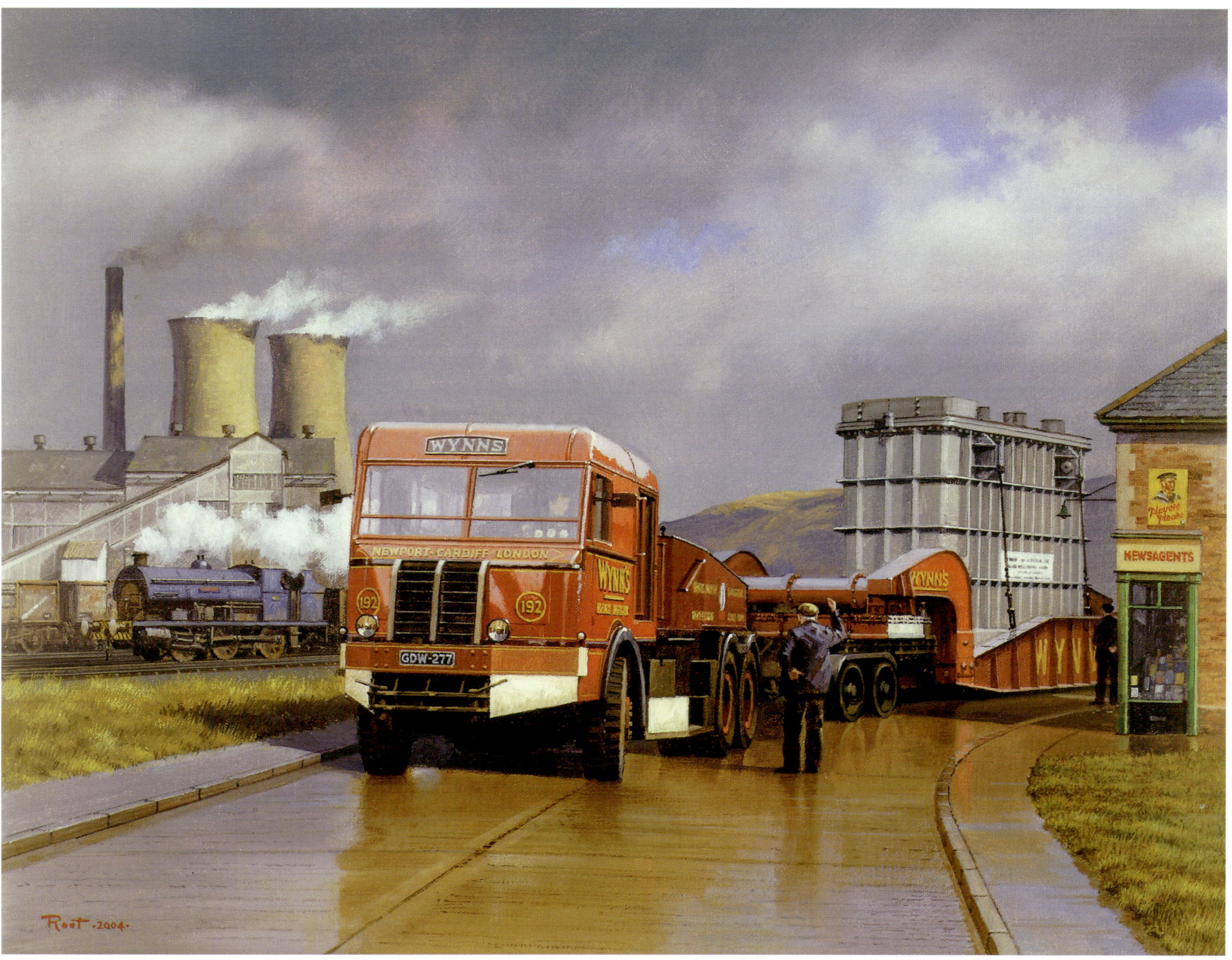
WYNNS
NEWPORT · CARDIFF · LONDON
WYNNS
192
192
GDW-277
WYNNS
Players Please
NEWSAGENTS
WYV
Root ·2004·

A Port for Winter

Painted 1994

Geography plays a huge part in determining development, but so do advances in transport. The natural route from London to the Continent was via Dover and Calais until the coming of the railways. Then the proximity of an east coast port like Harwich to the Dutch coast suggested an alternative, especially for those going to Eastern Europe. The railway link was easy, and Harwich was a natural deep-water port, and today the ferry services from Harwich, and the cargo services from adjacent Felixstowe, are considerable. From an early point the railway companies spotted the advantages of combining railways and ferries, and started to provide their own ships. In 1860 the South Eastern Railway Company commissioned paddle steamers to provide a Folkestone to Boulogne service, and other companies provided steamers to sail from Heysham, Dover and Stranraer. In the period before car ferries took over, between 1920 and 1980, many routes were served by steamers owned by the railway companies and later by British Railways.

The *Arnhem* and her sister ship, the *Amsterdam* were ordered from John Brown's shipyard on the Clyde by the London & North Eastern Railway, and were launched in 1947 and 1950 respectively. The order for the second ship was confirmed by the newly-formed British Transport Commission. *Arnhem* was 4891 gross tons, and both ships were to serve on the Harwich to Hook of Holland route. This was a night crossing, and the ships had first class sleeping accommodation in 1 and 2 berth cabins, and second class accommodation in 2 and 4 berth cabins. Night life would have been quite cosy at times! *Arnhem* was given a refit in 1954, but by the mid 1960s the competition from the large faster car ferries was too much, and she was sold for scrap in 1968. The *Amsterdam* had a happier destiny, being sold as a Mediterranean cruise ship in the following year.

In this painting of *Arnhem* on a chilly winters day, she is being kept company by an ex Great Eastern Railway 0-6-0 tank engine which is busy positioning wagons on the quayside. There are very few footprints in the snow, and even the imposing cranes have a frozen look about them. The crane operator had an unenviable task on days like these.

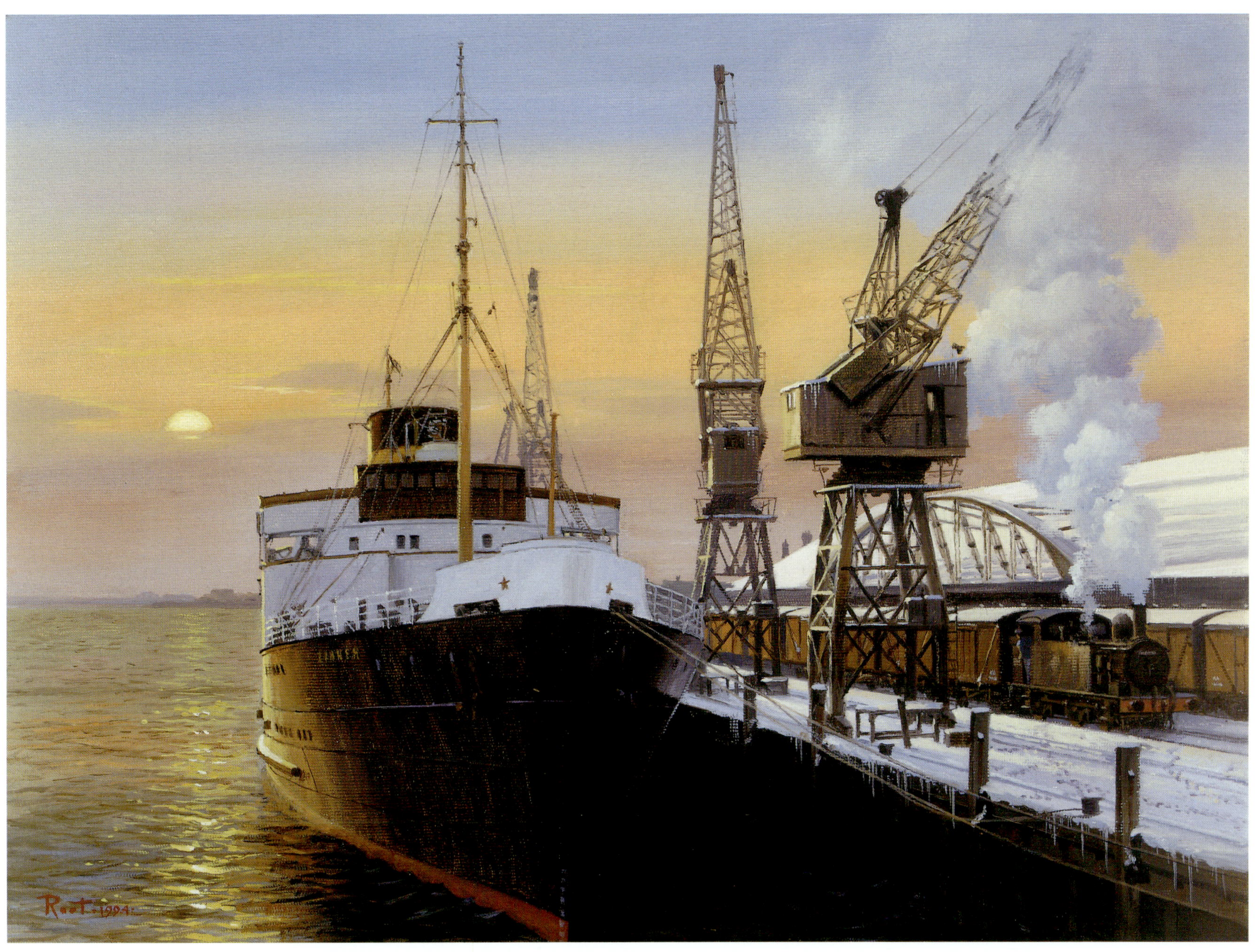

Collecting Churns
Painted 2002

One of the most interesting aspects of Malcolm's paintings is the way he shows us everyday routine tasks from a past era, with the people and their vehicles who carried them out. Here is another link in the chain which made up the huge and vital dairy industry in our country. During the war I remember our milk at home was delivered by the two White girls, using a tractor with a carrying platform on the back, which accommodated two churns. We went out into the road with our jugs, and the milk was ladled into them using a metal dipper with a long handle. The milk was often still warm from the cow, and the cream which formed was marvellous on strawberries and the like. By the 1950s the industry had to be better organized, and anyway two churns of milk wouldn't go far in a town! In this scene the milk lorry owned by Collett & Sons is doing its round of the farms, picking up the full churns and dropping off the empties, which because of the weight factor were carried on the top deck. I think this is a Yorkshire scene, as the town on the lorry's door is Halifax, but the vehicle has a Gloucestershire registration number, so has travelled north in its lifetime.

This operation needed a strong man, and the trick was to roll the churns on the bottom rim whenever possible, though this might convert the milk into butter if done too enthusiastically! They did have two carrying handles, but must have weighed nearly a hundredweight when full. The farmer has constructed a platform to help with the operation, both for unloading the churns from his trailer when brought down the drive from the farm, and also loading them on to the milk lorry. It looks as though it has been built with the ever-useful redundant railway sleepers.

The smart lorry in use is a Bedford O Type, first introduced before the war, but produced afterwards until superseded by more streamlined looking vehicles in the 1950s. Incidentally, Bedford, which was a part of the Vauxhall company based at Luton, contributed over a quarter of a million lorries for military use during the war. This model was powered by a six-cylinder petrol engine rated at about 27 horsepower. Notice the large steering wheel which is a reminder that you had to be fit to drive a lorry before the days of power steering, even if you weren't throwing full milk churns about as well!

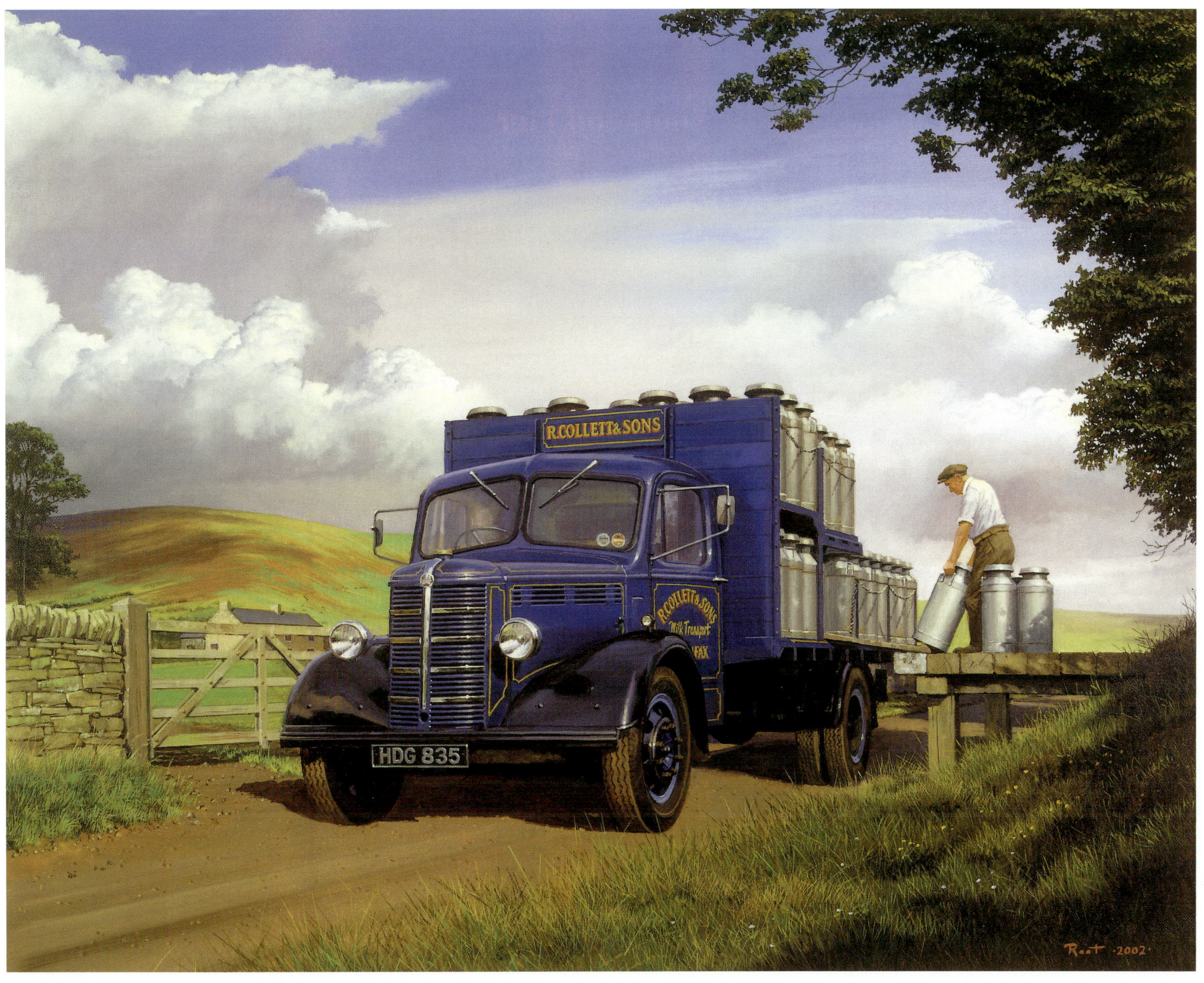
R.COLLETT & SONS
R.COLLETT & SONS
Milk Transport
FAX
HDG 835
Root ·2002·

Southend Pier

Painted 1989

Southend Pier, which is the world's longest pleasure pier, was first built of wood and opened in July 1830. The first pier railway had wooden rails and a truck with mast and sail! It did have a serious purpose however, that of conveying the luggage from the steamers using the pier to the shore. This was followed by a horse-drawn train on metal rails, which went right through the entertainment tent, causing some disruption to performances. In 1889 the pier was rebuilt in iron, and an electric railway provided at a total cost of £80 000. The doubling of the line was started in 1929 due to increased traffic. The train journey took about 4 minutes, and was a very popular feature. The pier was now one-and-a-third-miles long, and the Prince George extension on the east side opened in 1929 and was 326 feet. On the south side of the pier were steamer berths which were a total of 540 feet long. There was accommodation for 5000 people on the pier, with every facility on its two decks. It has had a colourful and eventful history. The pier juts out far into the Thames estuary, forming a barrier and defining the 'gate' through which all ships entering London's river must pass. It could therefore be of great strategic importance.

On 25 August 1939, anticipating what was coming, the navy took over the pier. War was declared on 3 September but the public were still allowed to use the pier until 9 September. During the war the pier became a base for all three services. The army provided AA guns and gunners, and two hundred Pioneers to guard against invasion. The RAF operated a barrage balloon unit and platform. It was the navy, however, which used the pier to control the formation of convoys, monitor ship movements, and supply ships with every kind of necessity. During the war the electric trains covered about 300 000 miles, and carried about 1½ million service personnel. Some of the coaches were adapted for carrying stretcher cases. As early as 22 November 1939 the Germans attacked the pier from the air, but the defenders were ready, and the aircraft received such a hot reception that they never tried it again. As the war progressed those on the pier watched the huge preparations for D Day taking place in the Thames, until on the night of 5 June 1944 the river suddenly emptied. From then until May 1945, millions of tons of supplies were sent past the pier to support the advancing armies.

This great pier has had an eventful life in peacetime also. In 1959 a fire destroyed the Pavilion at the shore end of the pier, and in 1976 a blaze destroyed most of the historic pier head which had played such an important part in the war. In 1986 the MV *Kingsabbey* sliced through the pier between the old and the new pier heads, severing the lifeboat slipway and irreparably damaging the boathouse. In 1995 another fire destroyed the 1959 bowling alley, and severed thirty metres of railway track, stopping the trains. But on this occasion the pier was re-opened in three weeks. Finally on 9 October 2005 a massive fire destroyed 130 feet of the pier, including a pub and shop, about a mile from the shore. Doubtless, before much time has passed, this magnificent old pier will be back in all its glory.

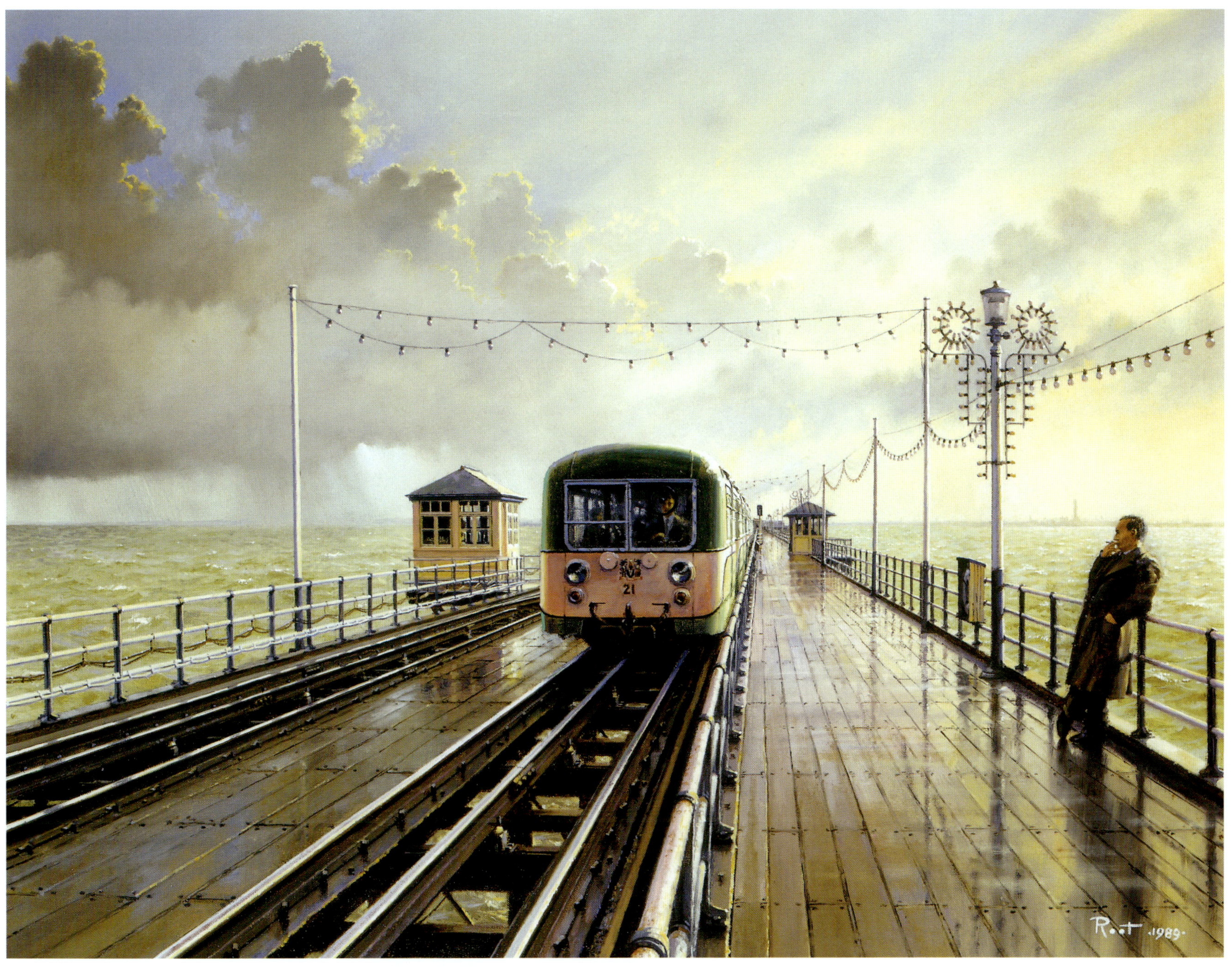

Steam Traction

Painted 2002

Glasgow has been an important city for centuries because of its position on the river Clyde, and it became a centre for industry thanks to the presence of coal and other essential raw materials nearby, also due to its communications, and principally the river. The North British Locomotive Company was established in 1903, and went on to build a large number of locomotives both for our own railways and for export round the world. The locomotive in this picture is destined for service on the Egyptian State Railways, so the scene probably dates from before the Suez Crisis of 1956. A railway locomotive with no fire alight, and no rails beneath its wheels, is something of a problem to move, but fortunately the North British Locomotive Co. works at Springburn were located just over a mile north of the docks, so the journey by road was not a long one. Once at the docks the locomotive would be swung on to the deck of a large cargo ship by a huge crane, and fastened down very securely to guard against bad weather on the voyage.

The two traction engines required for the task have been supplied by the same firm, Road Engines & Kerr Ltd, and both carry Breconshire registration numbers, so are a long way from home! The first in line is a Burrell, from Thetford (see page 72) and its partner is a Fowler engine from Leeds. Both had long lives in service. They were tight-coupled to each other and the 16-wheeled low loader trailer, and progress along the cobbled street would have been at a snail's pace, hence the excess steam being vented by both engines, which adds to the murkiness of the memorable scene.

The lorry on the right, like the bystanders, is also a local, having been first registered in nearby Greenock. It too is a pre-war design, but from 1933, and is a 3-ton Albion Model 47 which was built by Albion Motors at Scotstoun in Scotland. The company was founded as early as 1899, and produced a succession of fine well-engineered lorries with a good reputation for reliability. The company motto 'Sure as the Sunrise' led to the rising sun motif on the distinctive radiator.

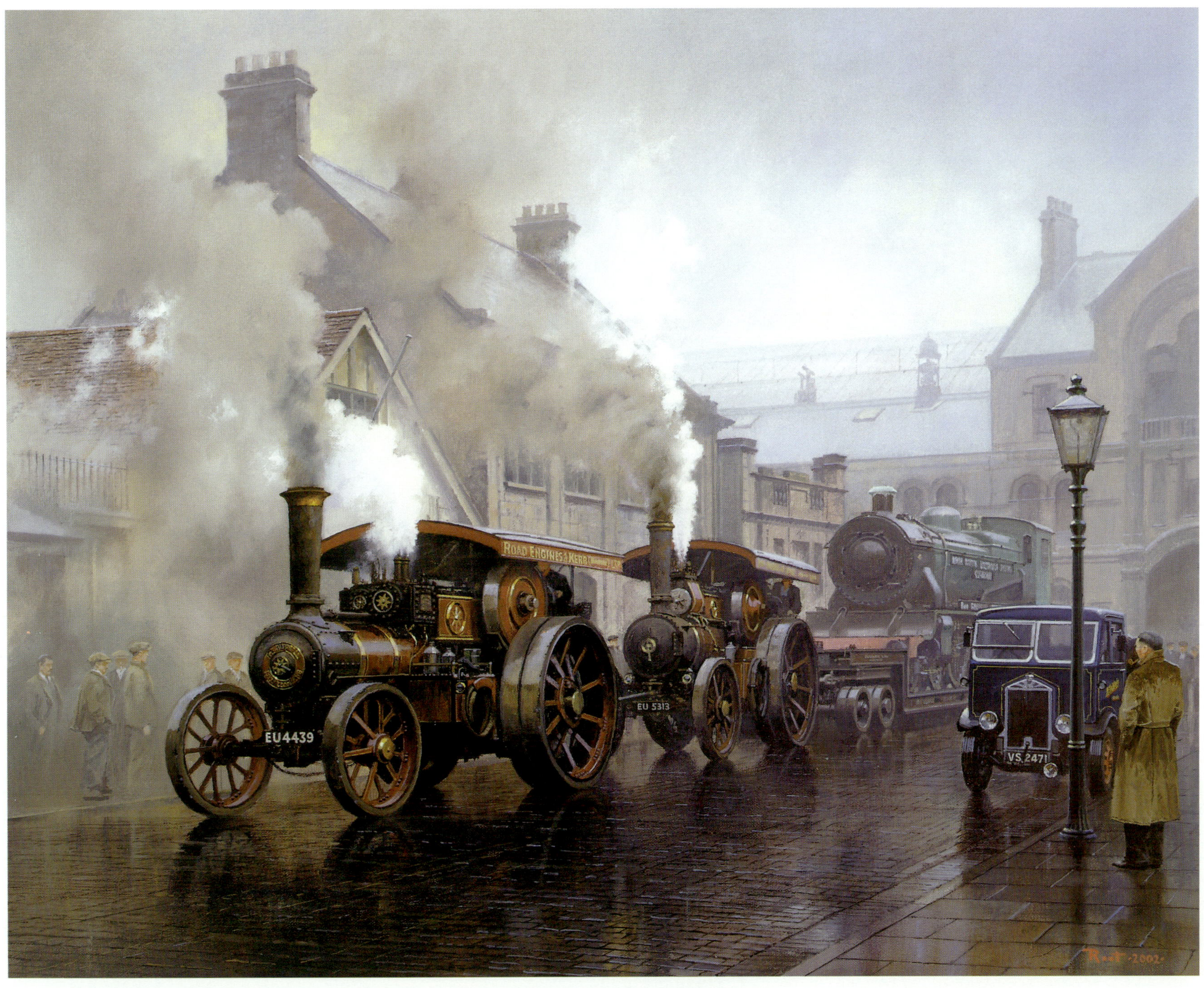
ROAD ENGINES & KERR
EU 4439
EU 5313
VS 2471

Footballer Highlights
Painted 2004

This striking picture could be captioned 'The Sunset of Steam' with the evening sun highlighting the exhaust smoke and steam from the speeding passenger train. This train is passing Marks Tey, south of Colchester in Essex, and is a down train probably bound for Ipswich or the Essex coast. It is hauled by a London & North Eastern Railway B17 class 4-6-0 , known as 'Sandringhams', but also named after football teams, in this case *Arsenal*. The name plate, a brass football flanked by the team colours, is over the central driving wheel splasher. These locomotives, introduced in 1928, were intended for express passenger traffic, and designed by Sir Nigel Gresley. The first batch was built in Glasgow by the North British Locomotive Company, with further batches built by the works at Darlington and by the Robert Stephenson Company. Ten of the class were later rebuilt by Edward Thompson and designated B2s. The B17 had a tractive effort of about 25 000lbs, and a total weight of less than 120 tons.

Sir Nigel Gresley was one of a small group of Chief Mechanical Engineers who had a huge influence on the development of the railways up to nationalization in 1947. He trained with both Stanier and Maunsell, and specialised at first on the design of carriages and express freight stock. He was superintendent on the Great Northern Railway from 1911 to 1922, and then CME of the LNER from 1923 to 1941, when he sadly died. He is remembered for many great locomotives, with the A4 class perhaps the finest, and one of this class, *Mallard,* still holds the speed record for a steam locomotive.

Once again the detail which the artist has incorporated into this picture is wonderful. Beneath the traditionally decorative fringe of the station roof canopy can be seen the row of red fire buckets hanging in place on the wall, which are such a well-remembered feature of every station. There is a porter's trolley loaded high with impressive cardboard boxes, the elegant station platform lamp, and beyond it the wall noticeboard with the train timetable displayed on it. And as I recall the trains ran very well to time, even when there were leaves on the rails!

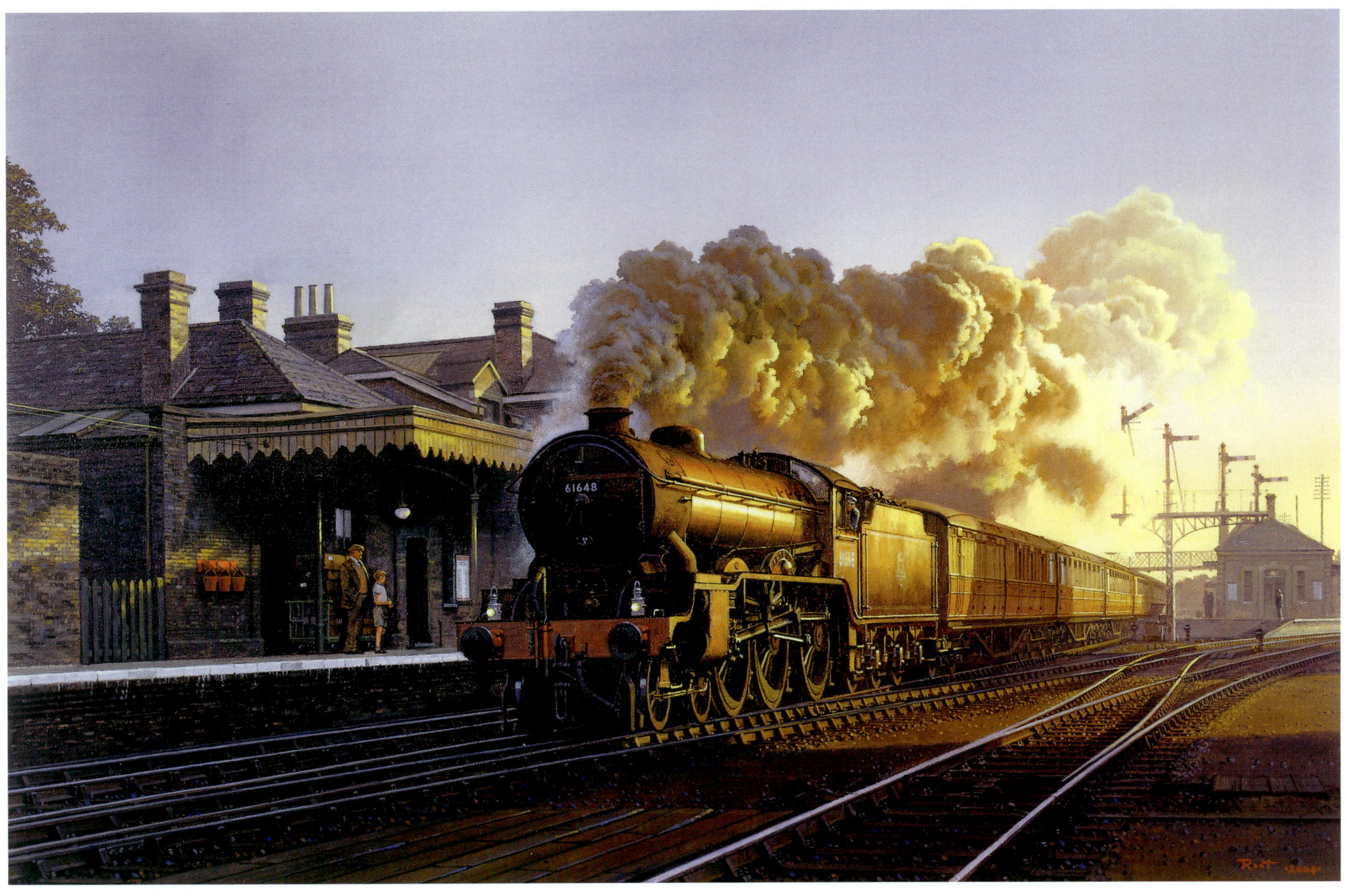

Drive Cottage
Painted 2002

This is a scene in rural Gloucestershire, and what an idyllic setting it is. I believe the house and its surroundings were painted from life, and what lovelier place to live in than one surrounded by woodland and a carpet of bluebells. The cottage was built in the grounds of a much larger house for one of its workers and his family, just before the Second World War. Its design is traditional – simple yet full of character. The garage seems to be a later addition of weatherboard with a chestnut shingle roof, very appropriate to such a woodland setting. It is interesting to note that no planning permission has been given for houses to be built in the middle of woods for thirty years, with one notable exception, and that was built largely with wood, straw, and clay. It is difficult to tell how long a lane the postman has had to travel to reach the house, but he has the time, and the tact, to make a very personal delivery of birthday cards to a young lady on her special day! My own postman delivers the letters between 5.30 and 6am and nearly at the double, so you wouldn't see such a scene round these parts!

The postman's van in the picture is a Morris J Type, delivered to the Royal Mail service in large numbers in the 1950s. It was the successor to the Morris Y Type, shown on page 71, and was a more streamlined model with a larger carrying capacity and a forward control steering position offering better visibility. It always seemed a pity to me that its radiator grille gave it a rather mournful hangdog expression! It was certainly ideal for the task, and was in service for many years. It was powered by a four-cylinder petrol engine beside and below the driver's seat, and had a very modest and rather thirsty performance.

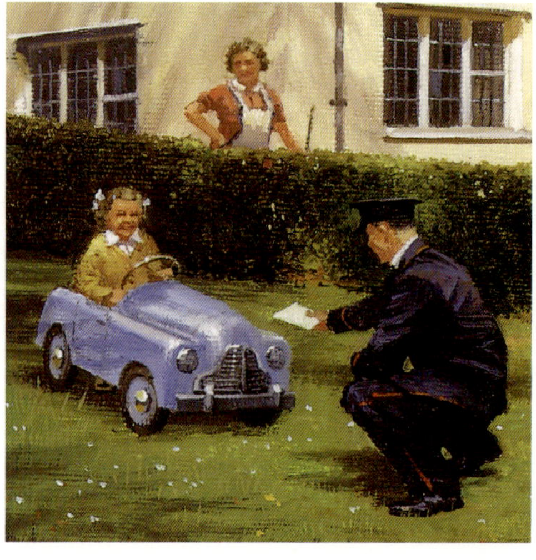

It appears that the young lady may have received her first car as the special birthday present, which explains why she is so attached to it, and it is so bright and shiny, and devoid of dents! I remember as a child poring over the Army & Navy Stores catalogue, which featured some lovely early pedal cars. After the war a friend had an Austin Devon, which was much coveted. I made do with a cast off pram, which could not be either self propelled or steered, so needed a lot of imagination. 'High Calamity' was eventually converted with much optimism to be a donkey cart, and was efficiently kicked to pieces by Mary Jane, our donkey, on its maiden voyage! My own children had homemade pedal cars which did steer and pedal. I often think many of today's children should first learn to do three-point turns, reverse and park on these vehicles, before progressing on to go-karts and the like.

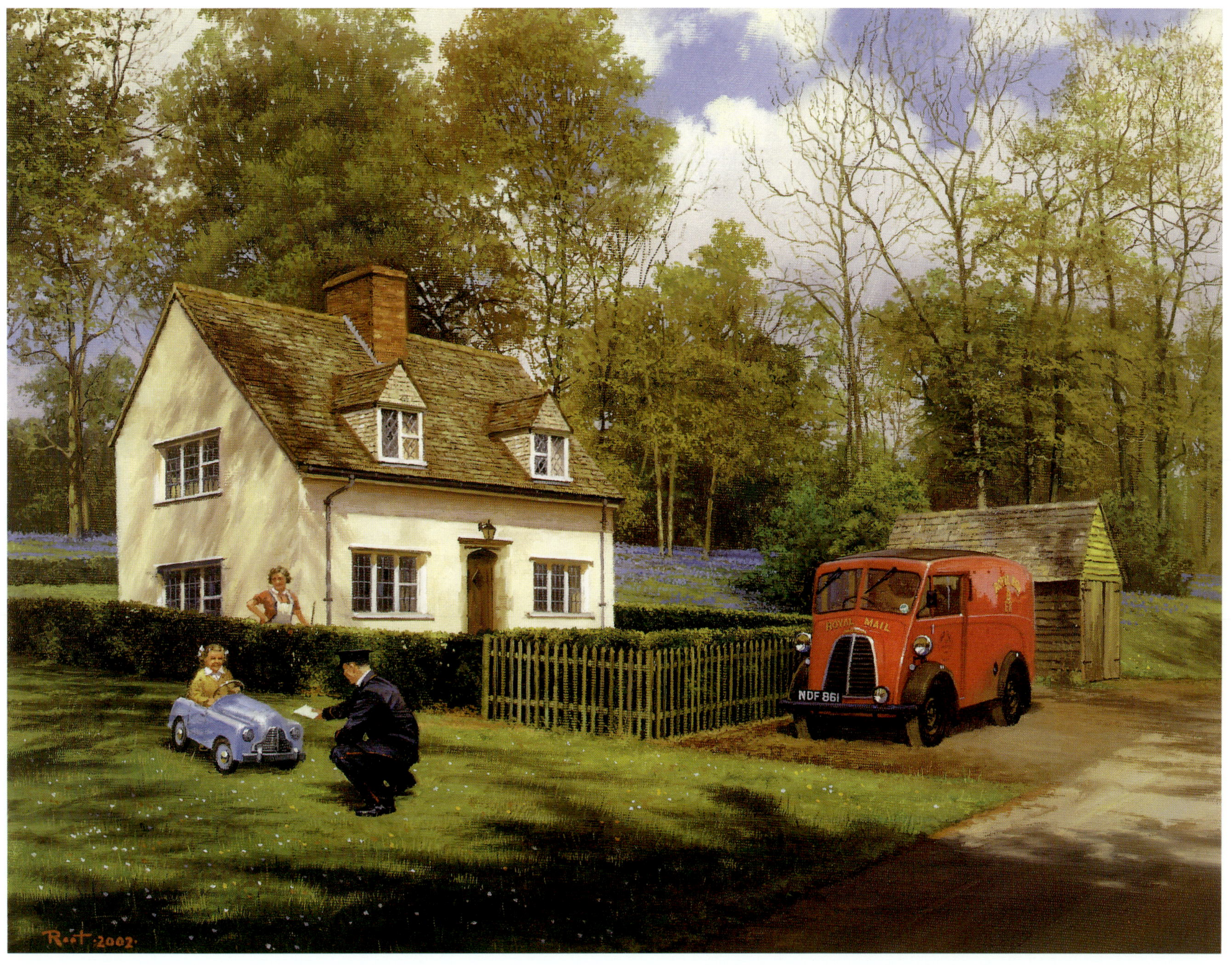
ROYAL MAIL
NDF 861
Root ·2002·

Torpoint Ferry
Painted 2003

The river Tamar makes a very considerable boundary between Devon and Cornwall and for many centuries the lowest bridging point was at Gunnislake, on the Tavistock to Liskeard road. Then in the mid nineteenth century Isambard Kingdom Brunel built the famous Royal Albert Bridge to take his Great Western Railway on its way to Penzance. As motor traffic grew, the Torpoint ferry provided a crossing just downstream of the railway bridge and for most of the twentieth century this was the only means of crossing until, in 1961, a new road bridge was built to take the main road across from Plymouth to Saltash. Crossing on the Torpoint ferry was always fun, as to us Devonians it seemed like going abroad, and the Cornish certainly regarded us as foreigners! There is quite a tide at this point, and it was a great help that the ferry was a chain ferry, so had no problems of navigation. Passing boats also had to keep well clear on pain of getting a chain round their propellers. This is a very still evening scene, with a lovely sky and a number of ever-hopeful seagulls!

Disembarking from the ferry is a coach operated by Plymouth Co-operative Society, with a local registration, which has been on a day trip to Cornwall. It is a 41-seater Leyland Tiger Cub, with a very smart Duple Elizabethan body, and it was first introduced in 1954, so would have still been very new. Fortunately it has a good road clearance, and the ferry ramp is not steep, so there is no risk of grounding. This could and did happen with some vehicles, but I suspect the smart driver has done this trip many times and knows the ropes. If the coach is first off, and that was often the way they loaded the ferry, then the ferry was by no means full of vehicles for this voyage.

Keeping company with the coach are a number of cars, but I can only identify three, and one of those is a 'probable'. Right behind the coach appears to be a blue Hillman Minx, the Mark III model first being introduced in 1948. This was a popular car of the day. Behind on the right is what seems to be an Austin 10 from the period immediately after the war, the model which preceded the Devon. This was very much a 'stopgap' car, with largely pre-war styling, and a sidevalve engine rated at 10hp. Next to this car is a Standard 10 saloon, like the coach dating from 1954. Powered by a 948 cc four-cylinder engine, it had good performance figures and quickly became a popular little car with its companion, the Standard 8. They competed well against the big three, Austin, Ford and Morris.

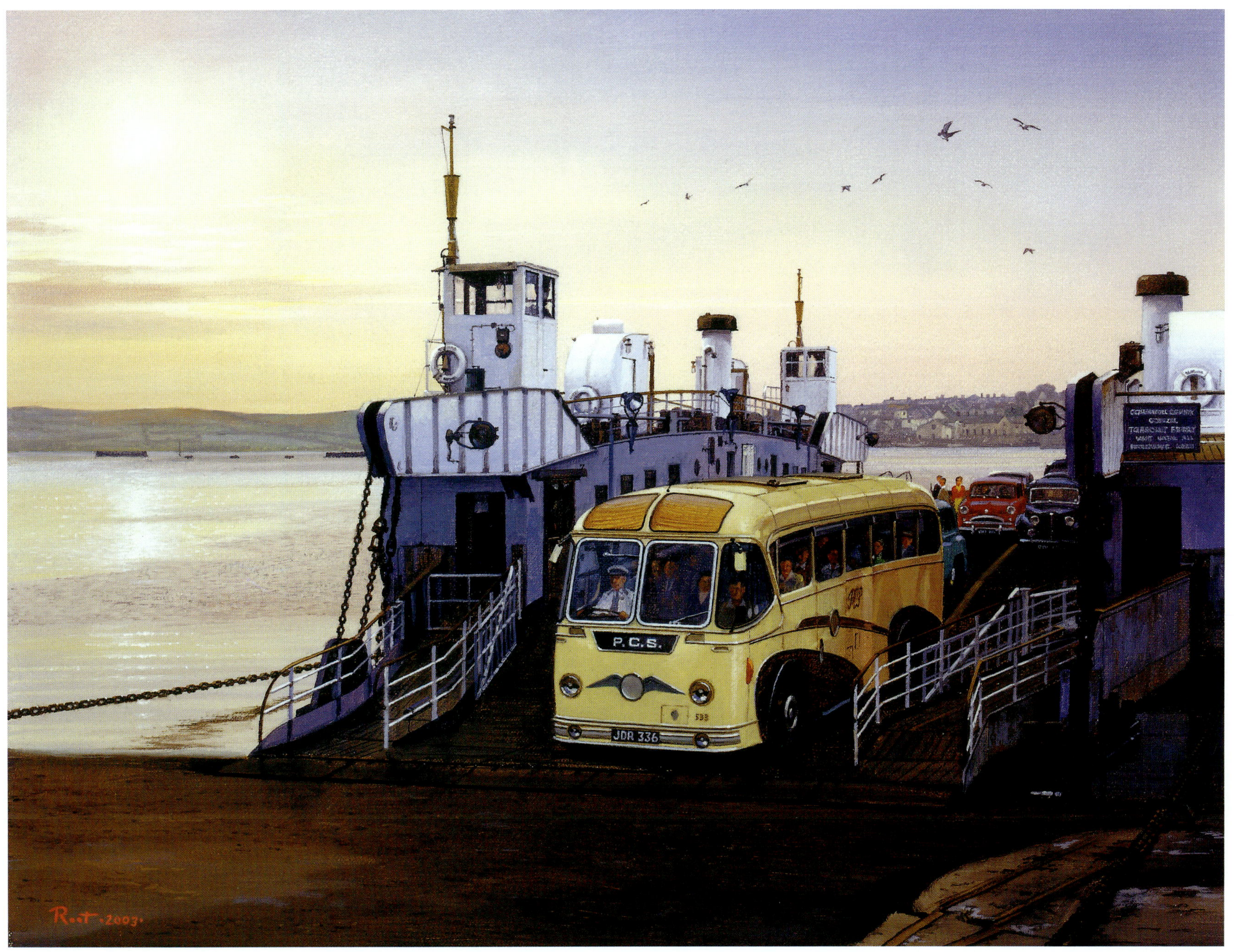

P.C.S.
JDR 336

Rural Connection

Painted 2004

Weybourne in north Norfolk is the scene for this picture, and it is situated just west of Sheringham, on the railway between Sheringham and Holt. Fortunately part of the original railway has been preserved, and is now the North Norfolk Railway, so this scene could be recreated today. A train has just stopped at the station, and an Eastern Counties bus is there to meet it. This bus is a 'Special', a service put on to meet the train and take its passengers to a number of destinations in the surrounding area. This sort of link was common at the time, and accounts for the small number of private cars in the station car park. Today we all drive to the station, and require huge car parks, while such bus service links have declined, especially in rural areas. As it was often just as easy to do the whole journey by car, many of the branch lines were closed by Dr Beeching because of lack of passengers. Speed of travel, rather than road congestion and air pollution became the requirement, and we are now seeing the results of our choice.

In this typical station scene we have four interesting vehicles. The star is the Eastern Counties single-decker bus, a Bristol LL5G with a body built by Eastern Coach Works, and they were a popular model, rugged and dependable. A number of coach-body builders would supply bodies on the Bristol chassis. This model would carry 39 passengers, and had its entrance door at the rear. Eastern Counties Road Car Co. developed from the Thomas Tilling bus company, and then merged with three other companies to become the Eastern Counties Omnibus Co. Ltd in 1931. In 1948 they became part of the British Transport Commission, and today are First Eastern Counties Omnibus Co. This bus, KNG 718, is now preserved at the Eastern Transport Collection in Attleborough, Norfolk.

Behind the bus, on the right, is a migrant from London, the ever-useful Scammell Scarab, affectionately known as the Mechanical Horse. The earliest models were introduced in the early 1930s, but the one shown is the later more stream-lined version, in British Railways livery which coincidentally is similar to that of the Eastern Counties bus. Used for the delivery of railway parcels and smaller freight items, it was powered by a modest engine, located between the cab and rear tractor wheels, and had amazing manoeuvrability, especially in confined spaces.

On the left of the picture is the 1939 Hillman Minx saloon, one of which served our family of nine children from 1939 to 1952. When the rubber knob of the gear lever eventually perished, my father turned a new boxwood version on his lathe, which worked very well! The car had an 1185cc sidevalve engine, and a 4-speed gearbox. The over riders on the bumper were a new embellishment since the previous year, when the model was first introduced with new styling. It cost £163 new, and my father sold ours for £400 thirteen years and 150 000 miles later! The second car peeping our behind the rear of the bus is a model unknown to me

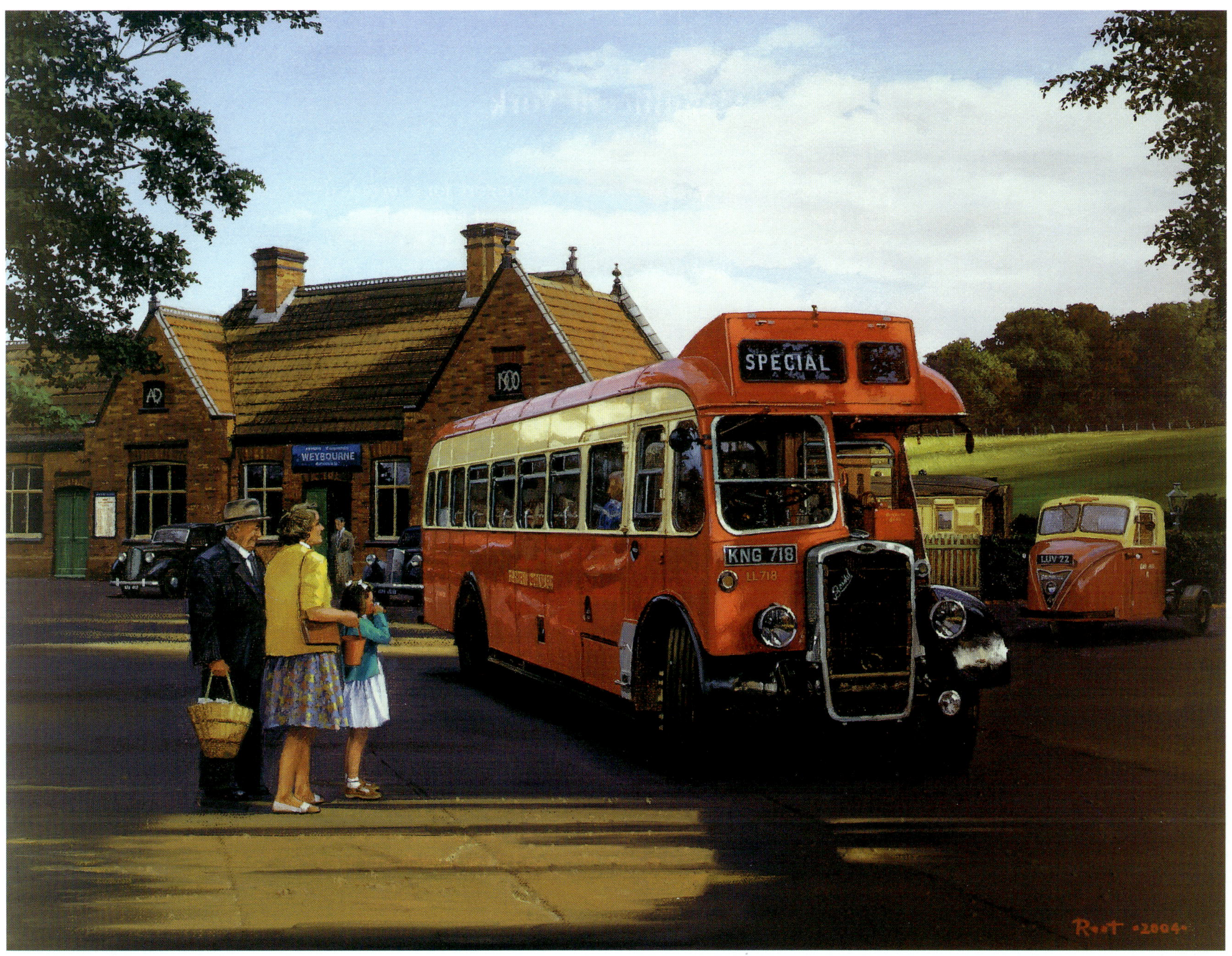
SPECIAL
WEYBOURNE
1900
KNG 718
LL718
LUV 22
Root .2004.

Magnificent York

Painted 1981

This powerful painting is an important milestone in our pageant of transport, for it records the change from steam to diesel on our railways. In fact this change took place over a period of at least thirty years, for the Great Western Railway was proclaiming the merits of its new diesel railcars as early as 1934. In fact they were not a success, and the steam locomotive thundered on for another three decades. However, by the 1960s the writing was on the wall for steam traction. Steam locomotives were large and heavy, and they required several hours of preparation before they were ready for work. They needed both water and coal in large quantities, and the latter was becoming increasingly expensive and hard to obtain in top quality grades. Overhaul of locomotives was lengthy and expensive. Each steam locomotive had to have a crew of two men, and driving them was a very skilled job especially on main line routes. Meanwhile diesel engines were being steadily improved and refined, until they offered a very attractive alternative form of traction for British Railways, who could not afford to be sentimental about the past.

As early as 1946, H.G. Ivatt had designed a diesel electric locomotive of 800 horsepower. Since then D. Napier & Son had developed a lightweight diesel engine for use in fast gunboats and the English Electric Co. adapted this to build the first Deltic locomotive, which they offered to British Railways, and which went into service in 1955. It was a powerful though expensive and complicated locomotive, and it was not until 1961, when faced with a crisis over future traction for the East Coast route, that BR placed an order for 22 engines. Most of these were delivered during 1961 and proved their worth very quickly. Weighing only 103 tons and with 3300 horsepower they had a top speed of over 100mph. Power came from two Napier Deltic diesel engines, each of which drove a 1100kw generator, which in turn powered six traction motors.

In this picture we see British Railways D9003, 'Meld' with an express train in York Station (see page 56 also). The train is the service from Kings Cross, and already the Deltics have reduced journey times considerably. The locomotives also demonstrated good track grip, and could be driven from either end like most other diesels. Hornby Dublo trains actually produced their model before the Deltic went into service, in December 1960, with a two-rail version called 'Crepello' and a three-rail version 'St Paddy' – both named after famous racehorses, and based on actual locomotives. I still run them, but their traction is hopeless without rubber tyres, and these stretch and are a real problem. Luckily the full size locomotives had no such handicap!

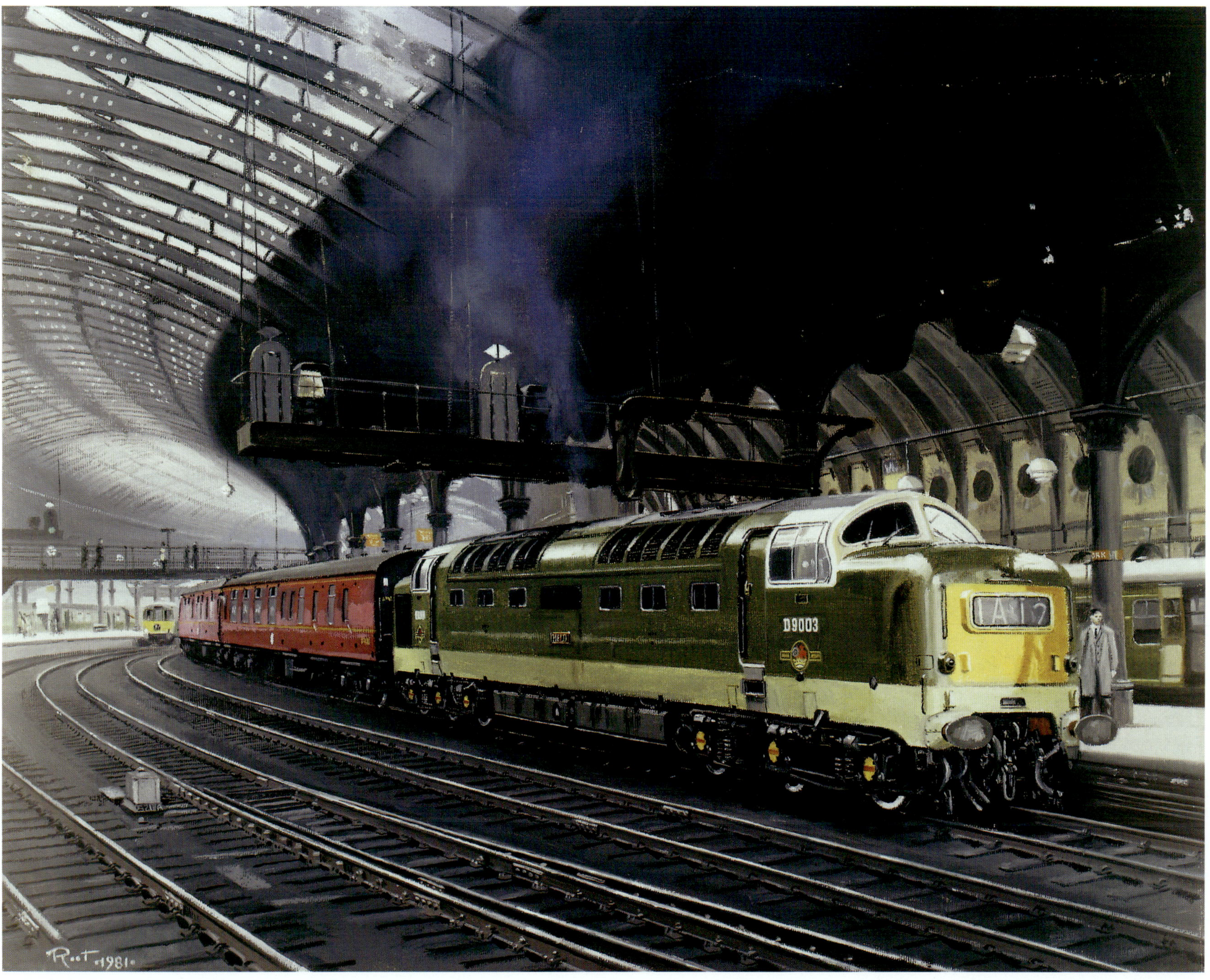
1 A
D9003
YORK

Motoring Icons
Painted 2004

This is a lovely scene from a bygone age, and two features at the garage point to a date in the 1960s. The garage is entirely devoted to Esso petrol, whereas in former times it might have boasted a variety of competing brands. Before the war the pumps might have been hand operated with a handle, hosepipe with tap, and a sort of goldfish bowl on the top! The second pointer to the date is the latest model of Austin Healey sports car being admired by two 'experts', a model introduced in 1963. The setting is in fact Cavendish in West Suffolk.

The story of Austin Healey cars is typical of the British motor industry. Donald Healey was born in Cornwall in 1898, and enjoyed success as a rally driver between 1928 and 1932. In 1945 he founded the Donald Healey Motor Company, and produced the first Healey sports model, an elegant car. In 1950 the company became Nash Healey, and developed the 100 Sports Car, powered by a four-cylinder engine of 2660cc, and producing 100bhp giving a top speed of about 110mph. The prototype was exhibited at the Earls Court Motor Show in 1952, and was such a hit that Donald Healey was persuaded to do an instant deal with the Austin Motor Company. The first Austin Healey cars were built at Warwick, but in 1953 the operation was moved to Longbridge. In 1952–53 some 94 cars were built. The next year this figure rose to 4424!

The Austin Healey 3000 Mk 2A was introduced in the early 1960s, and developed from the 100 Six. It had a six-cylinder petrol engine of 2912cc, giving 124bhp and a top speed of about 120mph which made it a very sporty car indeed. Meanwhile a smaller car, the Sprite, was also produced, and the first model became known as the 'Frogeye' Sprite because of the protruding headlamps! Alas, the days of the Austin Healey were numbered as greater mass production of standard models became the order of the day.

In the foreground can be seen an example of a popular mode of transport in the 1960s, a Lambretta motor scooter from Italy. This is the 1957 LD150 model. As petrol prices climbed, both Germany and Italy spotted the demand for very economical transport, and wartime names like Heinkel and Messerschmitt returned to the roads. Italy meanwhile produced Vespa and Lambretta scooters. Today we see Mercedes and BMW with Ferrari and Lamborghini, but the name of Austin has disappeared after nearly a hundred years. There must be a moral here somewhere! The scooter in the picture is registered in Suffolk, where the garage is located, while the Austin Healey is a visitor from Middlesex. One of the men, the vehicle owner, is perhaps discussing fuel consumption and negotiating a vehicle swap. Romantically the owner of the scooter in the picture met and married the man who was later to own the Austin Healey, hence the inspiration for the painting.

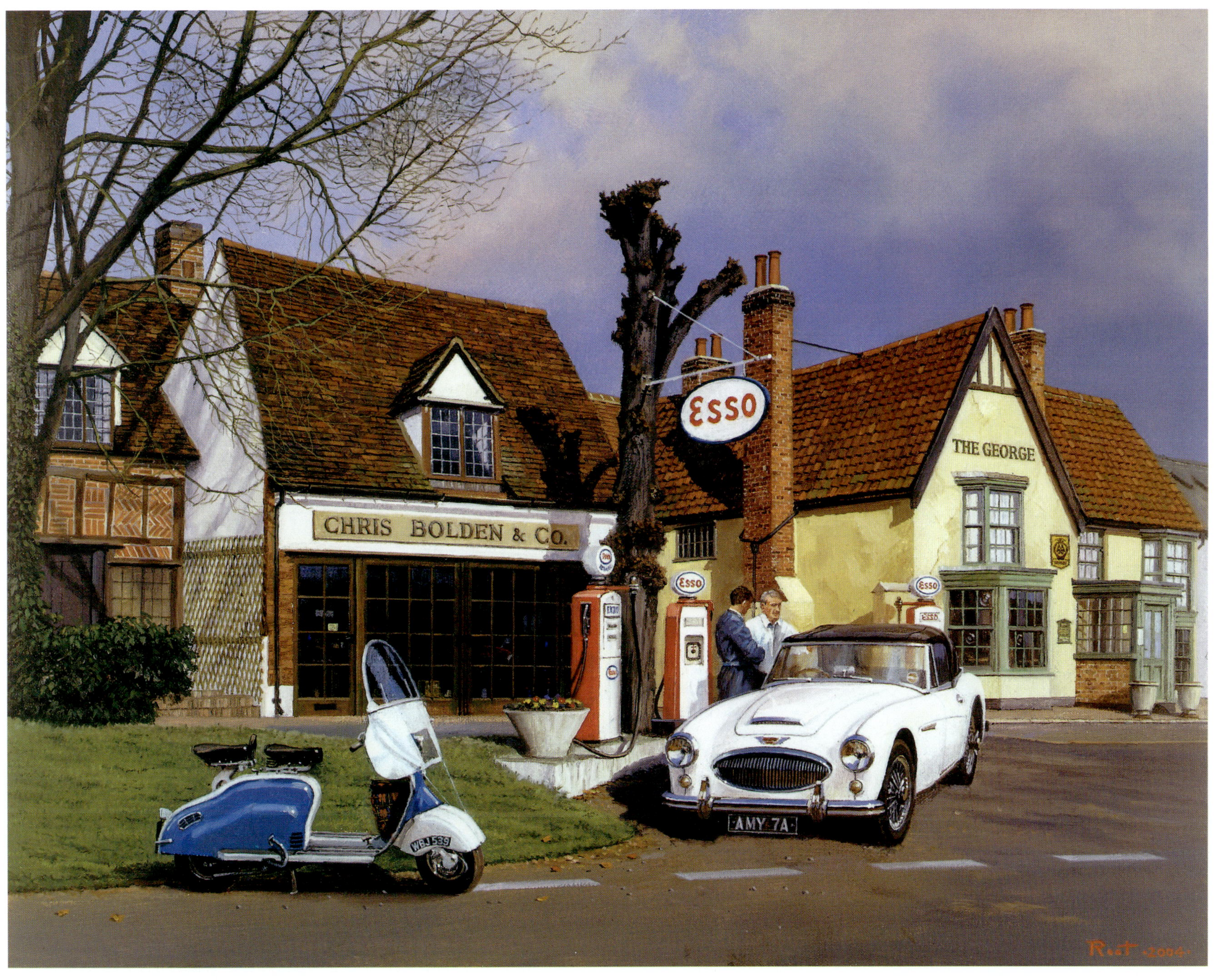
CHRIS BOLDEN & CO.
ESSO
THE GEORGE
ESSO
ESSO
WBJ 539
AMY 7A

Airport Activity

Painted 2003

This is a most interesting scene, and again adds to our pageant of transport in a number of ways. The airport illustrated is Southend, and the date the mid 1960s. In the early days of commercial flight in the 1920s and 1930s the London airport was at Croydon – you can still see the façade of the main terminal building from the A23 London to Brighton road. By the 1950s Croydon had been superseded by an ever expanding Heathrow, aided by Blackbushe and Northolt. When we flew from Gatwick in the early days, I seem to remember we parked our car in a field and clambered up an outside staircase to the departure lounge! (There were other routes, including one from the railway station). Meanwhile Lympne and Lydd had catered for cross-Channel flights, and many smaller city and regional airports also existed, including one in Ipswich where I now live. Gradually the three main London airports have developed and dwarfed all others (see page 114). At the same time, with a huge increase in air travel, many regional airports have expanded their facilities and their services and continue to do so.

This expansion over the decades has obviously gone hand in hand with the development of aircraft. Just as the First World War was the spur which led to the Atlantic crossing of Alcock and Brown (page 22), so the Second World War produced an even more significant development in aircraft design and production, which had a huge effect on commercial flying after the war. Many DC4s started as troop-carrying aircraft during the war, later to become very successful commercial airliners. Most carried between 44 and 52 passengers, but remarkably the aircraft shown here carried 88. They were powered by four Pratt and Whitney Twin Wasp engines rated at 1450hp each. It had a maximum speed of 280mph and a cruising speed of 246mph which was not so much slower than the cruising speed of the much newer Vickers Viscount. The aircraft was produced in different versions, including one with Rolls-Royce Merlin engines built in Canada and called 'The Argonaut'. The aircraft in this painting however was bought by Channel Airways from Riddle Airlines in 1962; a reminder that aircraft like coaches were often passed around!

The other two vehicles in the picture are also interesting. Today special purpose-built vehicles convey baggage to waiting aircraft, and lift it level with cargo holds. In the 1960s a Commer Karrier Bantam, made by the Rootes Group, does the task, being a flat truck with a small size and good manoeuvrability. The other vehicle originates from the 1930s, and is a six-wheel AEC Matador. These were originally used as artillery tractors, in a four-wheel version, and then the six-wheel version was developed and used as petrol bowsers for the RAF. The one shown may well be an ex-RAF model. I have never forgotten the experience of driving them across rough ground. It was best to stand, hanging on to the steering wheel and with the right foot on the accelerator. Gear changing with double declutching was a fantastic challenge!

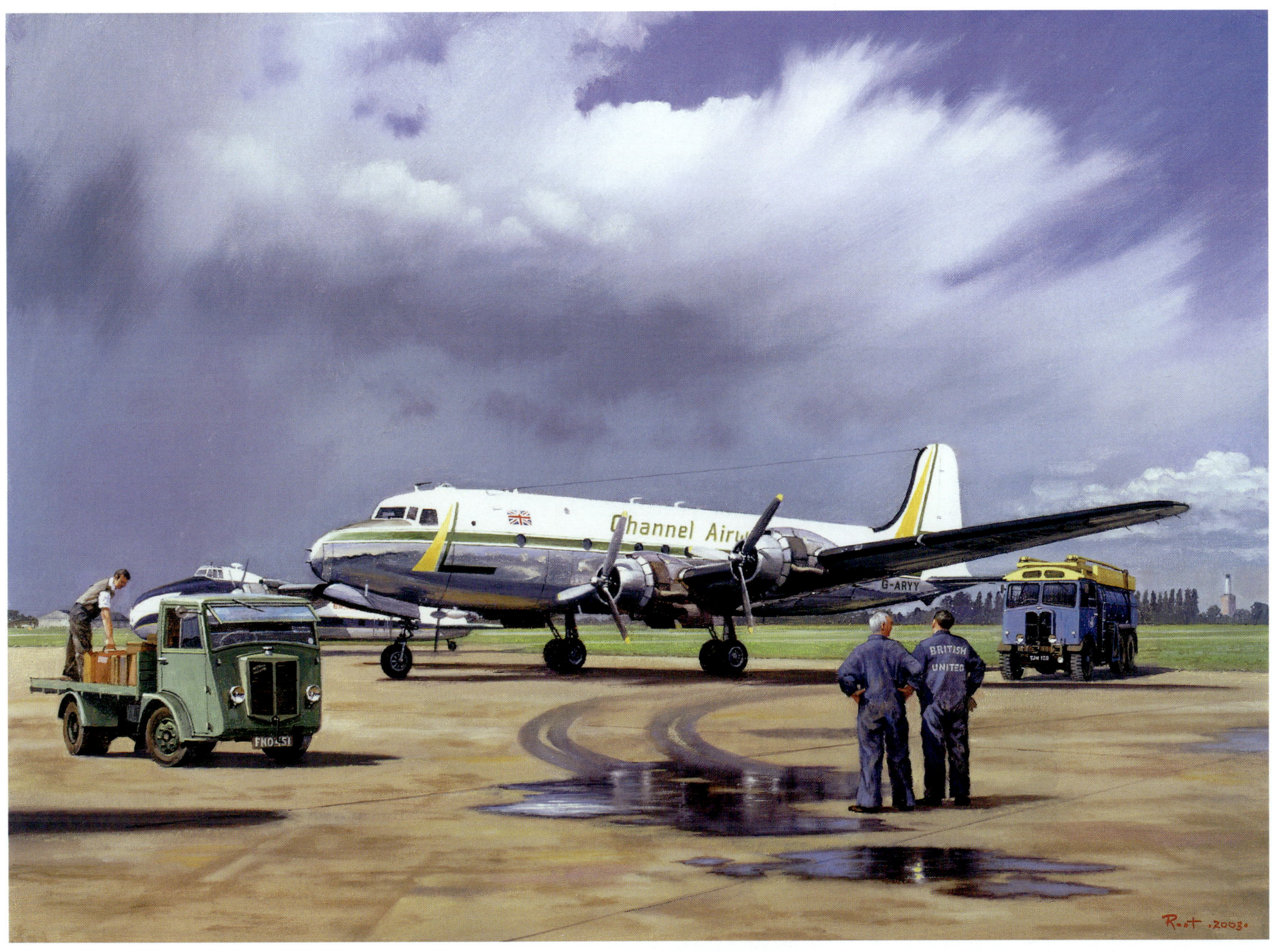
Channel Airw
G-ARYY
BRITISH
UNITED
FNO 451
Root .2003.

Searching for Nessie
Painted 2003

The world famous Loch Ness lies in north Scotland, between Fort William and Inverness, and the Caledonian Canal passes through it, so it sees a number of boats taking the short cut across Scotland without going right round the north coast. The Loch is just over 20 miles long, and has an average width of about 1½ miles, so is a considerable body of water. It is also surprisingly deep in places. Around 500 million years ago the earth's crust shifted and Loch Ness was formed. In the sixth century St Columba is supposed to have instructed a monk to swim across the loch to fetch a boat. In the middle of the loch the monster surfaced, and was just about to have monk for dinner when the saint bade it desist and begone. Since then, for 14 centuries, the monster has never harmed anyone. Sceptics might have an explanation for this remarkable fact!

The star of this picture, like many before and after him, is perched on the roof of his adapted van, armed with a cine camera with an impressive telephoto lens, and waiting for the 'moving of the waters'. He looks intent, and is getting a good suntan, but forever gazing at the waters of the loch could be very soporific! At least he has a well-equipped van, and has positioned it to get the best field of vision. The arrival of photography gave a great boost to the reputation of the Loch Ness Monster, with some notable photographs being taken, using a variety of types of trick photography, and various inflatable craft. At the same time the possibility of a leftover from the age of the dinosaurs could not be ruled out – a lonely Scottish Plesiosaur, perhaps – and the local tourist industry and gift shops thrived wondrously! I have passed Loch Ness on a number of occasions myself, and always scanned the waters with renewed hope. Sadly, the development of sophisticated echo-sounding used by recent expeditions has not found anything but a rather empty loch, but I do not anticipate that anything so crude will lay the legend to rest.

The Loch Ness Investigation van is a Bedford CA type, first introduced in 1947, and an excellent design with a large carrying capacity and powered by a sturdy four-cylinder petrol engine, as also used in the Vauxhall cars of this date. Bedford also produced the famous Dormobile on this chassis – the ancestor of all camper vans, and also a seven-seater minibus. My vicar in Surrey, John, had one, and used to hurtle down the A3 driving like Jehu! The coach passing the scene is on a tour of the Highlands, and is a Bedford SB, with a Duple Super Vega body – a very popular model of the time.

The painting reminds us of a period when people travelled for pleasure, or to further their hobbies, be they twitchers looking for rare birds, twister fanatics trying to catch tornados, railway enthusiasts spotting train numbers, or devotees hoping for a glimpse of the Loch Ness Monster.

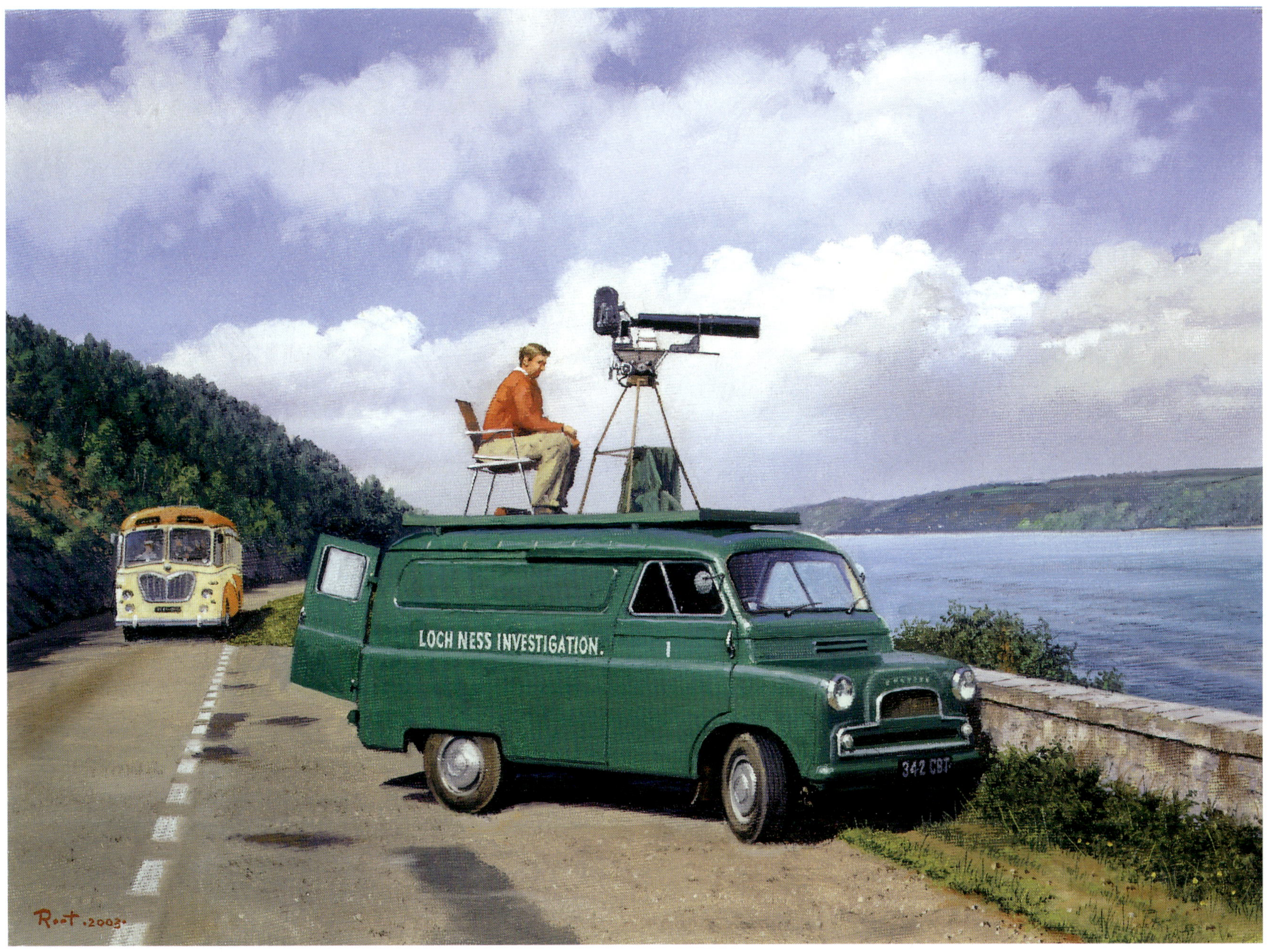
LOCH NESS INVESTIGATION.
342 CST

Ipswich Trolley Bus
Painted 2002

The trolley bus was introduced in this country as early as 1911, when the first vehicles appeared in Bradford and Leeds. They needed similar overhead wires as trams (see page 36), but no rails, so the capital cost was less, and maintenance also cheaper. Like trams they were cleaner and quieter than petrol and diesel vehicles, and in the period between 1920 and 1960 many towns and cities chose the trolley bus as a main public service vehicle, though usually supplemented by ordinary buses for less frequented routes, and out-of-town work. In Ipswich the trolley buses radiated from their town centre at Electric House, beside the Cornhill, and had their depot in Landseer Road, which is now the Ipswich Transport Museum. This painting clearly shows the web of wires needed to support the overhead power cables, and the intricacies of the points required at a junction. Notice how some of the posts also support telephone wires. When a bus pick-up arm became detached, or went on the wrong wire, the conductor was supplied with a long telescopic pole to hook it down and place it back in the correct position, so that normal service could be resumed.

Trolley Bus 126 has just come down Heath Road, past what in later years would be the new Ipswich Hospital, and turned at the roundabout into Foxhall Road, which will take it down to the town centre. The destination board does not record the number of this route, but I seem to remember it was 3A. I had to catch a 2A or better still a 2B to get home in the 1950s. This snowy scene, sparkling in the midday winter sunshine, is about a mile from my present home. This bus is a Sunbeam F4, with a Metrovick 95hp motor, and Park Royal bodywork. It was the last trolley bus to be bought by Ipswich Corporation Transport, and was sold to Walsall Corporation in 1962. In 1970 it came to the end of its working life, and was purchased for the Ipswich Transport Museum, where I had the privilege of sitting in the driver's seat. It has just accelerator and brake, a handbrake and steering wheel, so not difficult to drive if you remember to switch it on! It carried 30 passengers upstairs and 26 below.

The adverts on the bus may be a further piece of wishful thinking by the artist, - gin in front and beer down the sides! Tolly Cobbold (or in this case should it be Trolley Cobbold!) was a local speciality of the Ipswich area. The Ipswich trolley buses were eventually taken out of service on 23 August 1963. The Ipswich Transport Museum also has the first Ipswich trolley bus, dating from 1923, with solid tyres and powered by two 20 hp motors one on each rear wheel. It was built by Ransomes, Sims and Jefferies in Ipswich.

In the background, parked outside the shops is a 1947 Hillman Minx. This model superseded the 1939 model, having a trendier wrap-around radiator grille and a larger boot, giving the 'hump' shape at the back. It was a good sturdy car, but the Rootes Group replaced it with a new and very up-to-date Minx in 1952, with a 'mouth organ' radiator grille! (See page 90).

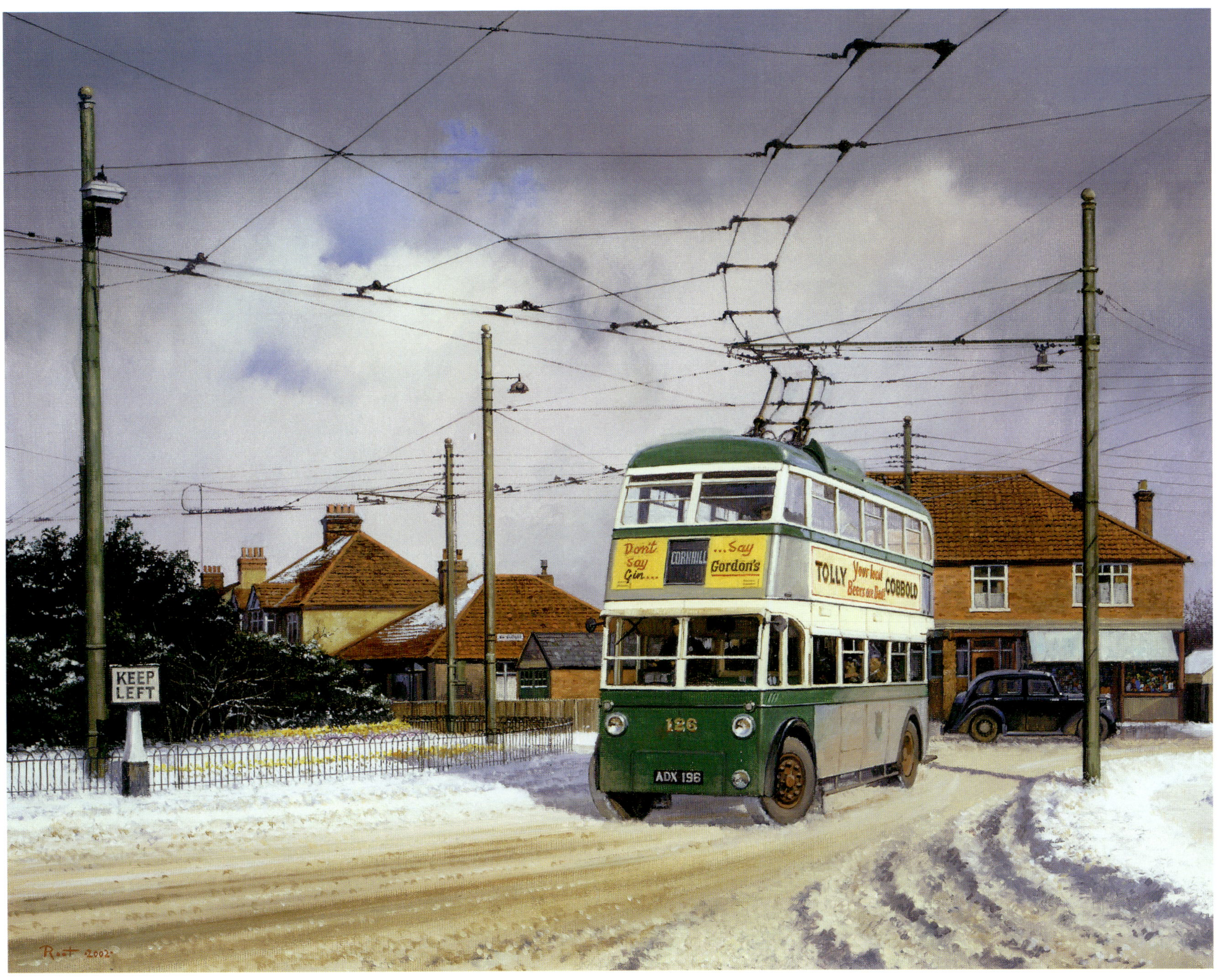
Don't
Say
Gin ...
CORNHILL
... Say
Gordon's
TOLLY
Your local
Beers are Best
COBBOLD
126
ADX 196
KEEP
LEFT
Root 2002

Confrontation at Witham Station

Painted 1988

Within a few years of its inception, British Railways was putting forward plans for twelve new locomotive types which would provide the motive power for the railways for many years to come. When the Big Four were nationalized, interchange trials were carried out to assess the locomotive designs of all four companies. The results were inconclusive, there being no definite 'winners'. It was therefore decided to produce some standard designs for ease of maintenance and uniformity of parts. With hindsight it seems strange that no one in 1950 had the ability to predict that in 18 years steam traction would be at an end, for by 1950 the signs were there to be read. The Britannia class, designed under the direction of R.A. Riddles, was the first of the new types to go into service in 1951. The locomotives had a tractive effort of 32 150lbs, and weighed about 141 tons. Fifty-five of the Britannia class were built, and many, in line with their patriotic class name, were named after great British literary and military figures.

In this magnificent but rather poignant painting we see two express trains, both headed by Britannia class locomotives, at Witham junction in Essex. Witham is on the London Liverpool Street to Norwich main line, and was also the junction for the Braintree–Bishops Stortford, as well as the Maldon branchlines. Coming towards us Britannia Class

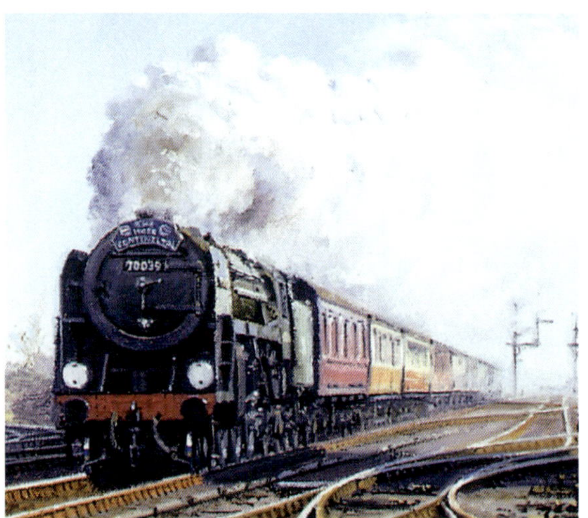

70039 *Sir Christopher Wren* heads the up Hook Continental travelling at speed, while number 70010 *Owen Glendower* waits impatiently for the all-clear so that it can resume its journey to Ipswich and Norwich. The unusual signal box between the two locomotives is designed to give maximum visibility, while allowing trains on the branchline to Braintree to pass underneath.

It is a still, clear sunny day, and the artist skillfully contrasts the steam and smoke patterns of the stationary and the fast moving locomotives. He also gives perfect detail to the near and distant signals, as well as remarkable detail of all the trackwork and points mechanism in the foreground. You can almost hear the hiss of venting steam, and the growing roar of the approaching express!

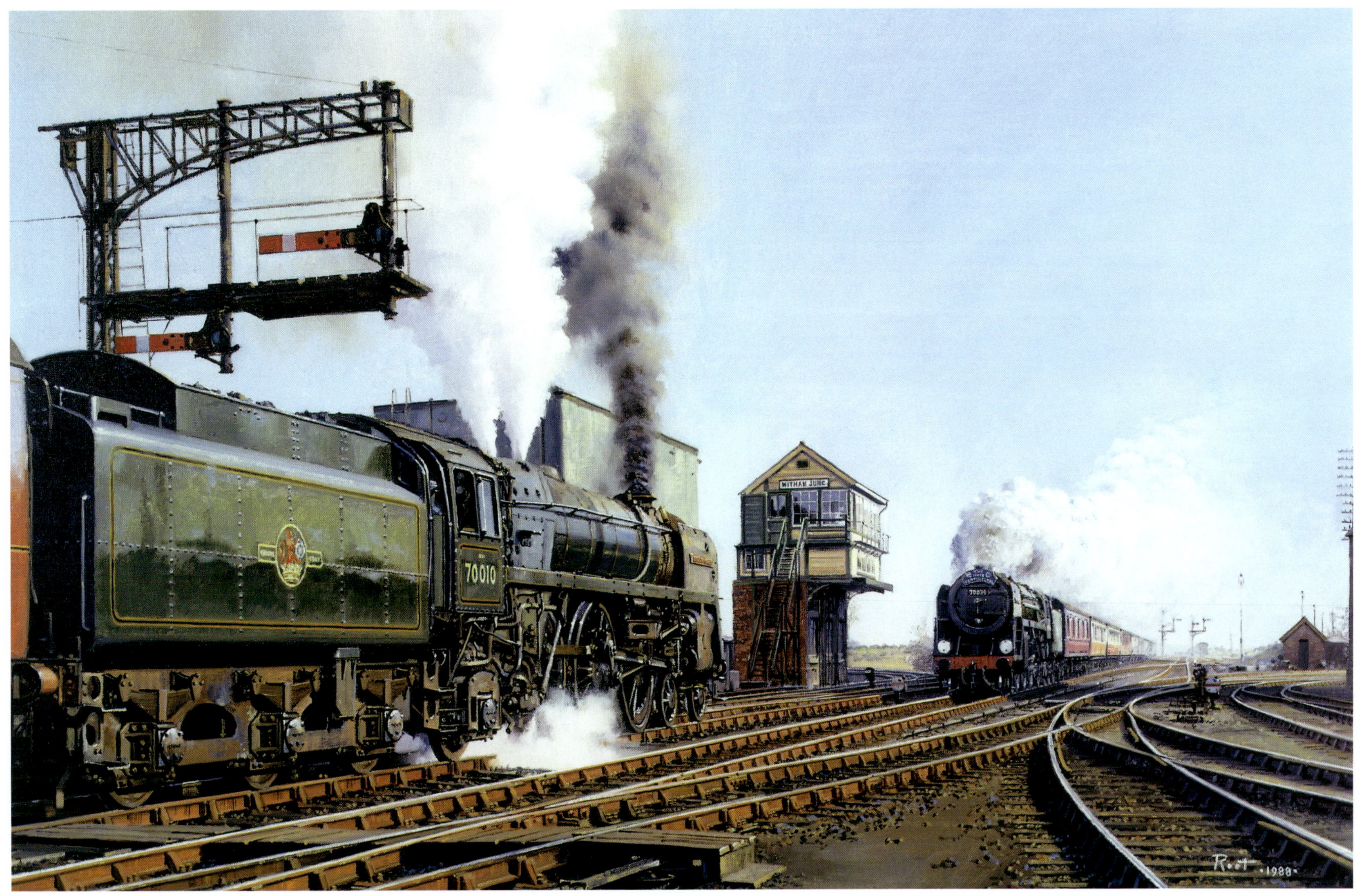
WITHAM JUNC
70010
70039
Root ·1988·

Road and Rail Services
Painted 2003

This painting shows just the sort of day a motorist thoroughly dislikes, with its promise of flying spray and mud, especially if you get stuck behind a heavy-laden BRS lorry! Malcolm has set this scene on the A74 at Beattock, high in the Pennines, so there is low cloud as well as rain to contend with, and headlights are in order. The Leyland Octopus lorry was being produced in the 1930s as an eight-wheeled forward-control lorry and I remember sitting in the cab of a derelict one in my Uncle's cooperage yard, and being amazed at the scale of the controls – there was no way I could reach the pedals! The model shown was introduced in 1953, and supplied new to BRS at the Doncaster depot. In 1965 it was sold on and was left to stand in the open for thirty years. It has now been lovingly restored to its former glory.

Leyland began building steam lorries in 1896, moving on to produce their first petrol vehicle in 1904. They recognized early on that size matters, and set about buying up much of the competition, including Albion, AEC, Austin, Guy, Morris and Scammell. The company became Leyland Motor Corporation, then on nationalisation just British Leyland, and it still makes a large range of lorries and vans today. The flat truck body shown has become increasingly useful over the years with the introduction of cargo containers.

Competing with the lorry, but more occupied in climbing the gradient to the summit at Beattock on the Carlisle to Glasgow main line, is an LMS class 5 locomotive, designed by Sir William Stanier and first introduced in 1934. With a weight of 125 tons, a boiler pressure of 225lbs per square inch, and coupled to driving wheels 6 feet in diameter it was a very useful mixed traffic locomotive.

The third vehicle in the picture is a Morris Y Type 10cwt van, dating from the late 1930s, and also produced just after the war (see page 70). It was very rugged, and popular with tradesman making deliveries. I remember the butcher, baker and grocer all had them. The butcher, Mr Lang, used to dispense a very interesting selection of meat from the back of his, and would skin rabbits on the spot with two cuts of the knife and a flick of the wrist. I wish I had got him to teach me how to do it!

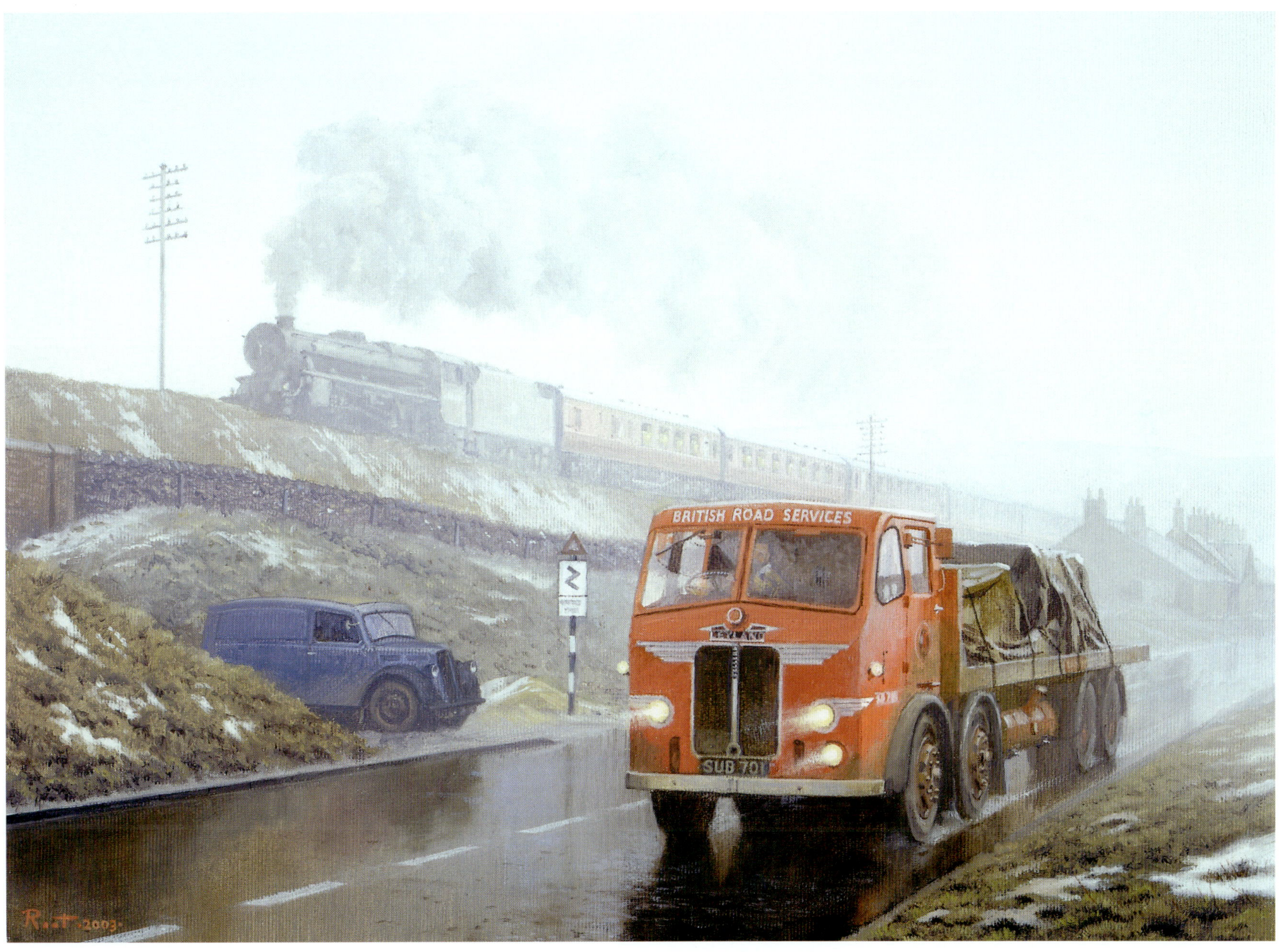
BRITISH ROAD SERVICES
LEYLAND
SUB 701

Canberra

Painted 1999

The Peninsular & Oriental Steam Navigation Company, known to everyone as P&O, originated in 1837, and merged with the British India Steam Navigation Company in 1914, so that by the mid 1920s they operated nearly 500 vessels. The fleet was requisitioned in 1939, and during the war 179 ships were sunk. In 1960 P&O merged with Orient Lines, but this was a critical time for liners, as the Boeing 707 Airliner had come into service in 1958, and that first year carried more passengers across the Atlantic than all the great liners combined. By 1960 two million passengers travelled by air, twice as many as by sea. But by 1960 P&O were committed to two large and splendid new liners, *Canberra* and *Oriana*.

Canberra was built by Harland and Wolff at Belfast, was of about 45 000 gross tons, and equipped with turbo-electric British Thompson Houston engines, placed aft. She cruised at about 27 knots, and could carry 2198 passengers in mixed class, or 1737 single class passengers for cruising. The intention was that she should serve the Australia run with world cruising as an alternative, and her maiden voyage included visits to San Francisco, Los Angeles and Sydney, returning via the Suez Canal, a distance of 42 000 miles! However, in spite of her luxury and impressive beauty it was a struggle to make a profit in the 1970s.

The spring of 1982 was to be a significant moment for the ship. When the Falklands Islands campaign was launched, *Canberra,* along with other liners, was 'taken up from trade' – a euphemism for 'requisitioned' and used as a troop carrier, or in the case of the P&O *Uganda* as a hospital ship. Helicopter landing platforms were hastily fitted to these ships, and in a record period of time they were ready for their new roles, which they all discharged with great success. *Canberra*, in her white paint, was nicknamed 'The Great White Whale' and was a great favourite with everyone. After several narrow escapes from attack, she went into Falkland Sound on 21 May 1982 and disembarked 3 Commando Brigade to begin the land war. After the war was over, *Canberra* ferried thousands of Argentine troops back to Argentina, and then brought British soldiers back to Southampton where she received a great welcome.

Sadly the economics of cruising did not improve and *Canberra* found herself competing with larger and more modern cruise ships. In 1997 she was withdrawn from service and scrapped. This lovely painting of her in happier times is a fitting tribute to a great ship and her brave crew.

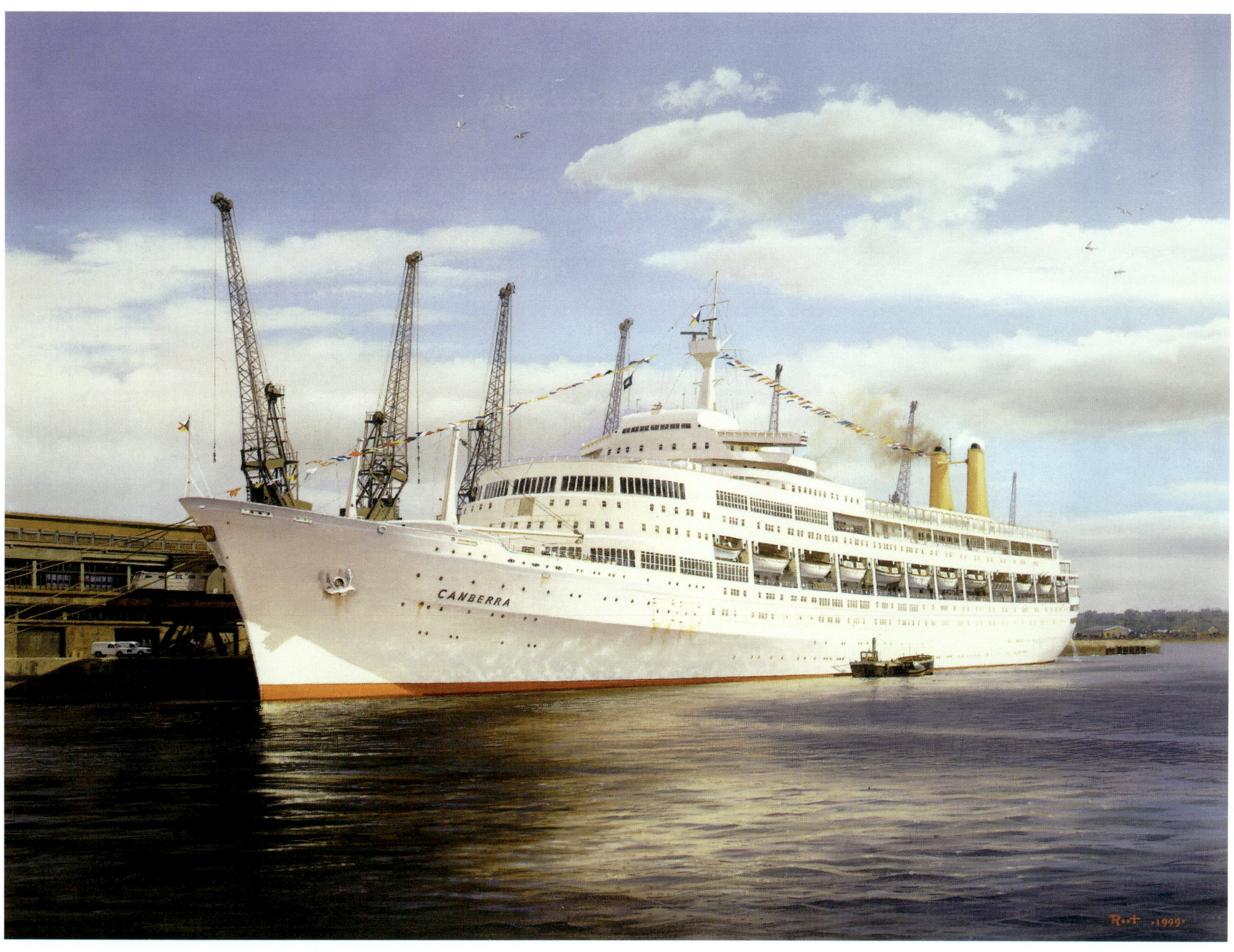

Crewe Rendezvous
Painted 2004

This is a magnificent portrait of a steam locomotive, and a very important one. Moreover, I have met this engine before, passing a 'twin' in a corner of very rural Wales! It is appropriate that this setting is the engine depot at Crewe North, for this was to the London, Midland & Scottish Railway what York was to the LNER (see pages 56 and 94). Six lines radiate out from Crewe, the most important of these being the West Coast route. This scene is close to the end of steam traction on British Railways, but the steam engines shown are refined and impressive machines which could carry on for many more years, given the chance.

The development and history of the 2-6-4 tank class is an interesting but complicated one. As this is not a technical book we will not go into it in too much detail here. Large passenger tanks had been used on the Southern Railway in London Brighton and South Coast days, and the 2-6-4 design was progressed by Fowler for the LMS in 1927. These were further developed by the great engineer William Stanier in the 1930s with the two- and three-cylinder designs. Fairburn carried on the development when he succeeded Stanier as CME of the LMS.

Flanking the tank engine are two most impressive locomotives from LMS days. On the left, just visible, is Stanier Pacific 46203, *Princess Margaret Rose*, and on the right is Princess Coronation Class 46233 *Duchess of Sutherland*. (see page 62). Both these great locomotives have been preserved, thanks initially to the foresight of Sir Billy Butlin. As the tank engine's crew get down from their cab, another railwayman stands and admires the locomotive. In the foreground can be seen the ash pit, into which clinker and cinders from the fireboxes was emptied. Both the cleaning of the ash pan and the emptying of the ash pit were dirty and physically demanding jobs.

Hornby Dublo made an excellent model of the Standard 2-6-4 tank, which was very heavy and pulled a long train. The model was produced in two- and three-rail versions numbered 80033 and 80054. Such is the world of collecting that they were much sought after and consequently very expensive. My brother spotted mine for me in London, and paid £10 for it a very long time ago!

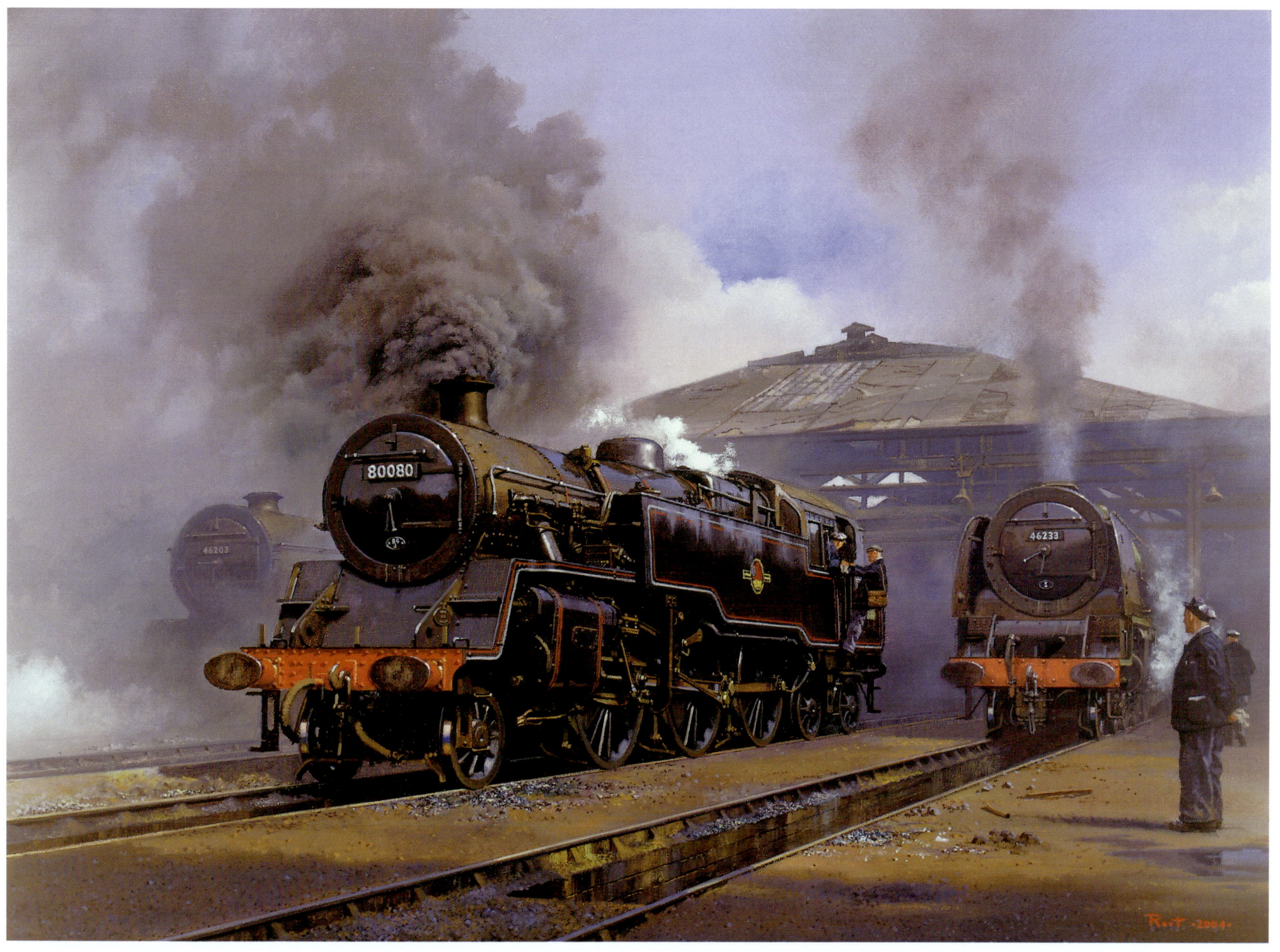

Lines of Communication
Painted 2003

This is very much a scene from the past, with the Post Office Telephones engineer perched atop a pole and going about his business! Post Office Telephones became British Telecom in 1980, but still part of the Post Office, and then the next year became a separate public corporation. Today most cables go underground, and pole climbing is not such a requirement. Climbing the pole could be quite tricky and especially transferring from ladder to pole. The angle irons on the pole were secured by bolts, which scuffed the inside of the engineers boots leaving telltale marks. Once at the top, and secured with his safety belt, he had both hands free to work. If a customer had reported a crackling line, the culprit was probably a corroded copper wire inside a connector – the tops screwed off for access. My telephone engineer friend, Harry, says that Malcolm has portrayed a party line going to two houses. This meant that either house could receive incoming phone calls, but only one could make an outgoing phone call at one time. If the other picked up the phone they could listen in on their neighbour's conversation. Thus if someone reported to the telephone engineer that there was 'heavy breathing' frequently on their party line, it was not the connector at fault but the neighbour!

The telephone engineer was supplied with a van, in this case a Morris Minor. The van would be fully equipped with

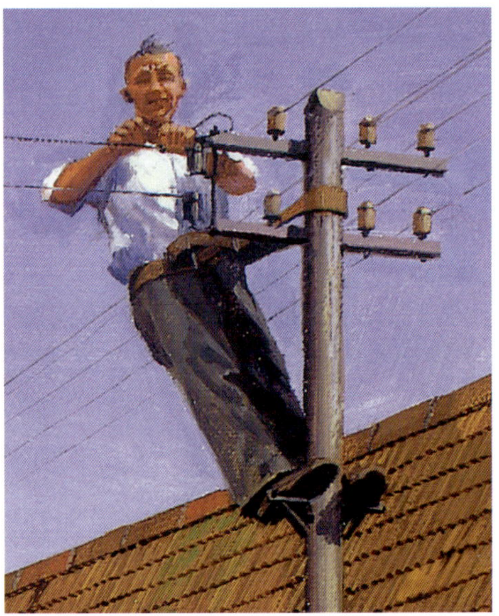

tools, a stepladder inside and a ladder carried on the roof. Pruning rods could be fitted inside, on the floor between the equipment racks. Every detail was covered in the Post Office instructions. The van in this picture, though registered in London, was supplied to a telephone manager in East Anglia.

The Morris Minor, on which this van is based, was an interesting car, as it was produced from 1948 to about 1970, with relatively minor modifications, at a time when car design underwent enormous changes. A 918 cc sidevalve engine was originally supplied, later to be upgraded for improved performance. The amalgamation with the Austin company to become BMC produced some changes of a mechanical nature, but fundamentally the car remained the same. The millionth model was produced in 1960. However there was always a devoted following of people who didn't want to pay extra for the latest trend in car design. You still see a lot of examples of this fine car in use on the road today.

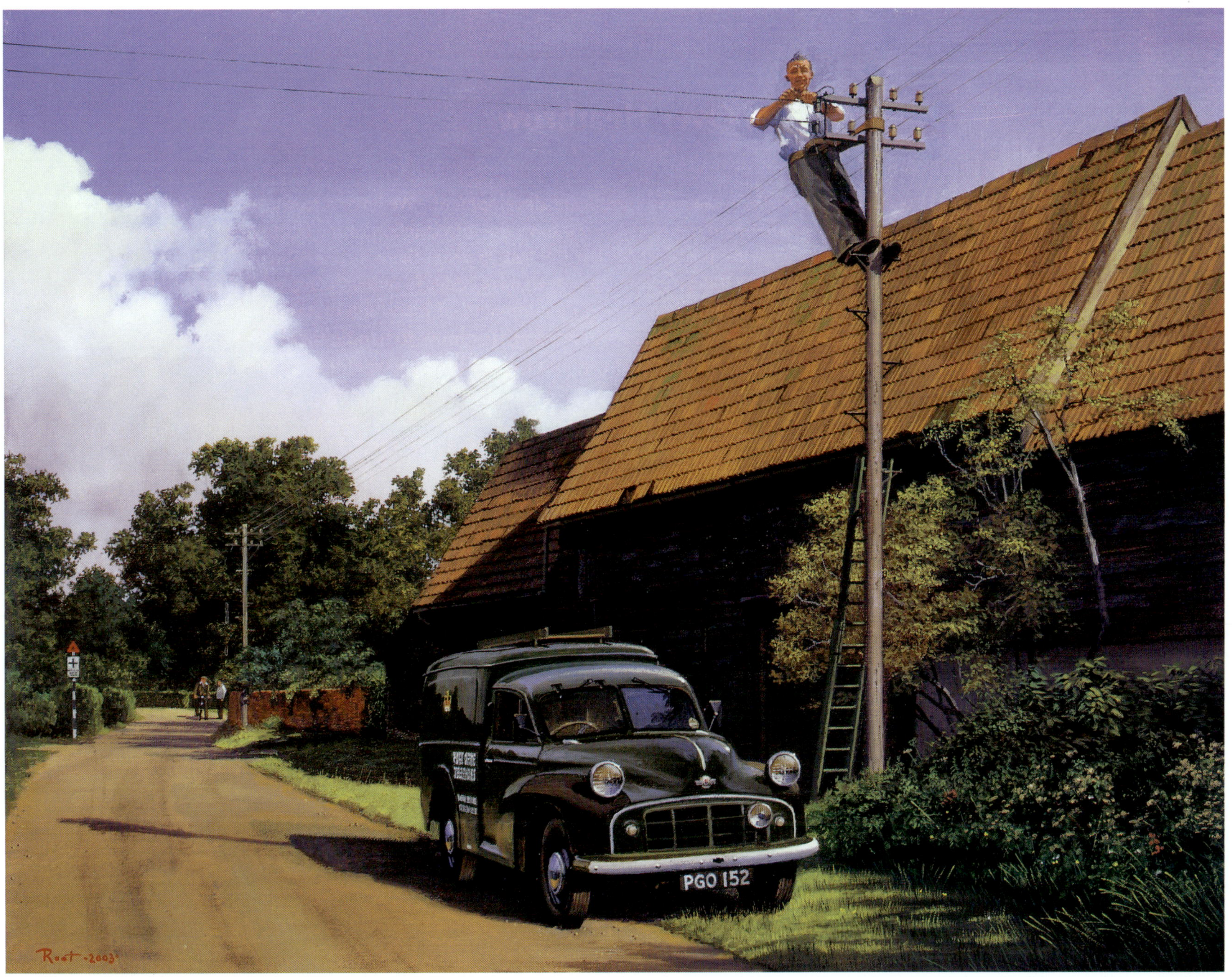

Over Heathrow
Painted 1998

We move now in our pageant to the 1970s, and a very significant development. We have already seen on page 108 what affect the Boeing 707 had on international travel. Now we have the introduction of the Boeing 747, the Jumbo Jet, which carried nearly three times as many passengers. For the last 35 years these airliners have dominated the skies, forcing other aircraft manufacturers to follow suit in their designs in order to remain competitive. In addition, the arrival of these aircraft necessitated the enlargement and development of many international airports such as Heathrow, pictured here. On 2 June 1970 Terminal 3 was extended at Heathrow to handle these larger aircraft, but even today the sudden arrival of over four hundred passengers can cause a long queue at immigration control!

The Boeing 747 has been constantly developed and adapted for particular airlines and tasks. The aircraft seen here is the 747-136, with a wingspan of 195 feet, and weighing in at about 325 tons. It can carry 404 passengers, cruising at 550 miles per hour, and has a range of about 5000 miles, with a useable fuel tank capacity of 120 tons. The picture shows the airliner in the livery of British Overseas Airways Corporation, later merged with British European Airways to form British Airways. BOAC took delivery of the first of these aircraft in April 1970. These 'wide bodied' jets can have 9 or 10 passengers sitting abreast, with two aisles, and unusually there is an upper deck as well. Seating can either be arranged for first and economy class passengers, or for economy class only, in which case about 70 extra passengers can be accommodated. The 747-100 version was powered by four Pratt and Whitney JT9D-7A turbofans which were located in the traditional position for Boeing aircraft, beneath the wings.

A special feature of this painting is the way the artist has captured the appearance of the clouds seen from above, with glimpses of the ground beneath showing through. Anyone who has flown will recognize what a brilliant interpretation this is.

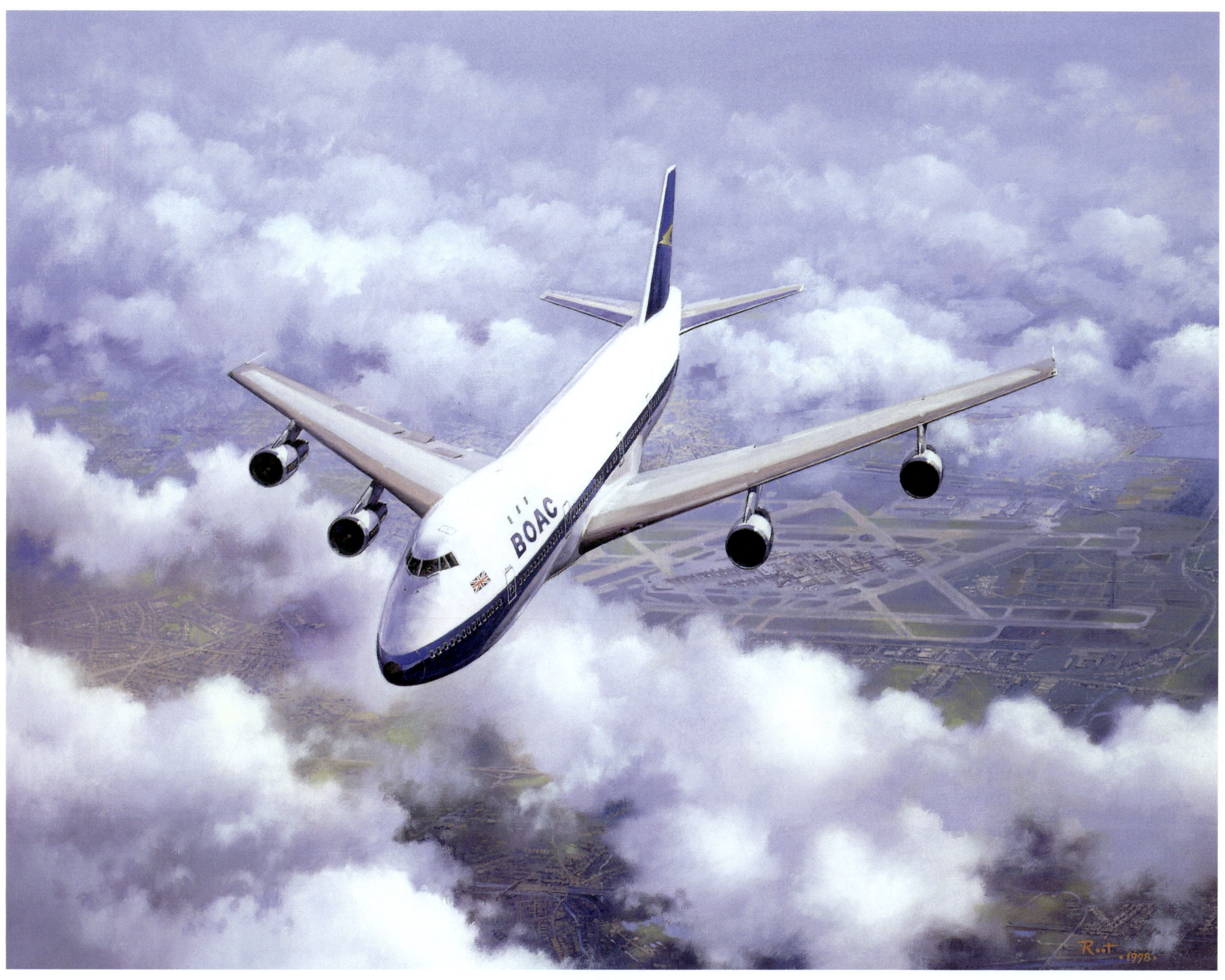

Yule Logs
Painted 2005

This is a different view of the church in Malcolm's home town of Halstead (see page 38), but also portraying a snowy day, with slushy conditions underfoot. Once again it is an example of heavy haulage, but this time the traction engine has given way to the heavy haulage tractor (see pages 40 and 76). It was often the case that timber and builders' merchants were located close to docks and railway stations, but in this case the heavy vehicle is labouring up the hill to the local woodworks. The lorry shown has the name Halstead on the cab door, so it seems unlikely they have slowed to ask for directions. It is more likely that the people in the picture know one another. Whatever the reason, the large lorry is completely blocking the child's view of the tempting sweet shop across the road, which may be a blessing in disguise, although I suspect it may only be delaying the inevitable!

As vehicles grew bigger over the years, so loads could be heavier, and problems of loading large tree trunks on a trailer became more of a challenge. The trailer was kept as low as possible, and many heavy haulage tractors were equipped with a winch at the back, which was a very valuable piece of equipment, and could be used also for pulling the vehicle out of a sticky situation. If a lot of timber was being loaded from a particular location it was worthwhile bringing a mobile crane in to do the loading job.

The tractor, which looks so impressive in this painting, is an interesting one. Latil was a French vehicle manufacturer established in 1904, and their tractors were built in Britain under license from 1924 by Latil Industrial Vehicles Ltd. Most of the vehicles produced were four-wheel drive tractors, with an auxiliary gearbox, and either the Latil 20hp petrol engine, or a Meadows diesel engine. The width between the wheels of the tractor was similar to the standard gauge of the railways, and Latil adapted several tractors for shunting railway trucks by adding four small flanged wheels which could be wound down to guide the vehicle on rails, while power was transmitted via the normal road wheels which rested on the track. Ingenious, but it doesn't seem to have caught on in a big way!

When painting pictures of trains I prefer to use a low view point as this gives a better impression of size and power. Conversely a high view point can sometimes give the impression of a model railway. In this portrayal of a Latil log transporter the same technique has been employed, although the position would have been an uncomfortable one as the lorry passed. It is worth remembering that at the time this type of vehicle would have been among the largest using the roads. This is of course not the case today!

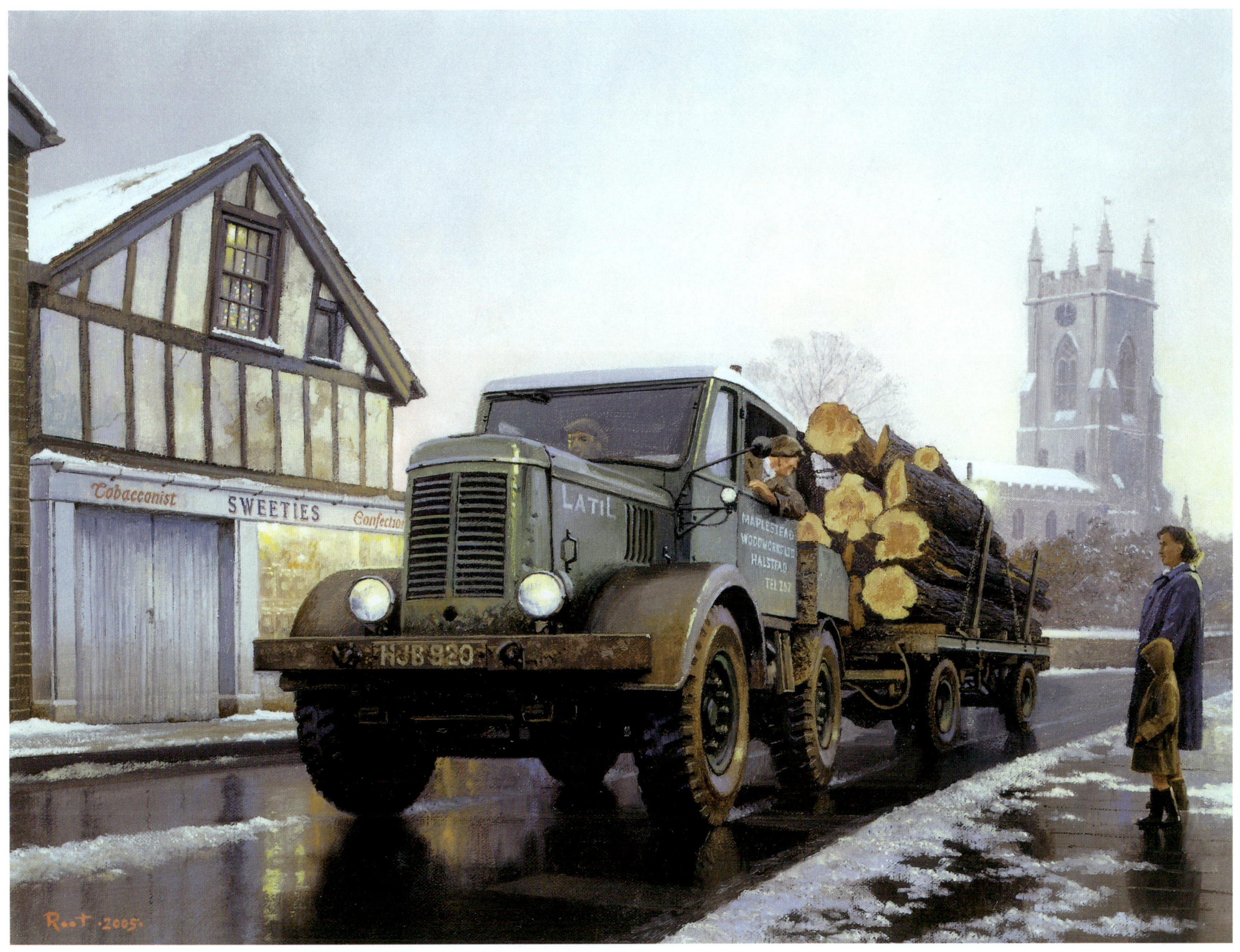
Tobacconist
SWEETIES
Confection
LatiL
MAPLESTEAD
WOODWORK LTD
HALSTEAD
Tel 262
HJB 920
Root .2005.

Victoria Bridge

Painted 1982

You might wonder why this painting is positioned here, as it appears to be a classic scene from the Great Western Railway of the 1930s. This is Victoria Bridge, on the GWR line which ran from Kidderminster via Bridgnorth to Shrewsbury. The railway followed the course of the River Severn, but only crossed the river once, near Upper Arley, and doing so via a magnificent bridge with a single 200 foot span high above the river. The bridge was built under the direction of a notable nineteenth century civil engineer, Sir John Fowler, and was completed in 1861. The painting well captures the majesty of the view, with the reflection of the train in the waters of the river beneath.

This branch of the GWR was closed, like so many, in the 1960s, but help was at hand, and soon after a preservation society was founded which worked to raise the necessary money to buy a stretch of the track. In 1970 the first section of the Severn Valley railway was opened, and in due course it was extended to connect Bridgnorth with the main line at Kidderminster once again. There was no possibility of continuing north to Shrewsbury as the land was now in private ownership. Over the years, this preservation society, like so many others, has put in an enormous amount of voluntary work, fundraising, restoring stock, and running the railway, so that today they have a very important collection of preserved examples of every aspect of GWR history.

When it was decided which locomotives should form the National Collection many were surprised to find no example of the GWR Hall class included. In all 329 of this classic locomotive (including modified Halls) were built, from 1928 onwards. They weighed about 120 tons and operated over much of the GWR system. However, GWR folk have always been of independent mind, and eighteen Halls were saved for preservation. Of these, number 4930, *Hagley Hall,* moved to live on the Severn Valley Railway, and is seen in this painting pulling classic GWR chocolate and cream coaches over the Victoria Bridge towards Kidderminster. I hope that steam locomotives at this classic location will long be a sight that many future generations will be privileged to enjoy.

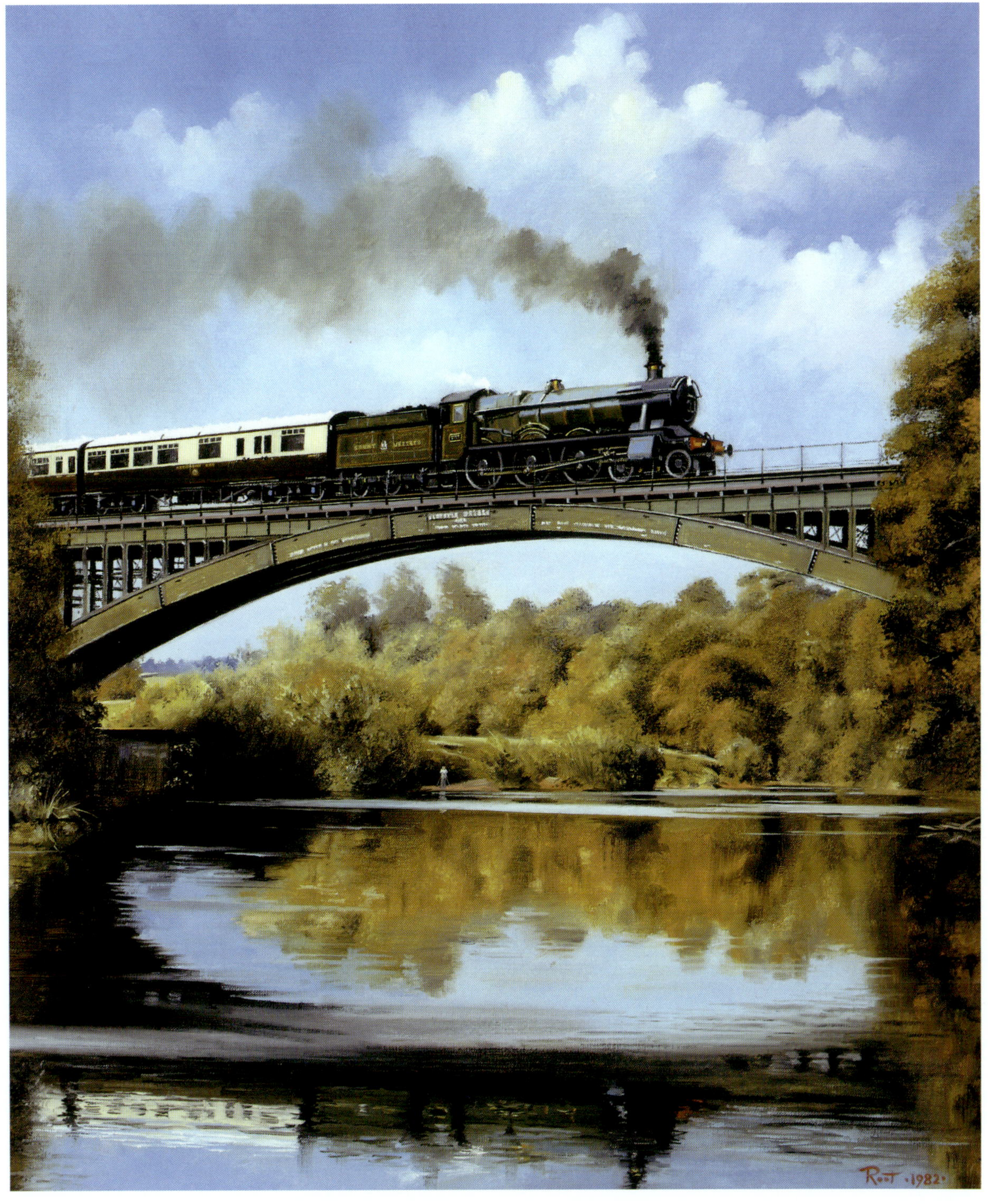

Victory Parade
Painted 2005

The Romans were great enthusiasts for victory parades. The preferred vehicle was a horse-drawn chariot, and the vanquished were required to follow on foot, and in chains, contrary to the Geneva Convention! Today, thanks to the victories of our Rugby and Ashes Cricket teams, we have had some victories to celebrate, and we are in no doubt that the open top double-decker bus, combined with a fine day, is the best vehicle for the celebrating team. These vehicles are usually to be found in cities or towns of historical importance, or by the sea side, and they are usually standard but out of date buses which have been converted in local workshops, and have a new but gentle occupation in semi-retirement. In general they are designed for sightseers to admire the interesting features of the city, from a good and mobile vantage point. When pressed into service for a sporting victory parade the situation is reversed, and the team stands on top of the open bus, while the crowd of onlookers are able to study their heroes.

The team celebrating on this momentous occasion is Colchester United, Malcolm's own team! In 1971 Colchester beat West Bromwich Albion in the final of the Watney Cup. This was Britain's first sponsored football competition, and was arranged with adapted rules to encourage goal scoring. Players could not be declared off side if they were outside the penalty area. It was hoped this would add excitement to the game, and it provided plenty of excitement for Colchester on this memorable occasion who won 4–3 on penalties after the match ended in a 4–4 draw. The prominent adverts on the bus are not to remind us of Malcolm's favourite lubricant, but the sponsors of the competition! The setting for the scene is Layer Road in Colchester, home ground of the victors.

The bus is an ex Westcliff Bristol KSW5G, powered by a Gardner diesel engine. With a cup on the radiator, and dressed overall in the team colours of blue and white, and complete with red barrels, it looks very smart. The other vehicle in the picture is almost a legend among family cars, the Ford Cortina, introduced in the early 1960s. First called the Consul Cortina to link it with the Ford Consul which it replaced, it soon became just the Cortina, and five different Marks were made, up to the 1980s. Shown here is the Mark I Super, with a four-cylinder 1498cc engine. The car was developed in conjunction with Lotus, and competed very successfully in the Monte Carlo Rally. My own Mk5 version did a quarter of a million miles of excellent and at times very arduous service, and then ended its career as a participant in the local Ipswich Stock Car racing!

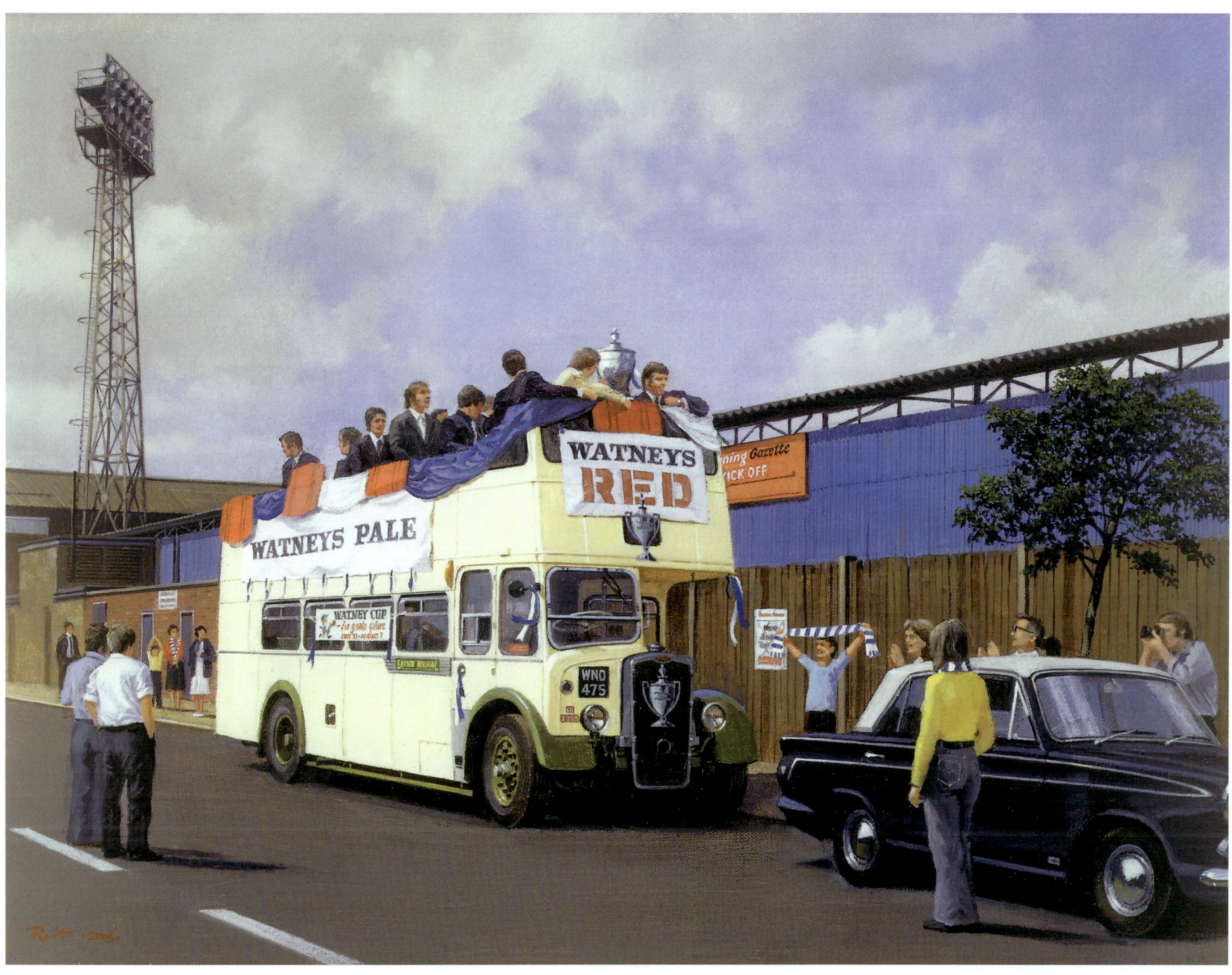
WATNEYS
RED
WATNEYS PALE
WATNEY CUP
WNO
475

Green Goddess
Painted 2005

Hythe, Dymchurch, New Romney and Dungeness are located by the sea in south-west Kent, in an area of flat land. The existence of the 15-inch narrow gauge railway which links these four places is due to three men: Count Louis Zborowski and Captain J. Howey were both drivers on the Brooklands racing circuit, and were also miniature railway enthusiasts. Before his premature death in a motor racing accident at Monza in November 1924, Zborowski involved the third man, Henry Greenly. He was an engineer and locomotive designer famous throughout the world of smaller gauge railways, and Zborowski ordered two locomotives of his design. Captain Howey decided to go ahead with the project that had fired their enthusiasm, that of building a main line in miniature, and Greenly designed the locomotives for the Romney, Hythe & Dymchurch Railway, which would be built by Davey Paxman & Co. of Colchester. The first locomotive, *Green Goddess* was tested on the Ravenglass and Eskdale Railway in Cumbria, where it had to cope with hills it would never meet by the sea in Kent. On 5 August 1926 the first passenger train travelled over the line, carrying the Duke of York (the future King George VI), Captain Howey, Henry Greenly, Nigel Gresley, and other notable railway enthusiasts.

During the Second World War the railway was closed to the public, because of its location, and an armoured train drawn by the locomotive *Hercules* was made up with armour plating and carrying anti-aircraft and anti-tank guns. The railway was also used by the Petroleum Warfare Department to carry materials for the building of the fuel line 'Pluto' under the channel to France. It took nearly two years to restore the railway to normal working after the war. The opening ceremony was performed by Stan Laurel and Oliver Hardy.

This lovely painting shows the first locomotive, *Green Goddess* on the turntable at Hythe. It was Henry Greenly's inspiration to produce an exact model of a full-size locomotive as far as possible, and *Green Goddess* was modelled on a Gresley designed 4-6-2 Pacific as run on the London & North Eastern Railway. The excellent design and workmanship of the locomotive made them extremely efficient in operation, so that they achieved a scale speed comparable to the Gresley Pacifics and are still steaming successfully 80 years after they were built. Eventually eleven steam locomotives were built for the railway, and all continue in service.

Shown with *Green Goddess* is the late George Barlow BEM who was the engine's driver for 31 years and was a legend on the RH&DR, and who was also Operations Manager for the railway. Captain Howey, who had to a large extent financed the railway, died in September 1963, but the railway has continued from strength to strength, and was a favourite haunt of mine in the 1970s. The standard of maintenance and care is outstanding, and it is well worth a visit. Trains run to a regular timetable all through the year, which can be accessed in advance.

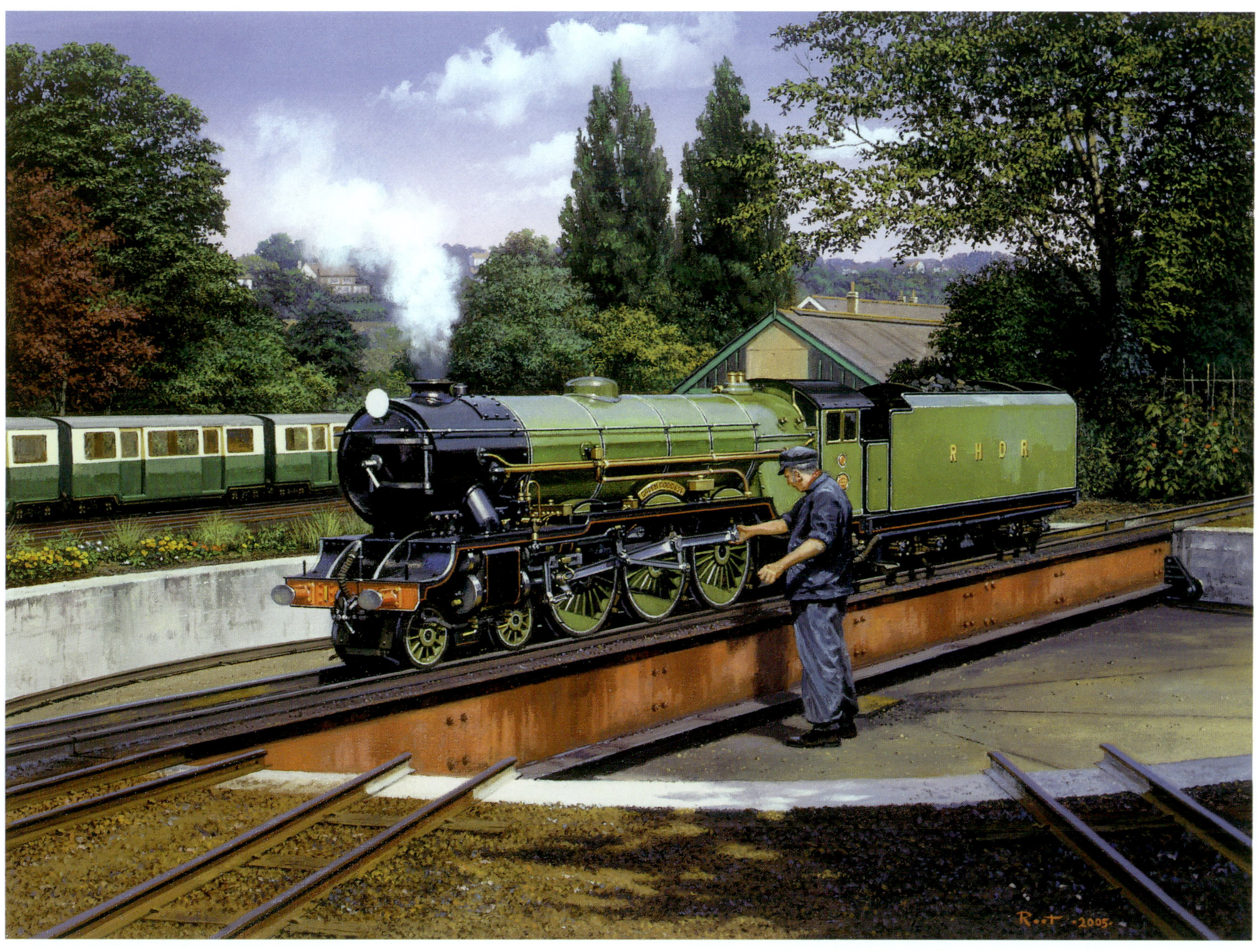

Sir Nigel Gresley

Painted 1985

Throughout our pageant of transport we have followed the development of different types of transport, and in particular the railways. However, if asked to name the most successful locomotive ever built, the choice would be a hard one. Each great company, plus British Railways, could submit a candidate, the Princess Coronation class from the LMS, the A4 Pacific from the LNER, a King from the GWR, a Bulleid Pacific from the Southern and a Britannia from BR. Each would have its own merits to put forward, and each was a development on what had gone before.

Though a GWR man, I think I have to give the prize to the Gresley A4. Nigel Gresley had already designed some notable locomotives when he was called upon to produce something special for the East Coast main line from London to Edinburgh. Gresley decided upon the Pacific design which he favoured, with an increased boiler pressure of 250lbs per square inch. (He learned a useful lesson when one of his locomotives was pitted against a GWR Castle). Most spectacular of all was the streamlined casing, which really was part of the locomotive, unlike the rather slab-sided equivalents on the LMS. This was a time when publicity and image were all important in the thoroughly modern 30s! The A4 was a true greyhound, and *Mallard*, one of the class, established the world record for steam traction at 126mph which still stands today and is testimony to the engine's performance.

In this spectacular and colourful picture we see the preserved A4 *Sir Nigel Gresley*, number 4498, in original blue livery from LNER days, heading a train on the famous Settle to Carlisle route. As usual the detail is wonderful – grass, tracks, drystone wall, and traces of snow remaining on the hill in the background. This picture, set in the early 1980s, shows the locomotive minus its valences, which covered the upper part of the driving wheels and valve gear, and much hampered maintenance. During the war these were removed and not replaced by harassed maintenance engineers, and were then probably collected up and turned into Spitfires!

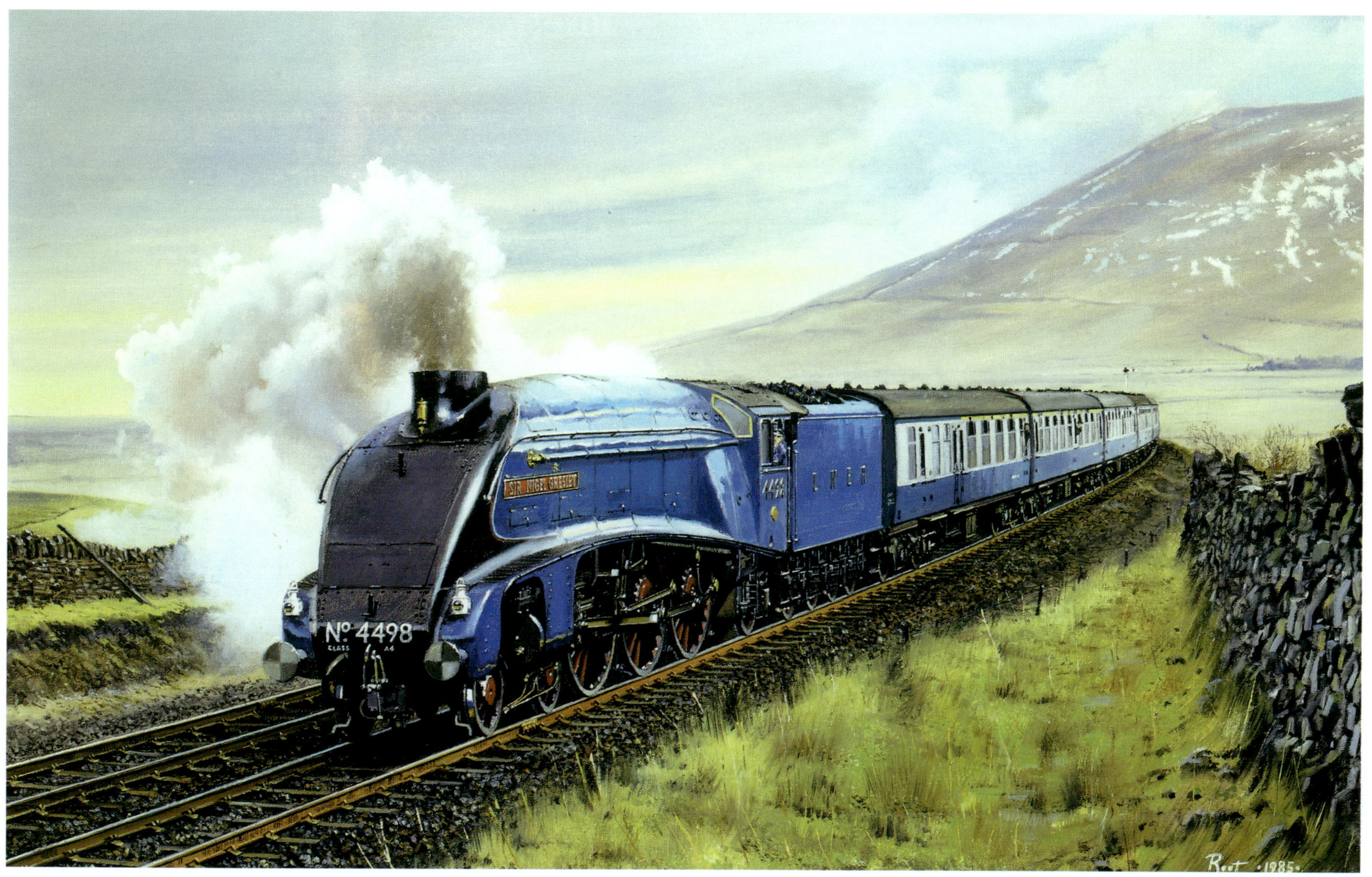

N° 4498
CLASS A4
SIR NIGEL GRESLEY
L N E R
Root 1985.

Waverley at Sunset

Painted 2005

We have discovered how Bournemouth became a noted seaside resort on the south coast of England (page 64), and like other resorts it took great pride in a spectacular pier, even if it was only one-seventh as long as Southend's! (see page 82). At Bournemouth a wooden pier was built in 1856, almost at the start of the town, but after several unsatisfactory attempts, a substantial metal pier was constructed in 1880, and added to in 1894 and 1909 to achieve the present-day length of about 1000 feet. The first pier cost £2600, but a restoration in 1979 cost £1.7 million! The presence of a pier put Bournemouth on the map for passing pleasure steamers, and it has been a favourite port of call with its multitude of seaside amenities for passengers to enjoy.

In this picture we see a very distinguished visitor, the paddle steamer *Waverley*, positioned off the pier on a fine summer's evening. The *Waverley* is the last ocean-going paddle steamer in the world, and carries the name of a former ship built on the Clyde in 1899. That first *Waverley*, of the LNER fleet, was requisitioned by the Admiralty at the outbreak of the Second World War and detailed for minesweeping duties. She was attacked and sunk during the evacuation of Dunkirk in May 1940 (page 44). After the war the Admiralty paid £15 125 in compensation, which helped towards the £107 725 cost of her replacement. The new Waverley was also built by A. & J. Inglis on the Clyde, and launched in 1946. She is a very handsome ship, of 693 tons, with a length of about 240 feet, beam of 30 feet and a

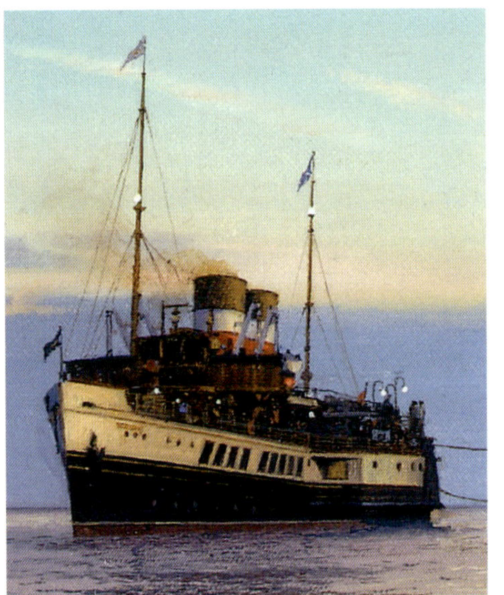

draught of only 6½ feet, making her ideal for shallow water. From 1947 to 1973 she was based on the Clyde, first with the LNER, then the Caledonian Steam Packet Co., and finally Caledonian MacBrayne.

In 1973 she appeared to have come to the end of her working life, but was sold very generously to the Paddle Steamer Preservation Society for £1, and they undertook necessary repairs and restoration, and a new life began for the ship. She still operated from the Clyde, but now also included cruises all round the British Isles, calling at over 100 ports and piers. She can do 18 knots, and her triple expansion steam engine is now fuelled by oil not coal. On this steamer passengers have a good view of the engine room and its impressive machinery. In 2000 the ship had an extensive rebuild, and continues today to delight passengers all round the coast, a living monument to those who built her and have sailed in her, and a tribute to those who give so much time and energy, not to mention money, to preserve such inspiring examples of transport from the past.

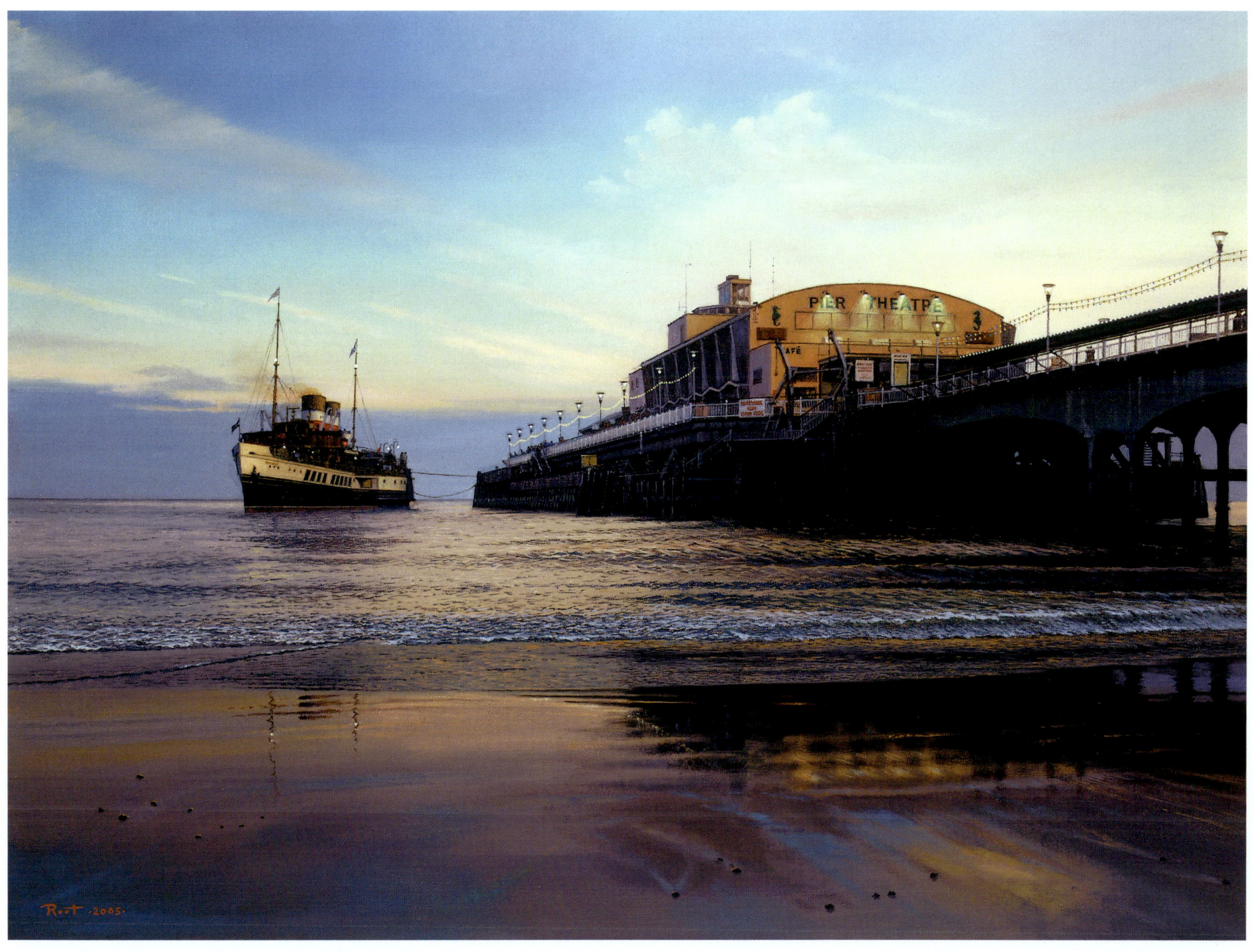
PIER THEATRE

Royal Train at Arten Gill
Painted 2005

This is a wonderful portrait of a splendid train amidst most impressive surroundings. This is Dentdale in West Yorkshire, and the train is crossing Arten Gill viaduct on its way to Dent, at 1150 feet above sea level the highest main-line station in England. Dent station is characterized by its snow defences, and is a cold and remote place four miles away from the community which it serves. In the background of the picture can be seen the dark forestry plantations from which the train has recently emerged. This viaduct carries the Settle to Carlisle railway over Artengill Beck. The massive structure, consisting of eleven arches, is made from locally quarried limestone. All these elements combine to make this railway one of the most impressive engineering achievements in the country. Again the different grasses, trees and stone walls are a distinctive feature of the landscape which the artist has captured to perfection.

The train gleaming in its distinctive livery is in fact the Royal Train, pulled by a classic locomotive, thus combining modern needs with preserved tradition. It was probably Prince Albert, Queen Victoria's husband, who gave the royal seal of approval to the newly established railways by persuading his wife to travel by train from Windsor to London on 13 June 1842. Victoria loved to be at Windsor, and also at Balmoral, and the train gave her the means to travel in comfort. The first Royal Trains were great examples of Victorian elegance, with separate day saloons for the Queen and the Prince Consort, though with an interconnecting corridor. Unlike the old road carriages, the trains had plenty of space for a large staff, and plenty of baggage. The future of the Royal Train has sometimes been in doubt, but it would be very sad if this special train were not available to any future Head of State of this great land. In my opinion such an attempt at economy would be small minded.

Pulling the train is a famous locomotive, the *Duchess of Sutherland* (see page 62). The painting depicts the occasion when HRH The Prince of Wales travelled on the Settle to Carlisle Railway in March 2005. This engine, like the *Waverley* is a living example of our country's famous industrial past, and it is due to immense work on the part of volunteers and fund raisers alike that such a magnificent locomotive has been available to haul excursion trains as well as Royal Trains in the recent past. One hopes this can continue for many years to come.

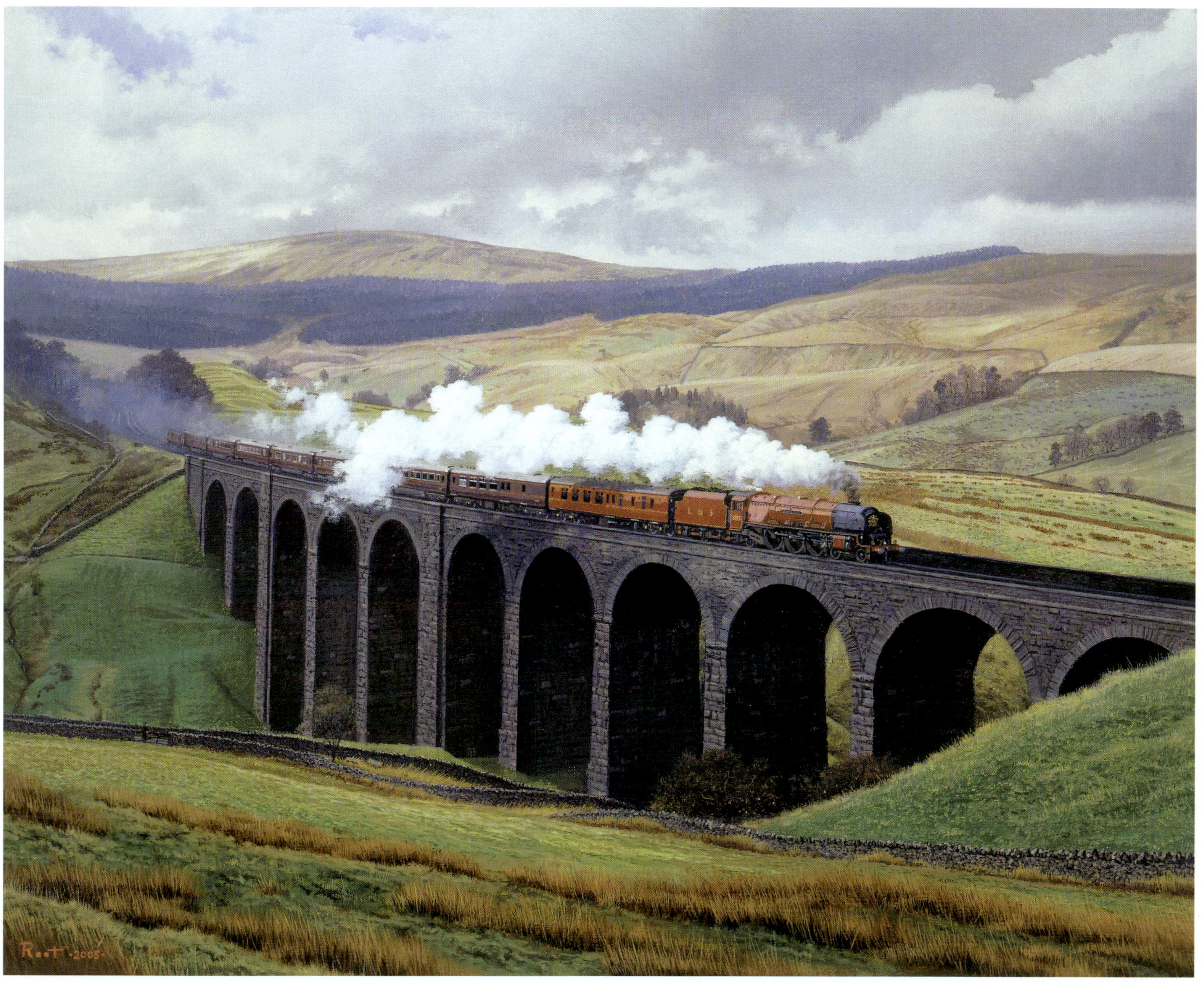

Halstead High Street
Painted 1999

Halstead, Malcolm's home town in Essex, is situated at the spot where horses or pedestrians descended into a gentle valley and splashed across the River Colne. As was usual the church was built on the higher ground to the east, and the town grew up between church and river. By the time the Domesday Book was compiled in 1086 there were 9 villagers, 78 smallholders, 22 freemen and 8 slaves, with three mills and 19 ploughs. A number of roads served the town from every direction, and in 1251 a market was established, though it was opposed by the powerful de Vere family, Earls of Oxford, who had organized rival markets at nearby Castle Hedingham and Earls Colne. By 1411 Halstead had a population of about 500, a woollen weaving industry was well established and so was the market. A bridge replaced the ford across the river, and travellers made the best of challenging roads and tracks.

In the later medieval period and beyond the town grew. A silk weaving industry replaced the wool weavers, and the thriving market moved to the top of the High Street as seen in this picture. In the 1850s the Courtaulds factory was the largest producer of black mourning crepe in the country, with 240 looms at work, and by 1891 there were 1400 operatives looking after over a thousand looms. After the death of Prince Albert long periods of mourning had become a social obligation! In 1860 the Colne Valley Railway opened Halstead station, giving much improved communications to east and west. For just over a century the railway served the town, the Colne Valley Railway becoming part of the LNER, and in turn British Railways. Finally in 1961 the railway closed to passengers, leaving the town to depend on road transport alone.

In this picture of the High Street at the end of the twentieth century, I can see eighteen cars and vans. This seems appropriate as we near the end of our pageant, for the car dominates everywhere. By 2005 there were 4½ million more cars on the road than in 1997! Roads easily become gridlocked, and parking is a constant battle with wheel clampers and traffic wardens. Many have problems even parking near their homes! One cannot escape the feeling that we should have managed our transport better, but who am I to talk?

This picture was almost certainly the largest and one of the most difficult I have undertaken. The vast amount of detail meant slow and sometimes frustrating progress. The lofty viewpoint was from a friend's bedroom, and with access limited sketches were made and photographs taken to lessen the inconvenience. The very first visit produced a wonderful lighting effect with contrasting shadows which I used in the painting. None of my further visits were as fruitful, although they were used to include the market and various figure studies. Studies of the individual buildings were also made from ground level.

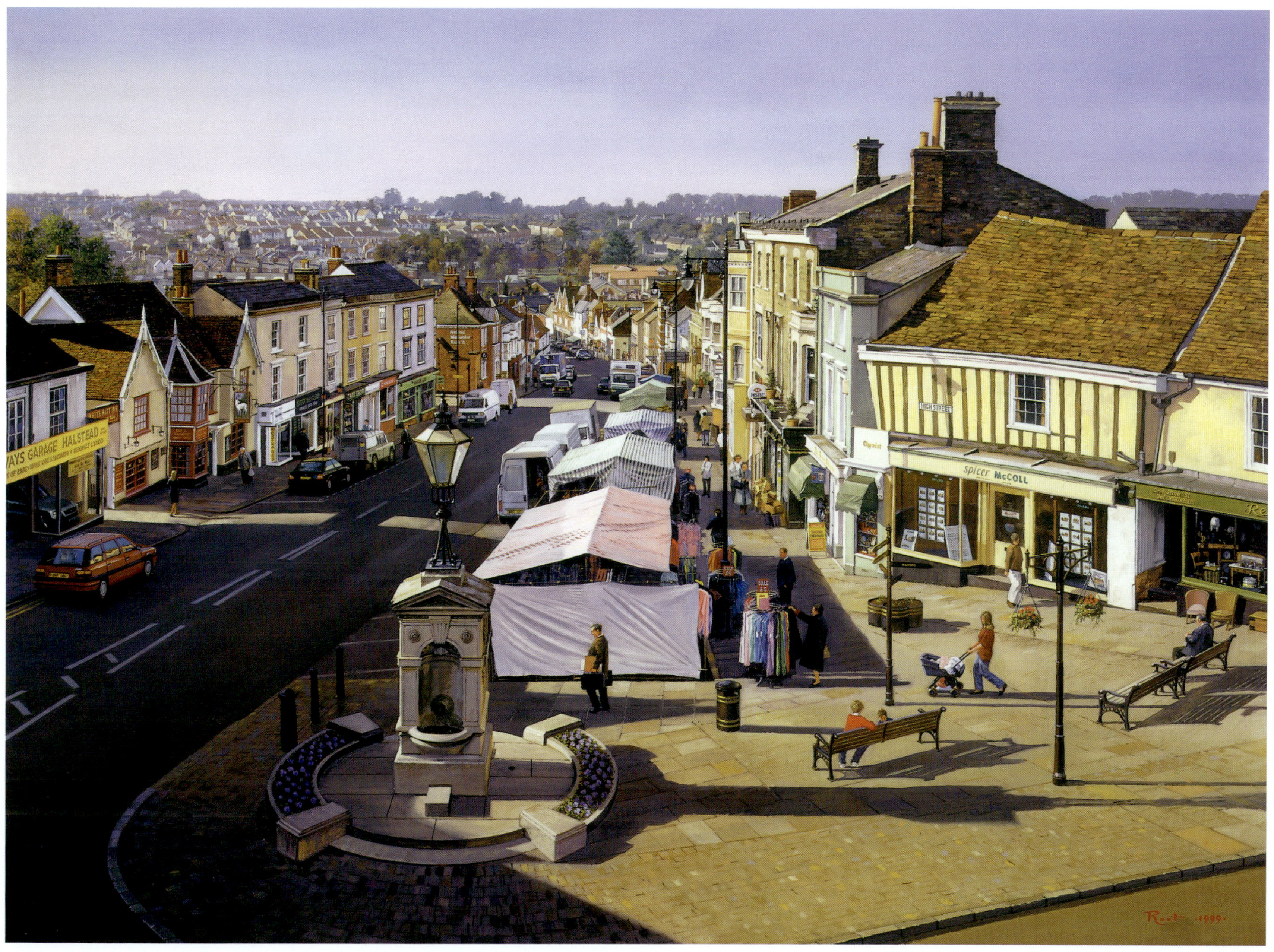

Royal Scot at Ais Gill

Painted 2005

In conditions like these – and I'm also writing on a very cold and frosty morning, it was a very good thing that loco-motive crews had a good fire nearby to keep them warm, though a fireman firing his engine up to Ais Gill did not have much opportunity to get cold! Once again Malcolm has captured the bleak majesty of this high Pennine area, with snow and drystone walls, and three people wrapped up well against the cold watching from a bridge as the train thunders by beneath them. From the comfort of warm carriages the passengers can enjoy the sunlit scenery passing their windows and thrill to the music of the wheels.

The locomotive hauling this train of maroon MkI coaching stock is 6100 *Royal Scot*. In the later 1920s the Chief Mechanical Engineer of the LMS, Sir Henry Fowler, was required to produce a design for a new locomotive to tackle the demanding West Coast route from London to Glasgow. After several designs were rejected a simple 4-6-0 three-cylinder locomotive was produced which proved highly successful, and the first of the class was 6100 *Royal Scot*. In 1933 it was decided to send one of the locomotives to the USA for the Chicago centenary celebrations, and number 6152 was selected. However, the unusual decision was taken to swap names and numbers with 6100, so that the pre-served locomotive which proudly carries the name *Royal Scot*, and a bell similar to that on the GWR *King George V,* is not in fact the original *Royal Scot* locomotive, the first in the class.

Here lies a paradox. Those who spend much time preserving the past tend not only to be experts but also purists. Their aim is to restore transport to its original state, down to the last detail. However, this is not always easy, as *Royal Scot* shows. Further, it is important for financial reasons to make an example that has been restored appeal to a wider public. The locomotive and train in this picture, a 'steam special excursion' at the start of the twenty-first century, would certainly do that, and few of the passengers would worry about small details of accuracy. It is the attraction of a majestic steam locomotive tackling the gradients for which it was built nearly 80 years ago which inspires the pas-sengers.

Perhaps we should be concluding our pageant with a high speed train on today's railways, but I for one would always back a great steam locomotive as a more fitting conclusion!

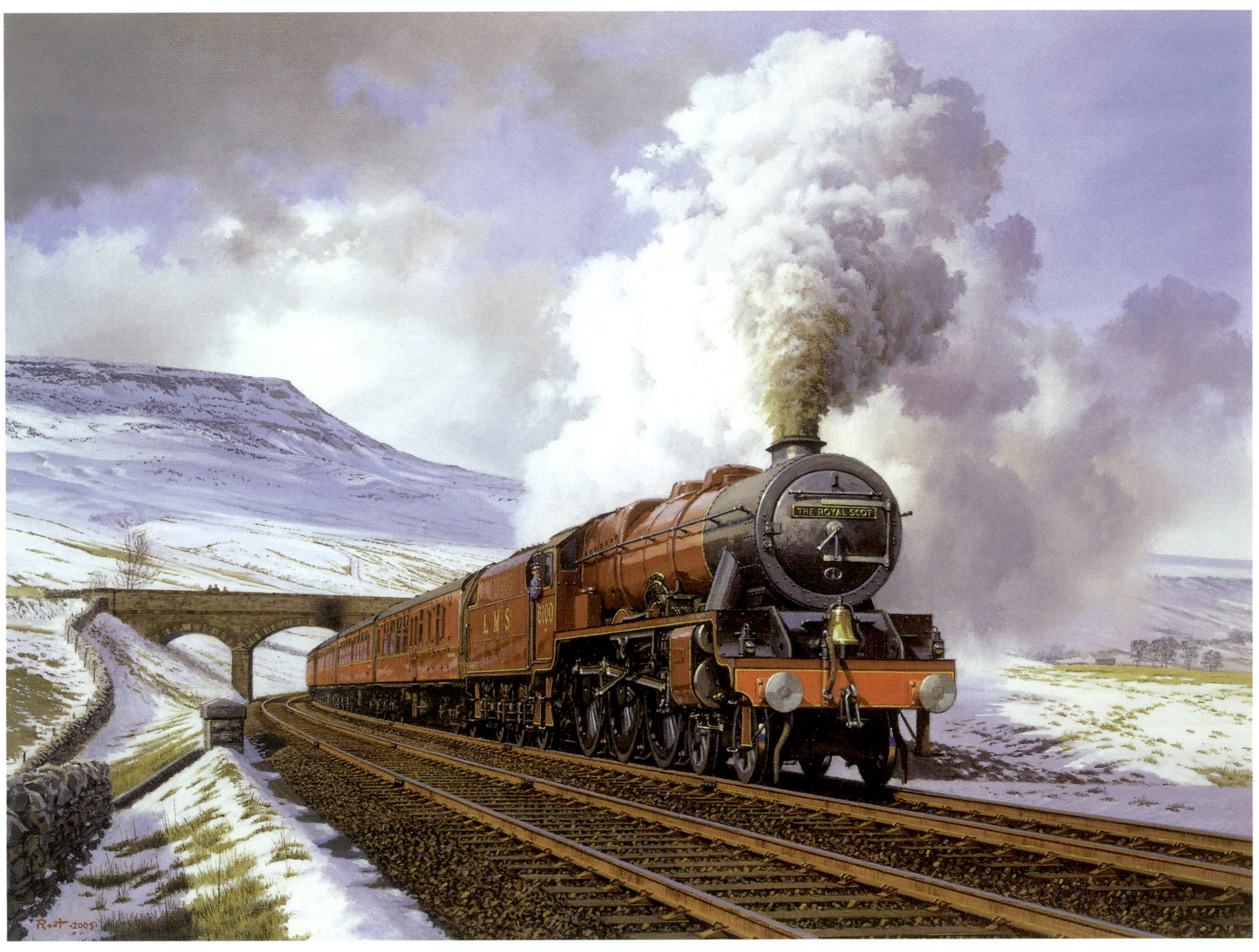
THE ROYAL SCOT
LMS
6100

Expanding Transport – Millennium 4
Painted 2000

This fascinating composite picture makes a fitting summary to our pageant of transport. The artist has woven together seven or eight scenes to create a whole. Notice how the smoke from the hot air balloon blends with that from *Mallard* and *Rocket* to become the clouds through which a Comet airliner is passing. Here we see a horse drawn stagecoach competing with a powered canal narrow boat, and both giving way to the Rover 12 saloon car. At sea are two mighty ships which both have a place in maritime history. The *Great Eastern* was Isambard Kingdom Brunel's ultimate achievement, and the 'ship too far' which hastened his death. Launched in 1858, she was 22 500 tons, six times the size of the largest ship afloat! Her size, and relative lack of power, made her very difficult to handle, and there were not enough passengers or cargo in the world to make her a profitable concern. In contrast the *Queen Elizabeth* had an illustrious career beginning as an invaluable troopship in the Second World War. The largest liner afloat, she carried over 2200 passengers. After the war she saw years of service until eclipsed by the airliners, was eventually sold, and allowed to catch fire and become a total loss in Hong Kong harbour in January 1972.

In the centre of this picture we see two of the most famous railway locomotives ever built. Stephenson's *Rocket* triumphed in the Rainhill trials of 1829, and paved the way for rapid railway development. Sir Nigel Gresley's A4 Pacific *Mallard* gained the world speed record for steam in 1938, which she holds to this day (see page 124). Both locomotives were produced by designers of genius, and have rightly been preserved for posterity.

It is in the air that the most rapid and spectacular development has taken place. In November 1783 the first manned flight in a hot air balloon took place (see page 12). The first aeroplane was flown by the Wright brothers in 1903 at Kitty Hawk, and the first Atlantic crossing made in a bi-plane in 1919 (see page 22). It took only 30 years and another World War for wood and wire bi-planes to become sleek jet airliners like the Comet. Finally in 1961 man first went into space, and in 1969 landed on the moon. Today the space shuttle, seen here blasting off on another mission, is the ultimate in transport.

Through Malcolm's paintings we have followed the great pageant of transport development down the centuries in our country, which is a country which has often led the world. Great engineers and designers have given us machines which were often superb examples of grace and power in their time. The pictures in this book capture the romance of developing transport over the last Millennium.

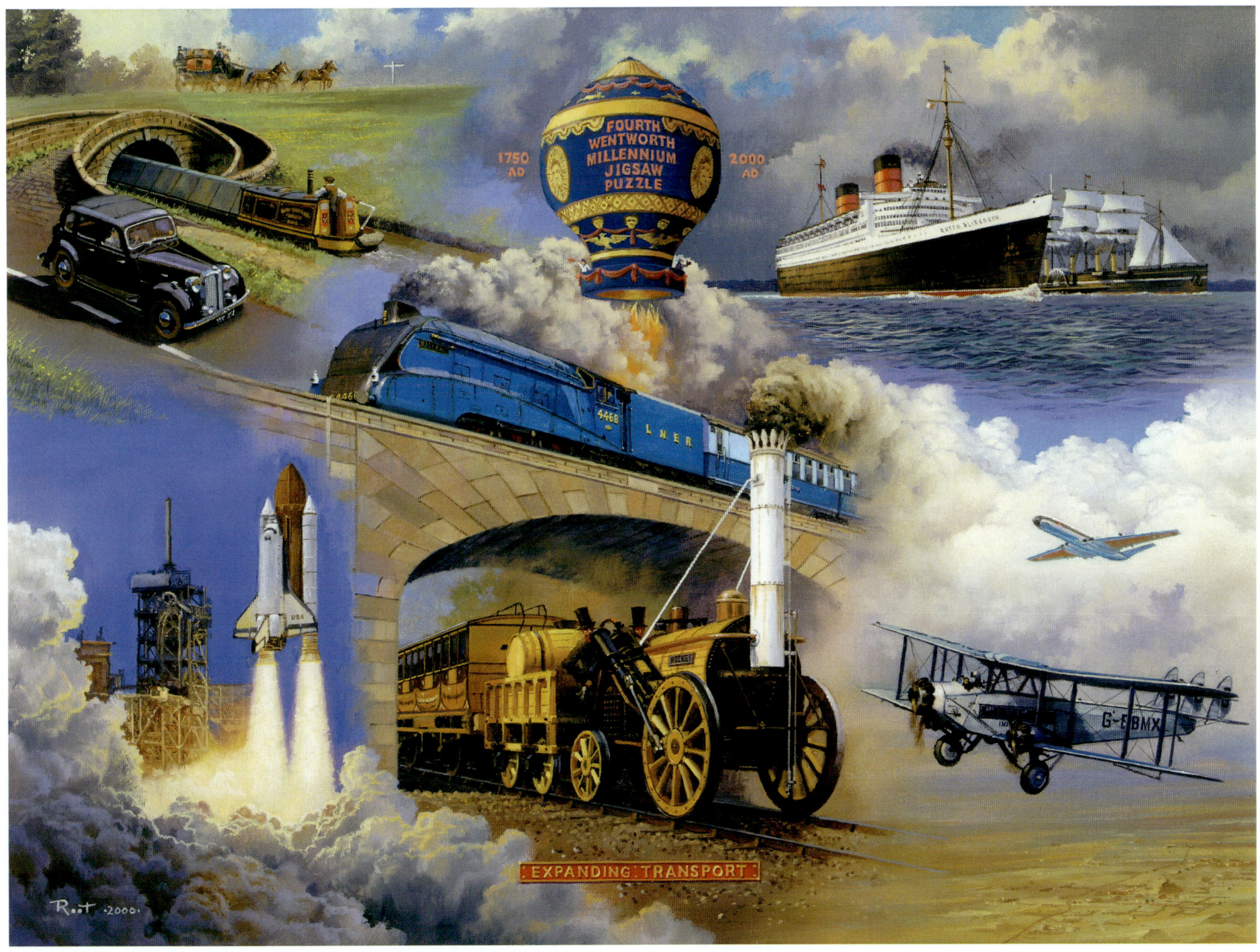
FOURTH
WENTWORTH
MILLENNIUM
JIGSAW
PUZZLE
1750 AD
2000 AD
EXPANDING TRANSPORT
Root 2000

Bibliography

Root and Tyler. *Malcolm Root's Transport Paintings*. Halsgrove. Companion Volume.
Root and Tyler. *Malcolm Root's Railway Paintings*. Halsgrove. Companion Volume.
Aceti and Brazendale. *Classic Cars*. Orbis Publications Ltd. London.
Michael Allen. *British Family Cars of the Fifties*. Haynes Publishing Group.
Ernest F. Carter. *Observer's Book of Railway Locomotives of Britain*. Frederick Warne & Co.
H.C. Casserley. *Observer's Book of British Steam Locomotives*. Frederick Warne & Co Ltd.
John Chalcraft and Steve Turner. *The Deltics*. Rail Photoprints.
Terry Coleman. *The Liners*. Penguin Books.
B.K. Cooper. *Great Western Railway Handbook*. Ian Allan Ltd. London.
Crowhurst and Scarth. *Locomotives of the Romney, Hythe & Dymchurch Railway*. Workshop Press.
Frank Dodman. *The Observer's Book of Ships*. Frederick Warne & Co Ltd.
Essex County Council. *Origins of Halstead*.
Nicholas Faith. *Classic Ships*. Boxtree Ltd.
T.G. Flinders. *On the Settle & Carlisle Route*. Ian Allan Ltd. London.
Michael Foster. *Hornby Companion Series. Hornby Dublo Trains*. New Cavendish Books.
William Green and Gerald Pollinger. *The Observer's Book of Aircraft*. Frederick Warne & Co.Ltd.
R.A. Harding. *Vintage Steam Owners and Operators of the Colne Valley*.
Edward Hart. *The Harness Horse*. Shire Publications Ltd
John Hamilton. *The Helicopter Campaign in the Falklands*. David & Charles, Newton Abbot.
Chris Harvey. *Austin 7*. Haynes Publications.
Paul Heaton. *The Wynns Fleet*. PM Heaton Publishing.
A.P. Herbert. *The War Story of Southend Pier*. Southend-on-Sea, Essex.
Norman Jacobs. *Clacton-on-Sea. Pictorial History*. Phillimore and Co Ltd
Patrick Kingston. *Royal Trains*. David & Charles, Newton Abbot.
Michael R. Lane. *Burrell Showmans Road Locomotives*. Model and Allied Publications.
L.A. Manwaring. *Observer's Book of Automobiles*. Frederick Warne & Co. Ltd.
G.R. Mills. *Hedingham Omnibuses*.
A. Morland and R. Pripps. *Ford & Fordson Tractors*. Motorbooks International.
Colin Morris. *Bournemouth Transport*. Ian Allan Publishing.
O.S. Nock. *British Locomotives of the Twentieth Century. Vols. 1 & 2*. Guild Publishing
Charles Ray Ed. *Romance of the Nation*.
S.W. Stevens-Stratten. *Light Commercial Vehicles*. Ian Allan Ltd. London.
S.W. Stevens-Stratten. *British Lorries*. Ian Allan Ltd London.
R.S. Summerhays. *The Observer's Book of Horses and Ponies*. Frederick Warne Ltd.
K. Turner. *Pier Railways*. Oakwood Press.
B. Vanderveen. *British Cars of the late 1930s*. Frederick Warne & Co Ltd.
Waverley. *The Golden Jubilee*. Waverley Excursions Ltd.
Archibald Williams. *Brunel and After*. Great Western Railway, Paddington.
John de S. Winser. *British Cross Channel Railway Passenger Ships*. Patrick Stephens Ltd.
W.B. Yeadon. *Named Trains on LNER Lines*. Book Law Publications.

Index